CYBERSPACE

JOB SEARCH KIT

Third Edition

The Complete Guide to Online Job Seeking and Career Information

Mary B. Nemnich

Fred E. Jandt

Send your comments to the authors via e-mail:
jobnet@aol.com

Publishing

Indianapolis, IN

D1530684

Cyberspace Job Search Kit, Third Edition

The Complete Guide to Online Job Seeking and Career Information

© 2000 by Mary B. Nemnich and Fred E. Jandt

Previous editions published as *Using the Internet and the World Wide Web in Your Job Search*.

Published by JIST Works, Inc.
8902 Otis Avenue
Indianapolis, IN 46216
Phone: 1-800-648-JIST   Fax: 1-800-JIST-FAX   E-mail: jistworks@aol.com
Visit our Web site for information on other JIST products: http://www.jist.com

Also by Fred E. Jandt and Mary B. Nemnich
  • *Cyberspace Resume Kit*
Also by Fred E. Jandt
  • *The Customer Is Usually Wrong!*

> *See the back of this book for additional JIST titles and ordering information. Quantity discounts are available.*

Editor: Lori Cates
Copy Editor: Sandy Doell
Interior Design: Aleata Howard
Interior Layout: Carolyn J. Newland
Cover Design: Honeymoon Image & Design, Inc.
Proofreader: Becca York
Indexer: Larry Sweazy

Printed in the United States of America.

Cataloging-in-Publication data is on file with the Library of Congress.

04 03 02 01 00   9 8 7 6 5 4 3 2 1

ISBN 1-56370-671-7

Acknowledgments

*The authors wish to thank and acknowledge
Lee A. Nemnich, who provided technical guidance,
insight, and support for this book.*

Contents

Chapter 1: Introducing the Internet....... 1

How It Happened 2

Why It Happened 2

Overview for the Job Seeker 4

Using the Internet in Your Job Search 4

Success Stories 5

Psychological Aspects of an Electronic Job Search 7

Frustration 8

Side-Tracking/Isolation 8

A Special Word to the Computer-Phobic 9

Chapter 2: Going Online 11

Web History 11

Getting on the World Wide Web 13

Commercial Internet Service Providers 14

The Most Common ISPs 15

The Largest ISPs 15

The Browsers 18

Search Engines 19

The Multimedia Web 27

Accessing the World Wide Web Through America Online 28

America Online E-Mail 35

**Chapter 3: Getting Job Information
from Corporate Sites
and Job Boards 39**

Corporate Web Sites 39

Popular Job Boards 43

Other Notable Job Banks 51

Even More Databases 55

Finding Even More Job Banks 59

Searching the Job Banks 61

Chapter 4: Usenet Newsgroups 63

What Are Newsgroups and How Do I Use Them? 63

Online Forums—Another Type of Newsgroup 64

Accessing the Newsgroups 64

Reading Newsgroup Postings 67

Job Posting Newsgroups 67

Sample Job Postings 69

Resume Newsgroups 78

Sample Resume Postings 78

Preparing Your Resume for Newsgroups 85

Submitting Your Resume 87

Chapter 5: Career Resources on the Internet 89

A Practical Example 90

Learning from the Competition 90

General Career Information 91

Researching Employers 92

Well-Known Sites for Employer Information 92

"Best Companies" Lists 93

U.S. Government Sites 94

Canadian Government Sites 96

Relocation Information 96

Chapter 6: Cautions: Job Search and Privacy Issues on the Web 99

Horror Stories 99

Applicants Don't Follow Instructions 99

Employers Don't Follow Instructions 100

Work-at-Home Scams 100

Other Scams 100

More Unscrupulous Activity 101

Headhunter Woes 101

What We Learned 101

Online Privacy in Your Job Search 102

Misinformation Can Be Duplicated 105

Recommended Precautions 105

E-Mail Security 106

Unwanted E-Mail 107

Unwanted Web Sites 108

For More Information 108

Chapter 7: Preparing Your Electronic Resume 109

The Audience 110

Building Your Resume 110
Resume Software 111
Resume ABCs 112
Making Your Resume Attractive 112
Making Your Resume Brief 115
Making Your Resume Clear 117
Resume Formats 119
The Chronological Format 119
The Functional Format 119
The Combination Format 120
Organizing Your Resume 120
Preparing Your Resume for Keyword Searches 121
Preparing Your Resume for Scanning 123
Online Resume Templates 124
Scannable Resume Tips from Restrac 124
The Summary Section 125
Applicant-Tracking Software 126
An Electronic Resume Template 126
Some Actual Sample Resumes 130
The Online Curriculum Vitae 135

Chapter 8: Preparing an HTML Resume for the Web 143

Why Have an HTML Resume? 143
Developing a Web Resume 143
Text 144
Links 144
Images 145
Other Things That Can Be Included 147
HTML Resume Layout 147
Linear 147
Hierarchical 147
Web 147
An Introduction to HTML 147
Building a Simple Resume in HTML 151
Tags 151
Inserting Links 155
In-Line Media—Images 156
Create a Test Version of Your Page 157
Publishing Your Web Resume 157
Commercial ISPs 157
Web Presence Providers 157
Resume Banks 158
Free Web Servers 158
Checking Your Web Resume 159
Publicizing Your Web Address 160

Adding Your URL to Search Engines 160
Linking Your Resume with Other Sites 161
Sample HTML Resumes 161

Chapter 9: Job-Hunting Netiquette 181

General Rules 182
Newsgroup Fundamentals 184
Follow the Employer's Instructions 184
Follow Newsgroup Usage Instructions 185
Networking 185
Choose Your Group 185
Surf the Net and Find Your Own Niche 186
Postings Are Public 186
Writing Tips 186
World Wide Web Netiquette 191
Keep Your Page Simple 192
Limit Your Links 192
Respect the "Low-Tech" 192
Include Your E-Mail Address 192
Send Them Home 192
Update Your Page, and Keep It Simple 192
Be Respectful of Others 193

Chapter 10: Internet Interviewing: By E-Mail, Phone, Videoconference, and in Person 195

The E-Mail Interview 197
Clarifying Your Resume 197
Exchanges Can Be Conversational and Friendly 198
Be Careful, Positive, and Polite 198
Tips on E-Mail Interviewing 199
Declining a Position 201
The Telephone Interview 201
Be Prepared 202
Phone Interview Tips 203
Desktop Videoconferencing 204
CU-SeeMe 205
Other Videoconferencing Programs 206
It Could Happen to You: Videoconferencing Tips 206
The Face-to-Face Interview 207
Evaluating the Interview Situation 208
Sizing Up the Interviewer 212
Hypothetical Interview Situations 213

Questions in Context 216
Evaluating Yourself 219
Negotiating a Salary 219

Chapter 11:   Advice for College Students 223

Places to Look 223
Entry-Level Jobs 223
Jobs by Discipline 224
Internships and Summer Jobs 225
College Placement Offices 226
University of South Florida 226
Online Placement Information: JOBTRAK 231
Major Online Career Services 232
College Grad Job Hunter 232
BridgePath 234
Insider Tips from a Professional Recruiter 236
Tips for a Successful Student Job Search 239
Resume Tips 239
Interview Tips 240
Keeping the Job 248
Job-Related Tips 248
General Tips 249

Chapter 12:   Advice for Employers 251

Electronic Recruiting 251
Newsgroups and Online Employment Services 252
Newsgroups 252
Commercial Online Recruiting Services 257
The Advantages of Online Recruiting 266
E-Mail: More Details, Less Time 266
Getting to the Right People 267
Your Computer Becomes "The Lobby" 267
Less Time on the Phone 268
Cutting-Edge People 268
You Control It 268
Legal and Ethical Aspects of Electronic Recruiting 268
Limitless Recruiting Opportunities 271

Summary 272

Glossary 273

Index 287

Chapter 1

Introducing the Internet

I f you're looking at this book, we assume you want to learn more about using the Internet and World Wide Web to either search for a job or recruit employees. We hope this new book meets those needs.

In 1995 we published *Using the Internet in Your Job Search*. It was one of the first books about online job search. When one of us was interviewed on CNN, we were asked how many job announcements were on the Internet. We said "tens of thousands" and worried that we might have overestimated.

In that first book we devoted just a few pages to the still new World Wide Web. Job search on the World Wide Web grew so quickly that our first book was soon out of date. So in 1997 we published *Using the Internet and the World Wide Web in Your Job Search*. This time we were prepared for that question about the number of job announcements on the Internet. We had identified more than half a million.

By this time the advantages of using the Internet and World Wide Web had become so great for both job seekers and employers that what once had been largely used only in high-tech industries became commonplace for most employers. What we found is reflected in our third book, *Cyberspace Resume Kit*, published in 1999. We found that over three million people had their resumes online.

This is now our fourth book. It represents our years of experience with online job search and gives you, the job seeker or employer, the most comprehensive and up-to-date information we can provide.

How It Happened

We're often asked to do interviews, speeches, and workshops for job seekers, employers, and career counselors. A commonly asked question has been "How did this all happen?"

The Internet was originally designed to link the military, defense contractors, and universities to make it possible to send computer data over telephone lines. More and more computer networks at universities and research centers were established and made a part of the Internet. Most of the information available on the Internet at that time was research oriented, but it also included notices of job vacancies of interest to the research and computer communities.

Over time, some connections were established by computer networks not located at universities or research centers. It was, however, only after the giant commercial online service providers, such as CompuServe and America Online, began to provide Internet connections to their users that the Internet became available to anyone who could afford the commercial providers' charges. As more and more people with all sorts of backgrounds and interests connected, the Internet became increasingly diverse in the types of information available. Instead of being just research- and computer-related, the job vacancies exploded to include all types of jobs—from gardeners to youth ministers, and from weekend sports television anchors to nurses—from full-time jobs to part-time jobs to contract jobs. Today you can find job vacancies for any type of job in your city or worldwide!

Why It Happened

Job search and recruitment on the Internet continues to grow because it offers advantages to both employers and job seekers. Employers list the following advantages:

1. **Speed.** Traditional recruiting by publicizing a vacancy in print publications can be very slow. Some publications require that announcements be submitted thirty or more days in advance. Then there is printing and mailing time; and of course, applicants must be given time to apply.

   In contrast, a vacancy announcement posted on the Internet can receive a response minutes after being posted!

2. **Coverage area.** Newspaper classified ads have largely been limited to the newspaper's circulation area. Specialized publications, such as industry trade magazines, are limited to their mailing lists.

   In contrast, a vacancy announcement posted on the Internet can be seen worldwide by anyone with Internet access. It's impossible to know

exactly, but it is a fairly reliable estimate that some forty million people use the Internet regularly.

3. **Cost.** Traditional recruiting is expensive. Publicizing a vacancy using advertisements is costly. A one-time two-column by two-inch display ad in the Monday edition of the *Indianapolis Star,* for example, costs $332.00. A headhunter's fee can be 20 to 30 percent of the new hire's base salary.

   In contrast, a vacancy announcement can be posted on the Internet at no cost.

4. **Automated staffing software.** Not only does advertising cost, there is a cost to opening, sorting, filing, and refiling applications and resumes on paper.

   In contrast, automated staffing software programs have reduced personnel costs by providing access to resumes at online job boards, matching candidates to positions, and monitoring and documenting candidates' progress through an organization's hiring process.

Other advantages exist for employers today; we discuss those advantages in chapter 12, "Advice for Employers." For now, let's look briefly at the advantages for job seekers. They are the same four advantages as for employers: speed, coverage area, cost, and automated staffing software.

We've been guests on television shows during which the interviewer challenged us to find a job vacancy for a person. Once in Fresno, California, the host asked Fred to find a vacancy for a person the producers had brought to the studio. The individual said that because of family reasons, he was not able to relocate. That meant Fred had to find the individual a job in Fresno. The person also said he wanted a job as a cable engineer. Fred had fewer than five minutes but was able to locate jobs in Fresno and jobs as a cable engineer, but not jobs as a cable engineer in Fresno. Even so, before the five minutes were up, the individual had an accurate idea of what was available in Fresno. Let us repeat that: *Before the five minutes were up, the individual had an accurate idea of what was available in Fresno.* That's speed.

We've found that most job seekers think of using the Internet as a way to locate jobs in other states, provinces, or countries. That's true—the Internet does make it possible for us to locate jobs in other states and countries—but it also allows us to locate jobs in our own hometown and ZIP code. The Internet is both international and local!

The costs to the job seeker of searching the Internet, beyond getting Internet access, can be free. In the next chapter, we'll discuss ways to access the Internet for a fee, but it's important to note here at the outset that many public libraries provide free Internet access to their patrons.

Automated staffing software offers the job seeker advantages as well. We've heard this story more than once: A job seeker posts her resume in a resume bank. Within a day the person receives an e-mail from an employer asking if she is interested in being considered for a position. Some companies are able to automatically access resume banks, scan the resumes posted there, and match the qualifications they find on the resumes to job openings they have. The job seeker did nothing but post a resume. Automated staffing software did the rest.

So, for both the employer and the job seeker, the Internet has advantages. That's why the Internet job market will continue to grow and grow.

Overview for the Job Seeker

If you are a job seeker, this is what you'll find in this book:

1. **Internet Service Providers.** An overview of major Internet service providers and how to use them to find jobs and career information.

2. **Job banks.** A descriptive listing of the major job banks where you'll find jobs.

3. **Newsgroups.** How to use newsgroups and forums in your job search.

4. **Career resources.** Where to find career information help on the Internet.

5. **Cautions.** A discussion of confidentiality and proper cautions you should consider when putting personal information on the Internet.

6. **Resume preparation.** How to prepare a resume for use on the Internet.

7. **HTML resumes.** How to prepare a resume for use on the World Wide Web.

8. **Submitting resumes.** How to submit your resume on the Internet.

9. **The Internet interview.** How to be prepared for interviews conducted over the Internet.

If you are a student, chapter 11, "Advice for College Students," presents information specially written with college students in mind.

Using the Internet in Your Job Search

We've often been asked to explain exactly what the Internet is. What we say is to think of the Internet as a very large library, but with no librarians;

anyone can "visit" and leave material. Some people have left "trash"; others have left "treasures." While there is a wealth of up-to-the-minute information available, you must be able to find it among all the less useful information. Valuable information is available on occupation employment trends, the unemployment rates in different locations, housing costs in different locations, and guides for building a resume, but you have to know where to find it. Unfortunately, this "library" is unorganized and has no librarians to help users.

You'll find this book to be a guide to the valuable information on job search that is available on the Internet. We've evaluated what's there and point you to what we know is the best.

In a library, a book's "address" doesn't change. Unfortunately, on the World Wide Web, addresses change and some sites disappear. We can guarantee that every site in this book was accurate when the book was published, but be aware that a site may change its address or disappear.

If you do find an outdated address, please notify us by e-mail at our publisher (jistworks@aol.com) and we'll correct it in future editions.

Success Stories

Over the years we've received many e-mail messages from people who have found new jobs on the Internet. We've heard from people who had been searching for a job for several months and then found one over the Internet in a matter of weeks. One fortunate job seeker wrote us that he found his job, interviewed, and was hired all in the same day! Another wrote that she not only found her own job on the Internet, but continues as a recruiter to use the Internet for finding applicants.

We thought you'd enjoy reading some of our e-mail:

```
I found my current job on ba.jobs.offered. I was looking
on the USENET groups for several months before I found the
"pearl." I am not a software engineer, so it took a long
time to find the job I wanted. I was a video producer at
Ames Research Center, but wanted to move on. I found an ad
for an office administrator at a start up company. The
magic words "start up" enticed me to send my resume. To
make a long story short, I am the office manager for a
rapidly growing CD-ROM publishing company and have decided
to change my career path to focus on Human Resources.
Quite a change from a Video Production background. I am
the happiest I've ever been at work. I work with great
people, and have a great boss. I think the Internet is a
great way to find jobs.
```

I was ready, not only for a job change, but for a CAREER change. I was a systems administrator, but wanted to stop working with computers and start working with people.

I first started looking in the classifieds in the local newspaper. I would read the ads aloud to my husband: "Could I be a...Karate Instructor?? Pizza Chef??? How 'bout an inline skating instructor?"

"You can't skate, and don't even talk about your cooking!!!"

OK, so I went online and discovered job searching on the Internet. I saw an ad for a technical recruiter. I had the technical expertise, yet I would work with people! I replied to the ad and within the day I had a telephone number of the firm.

I am now a very successful recruiter and use the Internet DAILY for our searches.

I always tell our applicants that I found my job on the Internet, and send them a list of resume and job listing newsgroups and web sites.

I can truly say (even tho it is corny) that it has changed my life AND CAREER!

How about a success story?

I have more work than I can do. Pretty short sweet and simple.

GOOD RATES AND GREAT WORK!!!

I got a good contract as a freelance HTML author thru Usenet. I starting working with the guy for quite a while, via e-mail, before we ever met in the flesh.

This is short and sweet.

I am a freelance html/perl writer. I saw an ad in **uk.jobs.offered** at 10.30 a.m. I sent a reply by email including a CV and saying that I could do half what they

wanted to a very high standard, and didn't know a thing about the other stuff.

At 11 a.m. I got a phone call from the company asking if I could come over at 6 p.m. After talking to the woman hiring me for 15 minutes, we agreed on 300/week and I got the job.

Hardly earth-shattering but it sure beats buying the daily paper and waiting two weeks to hear that you have an interview in another two weeks, or dealing with shady agencies that are charging out at double your fees.

Hi, I graduated from the University of Maryland, Baltimore County (UMBC) in June 1991, with a degree in Computer Sciences. My first job was with a computer company in Rockville/Gaithersburg, Maryland. The late spring of 1994 was an extremely hectic time for over 1200 (employees in my company) since this was when the first wave of layoffs [attacks?] commenced. While my company was quite heroic in its efforts to place "surplused" workers elsewhere in the organization, its most noteworthy effort to move them met with failure. Those workers would become simply out of luck.

I made it past the first two waves of layoffs, but destiny would have my job, as well as everyone else's; it was only a matter of time. In the month I had to find work either within or without the company, I turned to the Usenet newsgroups for help, and found numerous opportunities. An employee (of a computer company) got hold of my resume and simply sent my account an e-mail. I responded, we met, and he hired me.

No doubt a success story for me. :)

Psychological Aspects of an Electronic Job Search

Before you use this book as a guide to information on the Internet, we need to warn you of possible distractions from an effective Internet job search. We've learned from our experiences with job seekers to warn you of two dysfunctional situations to avoid: frustration, and getting sidetracked or isolated.

Frustration

Frustration is a standard problem with job searches in general. It usually results from the just-missed opportunities, the "one that got away." Applicants often wonder just who that other "perfect" person is who is taking all the jobs. It is easy to let feelings of inadequacy creep in. Added to this problem is the fact that, in today's labor market, job seekers are constantly playing a numbers game. *So many* people are looking for work.

On the Internet, frustration is a constant companion. After all, the sheer vastness of the system is daunting. How can one possibly find all there is to find? It is easy to begin to feel like an infinitesimal speck in cyberspace, an armadillo smashed on the information superhighway.

Sometimes you find a wonderful site and go on to explore its links. After a while you'd like to go back to that first wonderful site. You can save time by "bookmarking" those sites you think you'd like to return to.

Of course, with "information overload," which is often experienced on the Internet, the question is where to look, what to consider, and what to ignore. When it comes to a job search, you can control for geographical area, occupation, even wage range. If you are an accountant seeking work in Minnesota, why search for jobs in the West? Similarly, don't waste your time looking at all the accounting clerk postings, which are clearly below your level of expertise. Remember, too, that you don't want to waste an employer's time by "going fishing" in San Diego when you only want to "reel in" a job in Minneapolis. Focus your attention on precisely what you want.

Side-Tracking/Isolation

One peculiar aspect of the Internet culture is that users—particularly new ones—tend to get hooked by the seemingly endless parade of information available. It is not unusual to log on at 6:30 p.m. "just to take a quick look," and find yourself turning off the computer at 2 a.m. Some people get so caught up in the Internet world that they become isolated after a while, spending days at a time online, chatting with this or that newsgroup, or playing some interactive game. Beware! You have a job to do. If you go on the Net twice a day, make sure that at least one of those times is dedicated to your job search. Promise yourself that you won't get sidetracked by some other seductive activity until you have made at least one productive contact or attempt at getting a job. Then, by all means, reward yourself.

Go play on the Web. Cruise around some completely frivolous sites. Check out the reviews of the newest movies, read up on your personal passions, download a sound clip of the latest release of your favorite group, or spend some time talking to a job seeker's support group. Just never lose sight of your main mission and purpose for using the Internet. Stay on track and get "hooked" on a job.

A Special Word to the Computer-Phobic

So you haven't been able to program your VCR or microwave. You feel intimidated and overwhelmed by technology. The following are some tips for learning to deal with technology:

First, find a teacher you feel comfortable with. Many computer "experts" have no empathy for the computer-phobic. They speak a language you don't understand and have no patience to show you what to do. Find someone who's good with computers and who is a patient teacher. It could be someone at work, a friend at church, or even a neighbor's teenage child. Don't ask them to teach you everything about computers; just ask them to show you something on the computer that they think you could use. Focus on learning one thing that you can use; don't even begin to try to learn everything that could be done.

Then find a class at a local community college or adult education center designed to help beginners learn about computers and software. You can find these classes in course catalogs and by asking at computer stores.

We tell computer-phobic students to explore as a child would. Don't worry about doing something wrong. Explore and see what happens when you try something. The odds are that you're not going to do any harm to the computer. So, try it. Just avoid the "know-it-alls" until you're ready for them!

There have been misunderstandings about the Internet, and there have even been abuses of the Internet. But in the area of the job search, the Internet is a win-win situation for everybody—except, of course, those who haven't gotten online yet!

Chapter 2

Going Online

Now that you know why you should be on the Internet, it's time to make your first forays into cyberspace and start looking around. The Web's history is short. In the early days of the Internet, this process of navigating was a bit more complicated. Initially, the Internet was primarily the province of computer scientists. As accessibility grew, the Internet became a friendlier environment, easier to access. But it wasn't until the advent of the World Wide Web that access to the Internet became smooth and virtually effortless. Its popularity makes it the predominant way people are using the Internet. You need to know only a few things to use this powerful means of retrieving information.

In chapter 1 we described the Internet as a very large library with no librarians. However, today's World Wide Web search engines are like very efficient "librarians," sorting through millions of pages to bring to your computer the information you request. In this chapter we prepare you to use the World Wide Web on your own.

Web History

The World Wide Web was born of the need to simplify the process of finding and using the vast amount of data on the Internet. The concept of an interconnected, hypertext-driven system originated at the European Particle Physics Laboratory in Geneva, Switzerland. Known simply as CERN, an acronym for the French *Centre European Researche Nucleare,* the lab was a brain trust of scientists, students, and researchers from all over the world. The physicists at CERN were looking for a way to share information efficiently and quickly. In 1989 physicist Tim Berners-Lee advanced a proposal for a system that would make the dissemination of data faster and smoother without having to sort through a mountain of unnecessary documents on the Internet.

Until this period, the information on the Internet existed in databases that were cumbersome to search. For example, *Gopher,* an early Internet search tool, was easy in the sense that it was menu-driven and presented data neatly organized in lists. However, a search through Gopher still required the tedious and time-consuming process of paging through countless screens to get to the desired information. *FTP* (file transfer protocol—a means of transferring files from one remote machine to another) consisted not only of lists, but lists of often unintelligible file names. Berners-Lee sought a way to bring order to the chaos.

What Berners-Lee proposed was a simple means of finding information by following a series of *links* from one piece of data to another. Prior to this time, the metaphor most often used to describe the Internet had been a "tree," where users made their way to information by going from branch to branch up a "trunk" of menus. The Gopher system used this hierarchical means of organizing information. Searches accomplished in this manner were time-consuming, because one often had to climb the same tree again and again each time new information was sought. Berners-Lee envisioned his more efficient process as a "web" of "information nodes" that CERN scientists could use to move quickly from one piece of information to another. He called this concept of interconnected links *hypertext.*

In his proposal, Berners-Lee laid out the entire picture of a web that could be interconnected among several different machines. As early as 1989, Berners-Lee conceived of a broad-based use for his system—a "world wide web." He also raised the notion of *hypermedia,* the idea that not just text, but also pictures, sound, graphics, and animation, could be transmitted across the web.

It wasn't until 1990, however, that the first World Wide Web browser—that is, the software that allows users to explore or "browse" the information on the World Wide Web (WWW)—was developed. By 1991, the Web browser was in wide use at CERN.

It was time to take the Web to a more generalized level. Word had been spreading on discussion groups on the Internet (known as *newsgroups*) about this remarkable new tool. CERN began to make its browser available to anyone via ftp. Software development rapidly followed, and by early 1993, fifty Web servers were in existence. By late 1993, that number grew to more than 500 servers.

The early part of 1993 saw the emergence of a new browser, developed by Marc Andreesen and Eric Bina, undergraduate students at the University of

Illinois at the National Center for Supercomputing Applications (NCSA) in Champaign, Illinois. It was called Mosaic, and it soon became almost synonymous with the Web itself. When Mosaic was licensed commercially, Web browsing, or what is popularly called "surfing," became available to a wider group, and traffic on the World Wide Web took off.

The next year, Andreesen and former Stanford University professor Jim Clark formed Netscape and, by the end of that year, released the Netscape Navigator. In the fall of 1994, the Mosaic browser accounted for 60 percent of all traffic on the World Wide Web. By the spring of 1995, Mosaic accounted for 5 percent of the traffic and Netscape accounted for 75 percent of all Web visitors.

Today, many different browsers are available. The two most popular ones are Microsoft Internet Explorer and Netscape Communicator. Through competition and continuous upgrades, these two companies have made it virtually impossible for any other browsers to get a toehold. Nevertheless, they are undoubtedly the best and make Web surfing easy and fast. We will examine both of these browsers later in this chapter.

With the explosion of information available on the Internet, the need for a standard location system became apparent. You'll see these unique addresses referred to as URLs—Uniform Resource Locators. The locations, or addresses for Web sites are URLs. The URL for CareerPath, for example, is

```
http://www.careerpath.com
```

The elements of a URL are these:

http Stands for *hypertext transfer protocol*—the type of application used to access the information. Note that these days, most browsers allow you to leave off the *http://* part when typing addresses.

www Stands for *World Wide Web*.

careerpath.com The domain name of the server you want to access.

Getting on the World Wide Web

You will need a few tools to get started on the World Wide Web. To begin with, you must choose a service that gets you access to the Internet. Then, you need software that will allow you to browse the pages on the World Wide Web. Finally, you need to use a search engine to find the specific information you are seeking. This section will discuss each of these tools.

Commercial Internet Service Providers

An Internet service provider (ISP) is a service that provides you access to the Internet. Commercial ISPs charge a monthly fee to furnish you with a host of services and various means of using the World Wide Web. Because many people gain access to the World Wide Web through commercial services, we'll take a step-by-step look at the largest of these, America Online. We are using this service as an example, but bear in mind that there are many other Internet service providers from which to choose. You may decide to use a large national ISP or a small local one.

The ISP you choose has a lot to do with the kind of service you want. If you go with a national company, you get technical support at all hours, unlike local ISPs with usually very limited tech support availability. Another irksome problem with local ISPs is that they don't generally allow you to stay online without getting disconnected after being idle for a short period of time. However, costs for local ISPs are often lower than the average $20 per month for large ISPs, and they commonly offer more personal service than the large ones.

The number of local ISPs available to you varies with the region in which you live. Large metropolitan areas often have many of these, and competition drives the monthly service fees down. If you live in a small town, you might have to use an ISP outside your local dialing range, thus incurring more expenses than the monthly service charge. Check your Yellow Pages for a list of ISPs in your area code.

The largest national ISPs provide access in languages other than English and in countries other than the United States. Countries outside the United States use their own ISPs as well. For example, check out this list of service providers that are available in Canada:

A+ Internet Services, Inc.
A+Net
AT&T
Bleu Avocado
Connect America
DomainMart
Econo-Web
Fiberlink Communications Corp.
FreeInternetAccess
GalaxyNet-USA
Getheweb
IBM Internet Connection Services
Infinity Internet Services

Inter-Tech
jjj.net
MediaLinx Interactive, Limited Partnership
NETlimited
PCstarnet
T1 America, Inc.
U.S. Web Institute
Unilat Systems and Technology
UUNET Technologies

The Most Common ISPs

There are many national ISPs. They vary in size and service. Internet.com provides a huge list of ISPs organized by country, area code, or country code. For more information on ISPs, go to their site at `http://thelist.internet.com`.

The following is a list of some of the most common national ISPs:

Net4B
`www.net4b.com/`

Offers a personal Web page at www.yourname.com with no setup fee and e-mail at YourEmail@yourname.com. They also provide unlimited e-mail accounts for your business.

ConnectAmerica
`www.connectamerica.com/`

Provides co-locations, secure servers, Web site design and implementation, plus LAN/WAN consulting, International New ISP Setups, and ISP consulting. They give a break on fees to seniors, although their regular access fees are about the same as other major providers.

Earthlink
`www.earthlink.com`

Offers Click-n-Build Web page construction with 6MB of Web space to build it. Earthlink has joined with Sprint, the long-distance carrier. By bundling Earthlink Sprint TotalAccess Internet service and Sprint long-distance service, they provide price breaks on both long-distance and Internet access.

The Largest ISPs

Let's look at four of the largest national ISPs.

Prodigy

`www.prodigy.com`

Prodigy Internet provides direct access to the Internet in 600 cities nation-wide. The information at their site is organized into channels for easy navigation. They boast of fast connections and page downloads, plus the absence of pop-up ads, a nuisance for frequent Web surfers. Prodigy charges $2 additional per month for up to five additional mailboxes. They use Internet Explorer 5.0 as their browser. Prodigy offers two other services besides Prodigy Internet. Prodigy Classic, first introduced in 1990, pioneered online shopping. Features included live chat, newsgroups, and bulletin boards. Prodigy Business Solutions offers Web hosting and Internet provider services to small and medium-sized businesses. Prodigy also has a complete version in Spanish.

Figure 2.1

Prodigy's home page.

AT&T WorldNet

`www.att.net`

AT&T WorldNet Service provides six e-mail IDs per account, up to thirty free megabytes of personal Web space, plus the usual instant messaging, chat, and newsgroup features.

Figure 2.2

AT&T WorldNet home page.

CompuServe

www.compuserve.com

CompuServe, an Internet pioneer founded in 1969, is now a subsidiary of AOL. CompuServe's strength is its industry-renowned Forum areas—over 700 of them. It also provides the usual news service and searchable databases.

Figure 2.3

CompuServe's home page.

The Microsoft Network (MSN)

www.msn.com

This is Microsoft's entry in the ISP wars. Among MSN's features is a community directory where you can search for friends and acquaintances. Their E-mail Finder allows you to search for e-mail addresses. The Intellisense™ feature provides automated features like AutoSearch, which permits you to quickly find pages you want. Content advisor sets limits on children's access. MSN uses Outlook Express for e-mail. It contains the Windows radio toolbar that allows you to tune in radio stations while you work. It offers personalization of its home page, allowing users to read their own horoscopes, track their stocks, check their local weather, and so on.

Figure 2.4

MSN's home page.

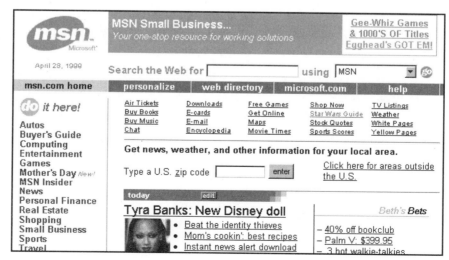

The Browsers

To "browse the web," you need a service provider and a software package. If you subscribe to a commercial online service, you can access the World Wide Web with the browser the service provides. Browsers contain many features that enable painless, point-and-click searching. These features are pretty much similar between the two main browsers, Internet Explorer and Netscape. Let's look at these two major full-service Internet browser software packages:

✔ **Netscape Communicator 4.5**   This is the major enhancement to Netscape's Communicator that enables faster and more efficient browsing, e-mail, and calendar and information-management features. It combines the browser Netscape Navigator with other Internet tools: Netscape Messenger, their e-mail tool; Netscape Composer, a Web-based word processor; Netscape AOL Instant Messenger, an e-mail feature that allows real-time conversation; and Netscape Calendar. Netscape Communicator 4.5 offers "Smart Browsing," an innovation that can "recommend" other Web sites and relevant information that might appeal to you based on the sites you visit regularly. This feature can also filter out pages with content you deem to be inappropriate. "What's Related," available on Communicator 4.06 and 4.5, helps you get ideas of where else to search on the Web for information that you are seeking. For more information or to download this browser, contact their site at **www.netscape.com**.

✔ **Internet Explorer 5.0**   Microsoft's browser has added the Intellisense feature that automates many of the functions available on IE. The Search Assistant has been improved and allows you to select a search engine and the type of search you want to use. AutoComplete provides a drop-down list of sites you have already visited. AutoCorrect automatically corrects typos you might have made in your search phrase that prevent you from getting to the site you want. AutoSearch helps you find the pages you want. IE also contains the Windows Radio Toolbar, so that you can listen to the radio online while you work. Outlook Express is the e-mail tool that comes with Explorer. You can download Internet Explorer 5.0 at **www.microsoft.com**.

With each of these browsers, you load the software on your computer. Your screen will show some of the available Internet service providers and charge information. You can enter your credit card number and be on the Web.

Search Engines

Today, the World Wide Web is a mass of information. How do you find what you want in this maze?

The popular phrase *search engine* refers to electronic directories on the Web that search for documents, pages, or sites based on keywords. The miracle of the Web is that you simply have to point and click to go to any of the sites ("hits") that the search engine gives you. Here are some examples of the search engines that are out there.

AltaVista

`altavista.com`

This search engine (see figure 2.5) was developed by Digital Equipment Corporation, and is now run by Compaq. AltaVista, which has been online since December 1995, is one of the largest of the search engines. It indexes an incredible 150 million Web pages!

Figure 2.5

AltaVista home page, with the keywords "disney jobs" entered.

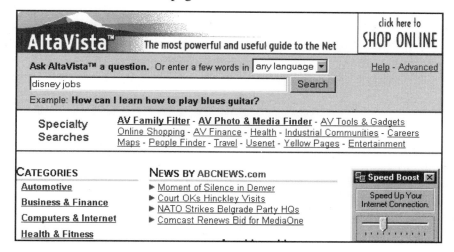

Figure 2.6

AltaVista results screen showing the first hit from your search.

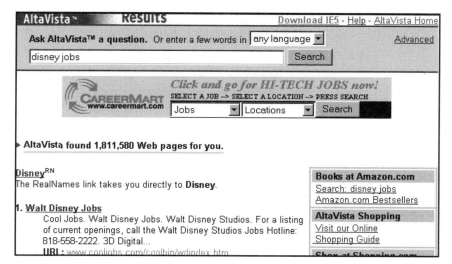

Lycos

`www.lycos.com`

Lycos is one of the oldest search engines (see figure 2.7). Its name comes from *lycosidae*, Latin for "wolf spider," a family of wandering ground spiders. It's one of the smaller indexes, but its Lycos Community Guides is an impressive directory of Web sites. You can enter a search string at the main box or narrow your search specifications by controlling several different fields in the search options area. Lycos searches yield comprehensive results (see figure 2.8).

Figure 2.7

Lycos' home page with the keywords "medical secretary job" entered.

Figure 2.8

Lycos' results screen, showing the first hit from your search.

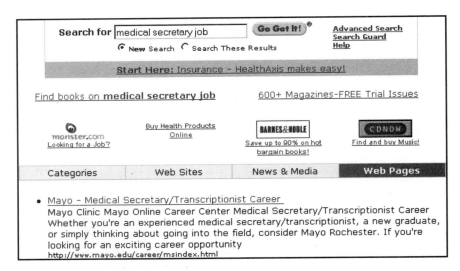

Ask Jeeves

`www.aj.com`

Ask Jeeves is a human-powered search service. It directs you to frame your queries in the form of commonly phrased questions. For example: "Where can I find an accounting job?" If Ask Jeeves can't answer your question from its own index, it brings you pages from other search engines. The results from Ask Jeeves also appear on AltaVista.

Figure 2.9
The Ask Jeeves home page with accounting jobs query.

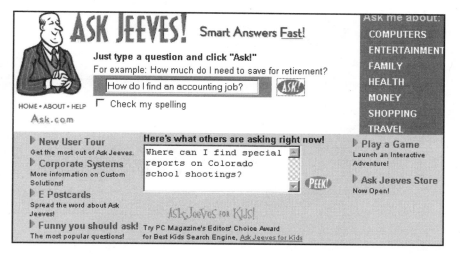

Figure 2.10
Ask Jeeves' results page.

Excite

`www.excite.com`

Excite has a full-text database of fifty-five million pages. It is a medium-sized index and contains Excite NewsTracker, a news search service. Excite is the search engine used by AOL. AOL calls its search engine AOL NetFind.

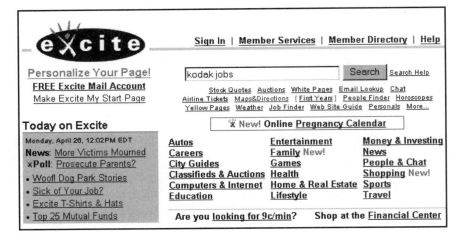

Figure 2.11

The Excite home page with "kodak jobs" entered.

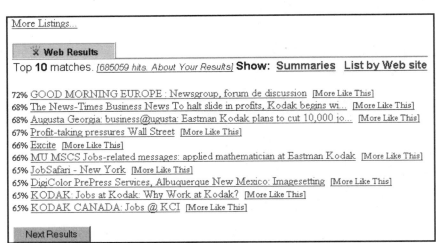

Figure 2.12

Excite's search results page.

GoTo

`www.goto.com`

GoTo is fast and very easy. Their home page is uncluttered, and the results page is often ordered in such a way that you don't have to scroll far for results. GoTo sells listings so that a company can get placed higher on the list of results. GoTo asserts that this improves relevancy, a key necessity for good search results.

Figure 2.13

GoTo's home page with "civil engineer jobs" entered.

Figure 2.14

GoTo's results page.

HotBot

www.hotbot.com

> HotBot has a very large index and power search features. Lycos runs HotBot as a separate service.

Figure 2.15

HotBot's home page with "dental assistant jobs" entered.

Figure 2.16

HotBot's results page.

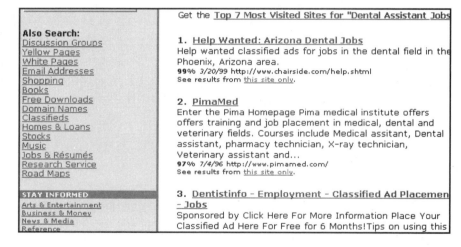

InfoSeek Guide

`http://guide.infoseek.com`

InfoSeek allows very detailed search requests. InfoSeek has a database of full text of about forty-five million pages. It offers complete displays of search results including the URL, the title of the Web page, the size of the file, and a summary.

Figure 2.17
Infoseek's home page with "journalism jobs" entered.

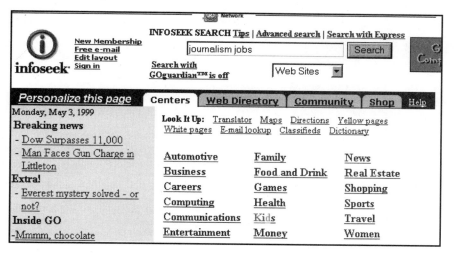

Figure 2.18
Infoseek's results page.

RESULTS 1 - 10 of 18,280,936 total results, grouped by site

Hide summaries | Sort by date | Ungroup results | Next 10

National Diversity Newspaper Job Bank
Comprehensive Internet listings of business-side and newsroom openings dedicated to increasing diversity in the newspaper industry.
93% **Date: 21 Jul 1998**, Size 1.0K, http://www.newsjobs.com/
Find similar pages

How to Find an Online Journalism Job on the Web
by Anne Hart, M.A. wfst@cts.com Online journalism is where all the journalism graduates are heading. It's the journalist's place to be. So how do you get a job in journalism on the Web? Head for the concept of publishing supported by advertising on the Web. It's a key theme in online ...
88% **Date: 10 Oct 1998**, Size 5.9K,
http://careermag.com/newsarts/jobsearch/1042.html
Find similar pages

K-State Journalism Jobs
We're converting this site to a combined job-openings site with our partners in K-State's A.Q. Miller School of Journalism and Mass Communications -- advertising, public relations, radio and television

Buy the book

Gifts for Mom in Our Gift Center
Win A Camera!
Mother's Day Contest
Spring Cleaning Books!

Classifieds
Jobs
Job

Northern Light
www.northernlight.com

Northern Light is the second-largest search engine, indexing some 125 million pages. In addition to its basic search feature, it also provides "special collection" documents from magazines, news services, and databases. Northern Light charges a fee to view these documents. Results of Northern Light searches are extensive.

Figure 2.19

Northern Light's home page with "architect jobs" entered.

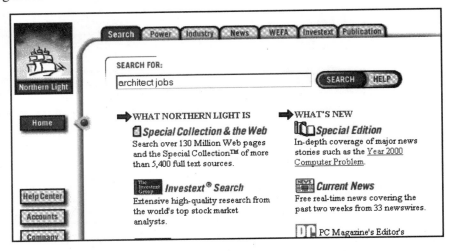

Figure 2.20

Northern Light's search results.

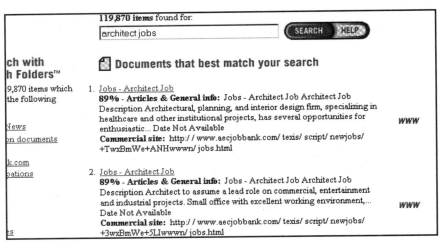

As this book goes to press, a newcomer to the search engine competition, Norway-based **fast search** (`www.alltheweb.com/`) has announced an index of 200 million pages, making it the largest of the search engines. With the incredible growth on the World Wide Web, it's impossible to say who will win the size contest among search engines!

We've shown you only a few of the several hundred search engines available on the World Wide Web. For a comprehensive, linked list of some of the better-known ones, go to one of the following two URLs: `www.home.co.il/search.html` or `www.tnl-online.com/infolink/topsrch1.html`.

The Multimedia Web

Why has the World Wide Web become the major way to visit the Internet? Think of a page of text that has a footnote. Imagine that just by pointing at the footnote, whatever is referenced in the footnote magically appears on the next page. Imagine that the second page also has a footnote. You could point at it and magically see what it referenced on the next page. This is the magic of the World Wide Web. It's called "point and click." Click on any highlighted text, and your Web browser magically takes you to that site.

The second reason is that the Web provides you multimedia. We've mentioned sound as an advantage of the World Wide Web. Sound on the Internet used to involve a three-step process: Download an audio file, decompress it, then play it. In 1994, former Microsoft vice president Rob Glaser developed software that received and decoded sound via modem. This software is called RealAudio. On the Web, RealAudio enables sound to play instantly while you're online, rather than you having to wait through a download and decompression. Since 1995, Glaser's RealNetwork, based in Seattle, has developed software products and services that enable users of personal computers and other digital devices to send and receive real-time audio and video media.

Real-time media is known as *streaming media.* Instead of having to download an audio or video file, streaming media files download as you use them. Today, you can capture real-time, or streaming, media online with a variety of tools. RealNetwork's RealPlayer and Microsoft Media Player, a multimedia streaming program, allow you to play and hear the more than 10,000 radio stations now broadcast over the Internet.

Video over the Internet has become so advanced that you can see live programs of near-broadcast quality right on your monitor. Even just a couple years ago, the quality of the video on the Internet was similar to surveillance video cameras. You can use either RealVideo or Media Player to view video clips from the major network news sites online. Streaming Internet broadcasting promises to make the Internet a player in the mass-media market. Now, you don't just read the top stories of the day on CNN; you actually view and hear them, just as you would on television.

You can download Windows Media Player for free at the Microsoft site: **www.microsoft.com**. You can download RealPlayer G2 with basic features for free at **www.real.com/products/index.html**.

It's also possible to use the Internet for your telephone calls—real-time conversation. The ability to place audio calls over the Internet is known as Internet Telephony (also known as Computer Telephony, Voice-over-IP, and VoIP). Some of the Internet telephone software programs available are

IDT's Net2Phone, Vocaltec Internet Phone, NetMeeting, Delta Three Internet Phone Lite, WebPhone, and Cooltalk. You and the person you want to talk with must have the same brand of software. With that in place, you can talk live to anyone anywhere in the world for no cost other than your service provider's regular access charge.

Sound, video, even real-time telephone conversations. The World Wide Web is truly a multimedia experience!

Accessing the World Wide Web Through America Online

To give you an idea of how ISPs work, we will show you a walk-through of the most common ISP, America Online. Keep in mind that procedures, features, and services for other ISPs will vary.

America Online (AOL) provides a CD-ROM for your first sign-on. It comes with a preassigned numerical userid and alpha password like this:

```
48-6284-5667

CUBS-CURIAE
```

Before you log on, you will be asked for your userid and password, and then you will be led through a series of questions, such as the baud rate of your modem, and personal information, such as your name, address, phone number, and credit card information. You will also be asked to enter a new password of your choosing, along with the name you want to use online. Your userid will then look like this:

```
name@aol.com
```

Generally, AOL provides a CD-ROM for several hours—as many as 50 or even 100—of free service as a preview. You can often find these CDs free in computer magazines. (We found ours in *PC World* magazine.)

For your first logon, the CD-ROM packet contains the following instructions:

1. Insert the AOL CD-ROM in your CD-ROM drive. The install program should start automatically. If it does not, go to step 2.

2. Click Start, then select Run. At the prompt, type **D:/SETUP** (or **E:/SETUP,** depending on which drive the CD is in) and press Enter.

3. When the installation is complete, click the America Online icon, and you're ready to go!

The first screen shows your name and a prompt for your personal password. Type your password. (For security reasons, your password does not show on the screen. Notice that asterisks are displayed instead.) From this point on, each time you log on, your screen will look like the one shown in figure 2.21.

Figure 2.21

The AOL logon screen.

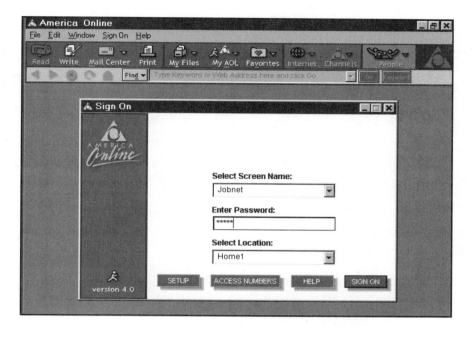

After you enter your password, you will see a dial-up screen that tells you that your modem is connecting you to AOL. Next comes a Welcome screen (see figure 2.22).

Figure 2.22

AOL's Welcome screen.

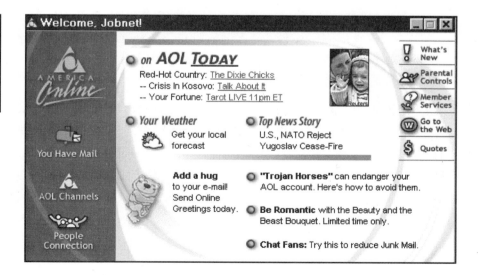

If your system has a sound card, you will also hear a voice say, "Welcome!" The same voice will also inform you if you have mail.

Notice that there is a toolbar at the top of this screen that contains several different icons. One of these icons is a globe. If you put your cursor there, the message "Access to the Web and other Internet features" is displayed. Click the icon, and it opens a drop-down box with a list of choices.

Figure 2.23

AOL's Web access drop-down box.

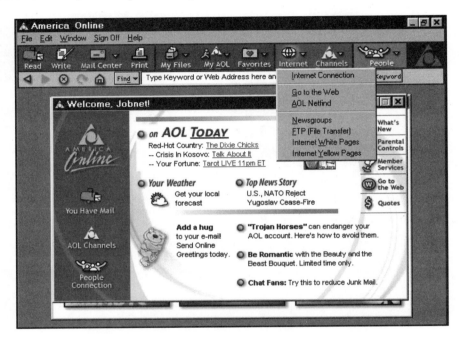

AOL uses Microsoft's Internet Explorer as its browser. However, Netscape Navigator is also available through AOL. If you plan to use Netscape Navigator, you will need to download it following very simple onscreen instructions. In the box at the top of the screen where it says Type Keyword or Web Address here and click Go, type the keyword Netscape. It will take you instantly to the download instructions for Netscape Navigator.

Once you have clicked Go to the Web, you will be at the Welcome to AOL.COM page. This is AOL's starting page for Web exploration.

Figure 2.24

AOL.COM— America Online's starting page for Web exploration.

Notice that below the toolbar is a long white box. If you know the URL (address) for a particular Web site, you can type it in here. Place your cursor at the start of the line and type the address, such as **www.microsoft.com**, and press Enter. This will take you directly to the site.

To search the Web for the information you want, you can type a keyword in the space next to where it says Search the Web Here. This screen also contains a large list of shortcuts that require only a mouse click for instant access to a site. We did a search using the keywords "account executive jobs."

Figure 2.25

Keyword search.

We clicked on Search and retrieved the screen shown in figure 2.26.

Figure 2.26	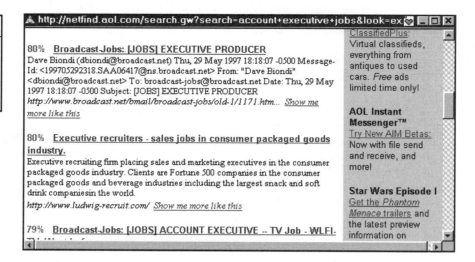
The search results screen.	

From the list of the first ten results, we selected number 1, Broadcast-Jobs. The percentage at the beginning of each item tells what chance the item has of exactly meeting the criteria you were searching for. That selection returned the screen shown in figure 2.27, a job in Minnesota.

Figure 2.27	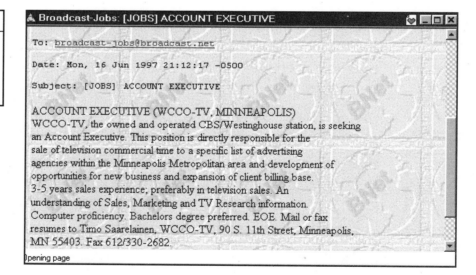
A job opening.	

We've shown you how to use AOL's keyword feature to get to a jobs area. You can also use AOL Workplace to find a job. From the AOL toolbar, select Channels. From the drop-down menu, select WorkPlace. You will arrive at AOL's extensive job search and career area.

Figure 2.28

AOL's WorkPlace.

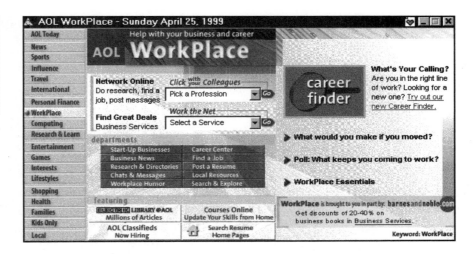

Click on Find a Job, and you will be taken to a screen that gives you many alternatives for your job search (see figure 2.29).

Figure 2.29

The Find a Job window.

One option at this screen is to go to Monster.com, a very large database of jobs and resumes. Or, you can choose from a list of what AOL calls the "Best Job Listing Sites on the Web." From this list, we selected CareerMart to find a nursing job on AOL.

We first accessed CareerMart's home page.

Figure 2.30

CareerMart's home page.

Then, we clicked on Job Search and were presented with the CareerMart search page, where we selected nursing jobs in Texas.

Figure 2.31

The search page with nursing jobs in Texas selected.

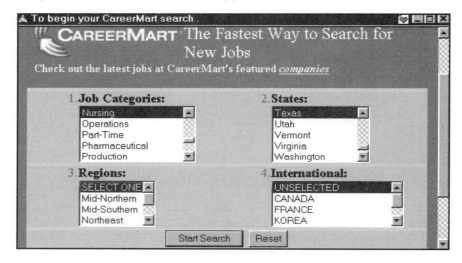

When we clicked the Start Search button, we were presented with the search results shown in figure 2.32.

Figure 2.32

The search results page.

Your CareerMart Search Results:

(Click anywhere on the appropriate row to view full job details)

State/Country	Company	Job Category	Job Title
TX	Integrated Health Services, Inc.	Nursing	CNA; LVN
TX	Integrated Health Services, Inc.	Nursing	CNAs; LVNs - Keller location
TX	Integrated Health Services, Inc.	Nursing	LVNs; CNAs - Dallas location
TX	Integrated Health Services, Inc.	Nursing	LVNs/CNAs
TX	Integrated Health Services, Inc.	Nursing	LVNs/CNAs at Plano

We clicked on the first option and retrieved the job shown in figure 2.33.

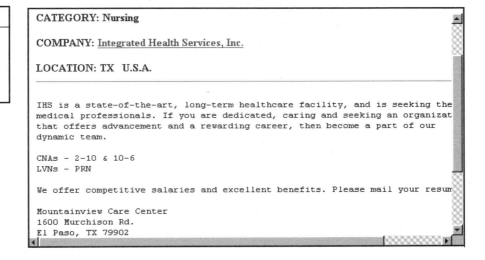

Figure 2.33

A job opening.

CATEGORY: **Nursing**

COMPANY: <u>Integrated Health Services, Inc.</u>

LOCATION: TX U.S.A.

```
IHS is a state-of-the-art, long-term healthcare facility, and is seeking the
medical professionals. If you are dedicated, caring and seeking an organizat
that offers advancement and a rewarding career, then become a part of our
dynamic team.

CNAs - 2-10 & 10-6
LVNs - PRN

We offer competitive salaries and excellent benefits. Please mail your resum

Mountainview Care Center
1600 Murchison Rd.
El Paso, TX 79902
```

At AOL WorkPlace, you can also:

✔ Post a resume

✔ Search for local employment

✔ Join an online Career Fair

✔ Calculate your salary (to compare the cost of living in hundreds of U.S. and international cities)

✔ Read job descriptions

AOL's WorkPlace feature is also accessible just by typing the keywords Find a Job.

America Online E-Mail

AOL has an easy-to-use e-mail system. When you first log on to AOL, you will see (and hear, if you have a sound card installed) a message telling you whether you have mail. Just click the mailbox icon and you will retrieve your new mail.

On the toolbar at the top of the AOL Welcome screen is an icon that says Write. To compose an e-mail message in AOL, just click on Write. You will get the screen shown in figure 2.34.

Figure 2.34

Write Mail screen.

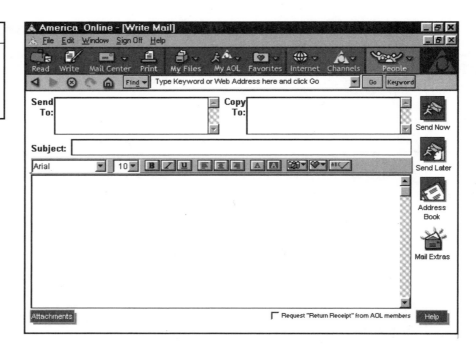

Simply type the information in the Send To, Copy To, and Subject fields, then type your message in the body.

Figure 2.35

An e-mail message using AOL's Write function.

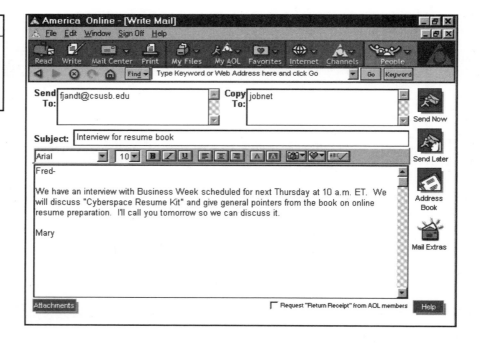

Click the Send Now icon and your message is on its way.

AOL's e-mail program also allows you to change font style, size and color, background color, and alignment. The program has a spell-check feature. You can even insert a picture or a favorite URL into the message. E-mailing on AOL is very easy.

Remember that commercial service providers differ in the amount and range of Internet services they deliver to you. Before you subscribe to any service, evaluate your needs and what the services can provide—and at what cost.

The Internet started to change the way job searches are conducted, and the ease of using the World Wide Web has made the change complete. You can use the ISPs and search engines we've described in this chapter to find job listings and career information on the Internet. In the next chapter, we identify and describe some of the major sites for job listings.

Chapter 3

Getting Job Information from Corporate Sites and Job Boards

Among the advertisements for American Express, Anheuser-Busch, Frito-Lay, and PepsiCo at the 1999 Super Bowl was a thirty-second ad for the two-year-old company called HotJobs.com. In the ad, a bored security guard clicks onto the job listings Web site and fantasizes about more prestigious careers. HotJobs.com isn't the only job listings Web site to advertise nationally. So have Monster.com and Careerpath. Job search on the Internet has come of age.

In this chapter you'll read about corporate Web sites and job boards. Today's typical Internet job seekers prepare resumes and post them on their personal home pages. Then they study the vacancies on job boards and post their resumes there. And they visit the Web sites of companies they are interested in.

Corporate Web Sites

Many companies and public organizations have established their own Web sites. And many of these organizations now include their vacancy announcements on their home pages.

You'll notice that many companies are putting their Web addresses in their newspaper display ads. Their home page typically has more information about the organization—its mission statement, product descriptions, recent press releases, and more. The typical vacancy announcement on an organization's home page has more detail than a classified ad would have.

If you have a particular employer in mind, use one of the Web search engines to search for that company's home page. (You read about using search engines in chapter 2, "Going Online.") Or use the Dun & Bradstreet service Companies Online located at **www.companiesonline.com/**, which has information on over 100,000 public and private companies, including links to their home pages.

You might want to visit some sample company Web pages. Let's say you have an interest in working for the global telecommunications giant Nortel Networks based in Toronto. First, you go to its home page at **www.nortelnetworks.com/**.

Figure 3.1
Note the link to "Careers" on the Nortel Networks home page.

Figure 3.2
The Nortel Careers page.

Clicking on Careers on the Nortel Networks home page takes you to its career information page with links to opportunities in North America, Europe, the Caribbean & Latin America, and Asia/Pacific, and links to more information about the company.

Clicking on North America on the Nortel Careers page gives you a window with three selections: students and recent graduates, professionals, and Bay Network jobs. Clicking on Professionals takes you to Nortel's job search engine where you can search by job category and by location. If you select Toronto, a list of current Nortel vacancies in the Toronto area appears. Clicking on one of these items takes you to the complete job vacancy announcement.

Figure 3.3

A vacancy announcement at Nortel.

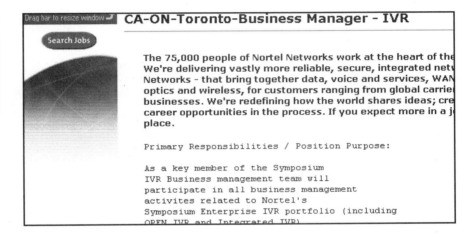

Vacancy announcements on a company's own home page contain more detailed information than they might if published in newspaper ads. An e-mail address and fax number, as well as a postal address, are provided. Notice that Nortel is one of those companies that scans all resumes into their job database. If you sent them a resume, you'd want to be sure it was *scannable*. See chapter 7 for more information about converting your traditional resume to a scannable resume.

Here's another example. The many companies, divisions, and departments that make up the Disney organization share their own careers site: `disneycareers.com`.

Figure 3.4

The Disney careers site.

Clicking on Career Search takes you to a search engine of Disney jobs. You can select a career field, geographical location, and other keywords.

If you select Creative on the Disney search page, a list of available positions appears. Clicking on one of the positions gives you the complete job vacancy announcement. The Disney job announcement gives you the option of submitting your resume online.

Figure 3.5

A Disney job announcement.

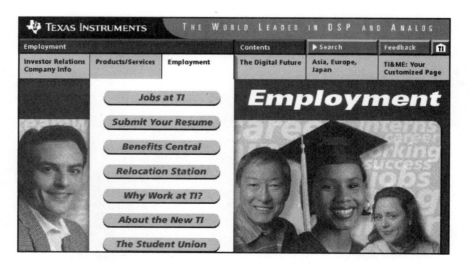

The Walt Disney Company and Affiliated Companies

Walt Disney Imagineering - Creative

Title
    Account Manager, Participant Services
Location
    Glendale, CA 91221, USA
Description
    Interacts with project teams, park operators, Corporate Alliances and sponsors to develop presence for theme park and resort environments. Prepares proposals for participant identity in prospective locations. Manages participant graphics projects by working with the sponsors and project teams to understand communication needs developing creative/brand briefs directing Graphics personnel, reviewing work with sponsors and managing

The Texas Instruments Web site at **www.ti.com/** links you to its Employment page, which lists openings at all of its major locations. It also includes a short diagnostic test, called "Fit Check," to help job seekers figure out whether their "wants and needs" mesh with those of TI. The Texas Instruments Employment page allows you to submit your resume by e-mail or by entering information into a form, which is directly imported into TI's resume database.

Figure 3.6

The Texas Instruments Employment page.

If you don't have a particular employer in mind, but you want to review corporate home pages, go to Yahoo at **www.yahoo.com/**. Select Business & Economy. Then select Companies and then the type of company. You'll be able to go directly to the company home page. As we've said, some will have their job opportunities posted there. BizWeb, located at **www.bizweb.com/**, has a similar, but smaller, directory.

Recruiting-links.com, located at **www.recruiting-links.com**, allows you to search jobs posted on employers' own sites that meet the job seeker's location, industry, and job requirements.

Local and state governments have their own home pages with job postings just like business organizations. The State of California official Web site has a page with links to California cities' and other states' employment Web sites. It is located at **www.ca.gov/s/working/employ.html**.

Popular Job Boards

In this section you'll read about six popular job boards. We're not saying these are the best for you—just the most popular at the moment.

America's Job Bank
www.ajb.dni.us

America's Job Bank (AJB) is a joint effort of the U.S. Department of Labor and the more than 1,800 public employment service offices of each state. Because America's Job Bank is run by the Department of Labor in conjunction with the Employment Service offices, neither the job seeker or the employer is charged a fee. All employers who register with America's Job Bank are verified as legitimate.

<table>
<tr><td>

Figure 3.7

At America's Job Bank's home page, click on Job Seekers.

</td><td>

</td></tr>
</table>

In 1979 the public employment service offices began cooperating with each other to exchange information on job listings. America's Job Bank became the computerized network that made it possible for the public to have access to one of the largest listings of available jobs from all over the United States.

Most of the job opportunities listed on America's Job Bank come from the private sector and are for full-time positions. Listed jobs come from a broad cross section of qualifications, wages, and types of work.

You can search the America's Job Bank job database by using a menu, keywords, and military code.

A Menu Search starts with twenty-two broad occupational areas and provides the capability to refine the search to a more specific predefined occupational group. There are also several optional search criteria, including job location, jobs entered during a specific time period, education and experience, job duration, and minimum salary required.

A Keyword Search provides the capability to choose skill words that are important for the position being sought. The words may be given equal weight or may be prioritized. The search will retrieve all jobs containing the words that appear in the Job Title, the Certificates/Licenses Required, or the Type of Education Required sections of the job listing. The same additional criteria used in the Menu Search are also available in the Keyword Search.

If you were looking for work as an accountant in Minnesota, you would enter the keyword "accountant" and select Minnesota from the drop-down list box. You would then be presented with a list of accounting-related positions in Minnesota, arranged alphabetically by city.

A Military Code Search allows job seekers who have a military background to enter their Military Occupational Code and have the system search for any equivalent civilian jobs that are open. The same additional criteria used in the Menu Search are also available in the Military Code Search.

In addition to the job search function, AJB offers links to state job sites, employer sites, and private agencies. Each of the states runs its own job-search site. Many use the same job searches as AJB; some use searches developed in-state. The list of job openings at the state level is not always the same as the orders submitted to AJB, and therefore if you are interested in working in only one specific state, you may benefit by doing your search at the state level. However, there are some orders that are entered nationally that do not appear on the state file, so a search of the national file will ensure that you don't miss any possible jobs.

Figure 3.8

At AJB's Job Seeker Services page, click on Keyword.

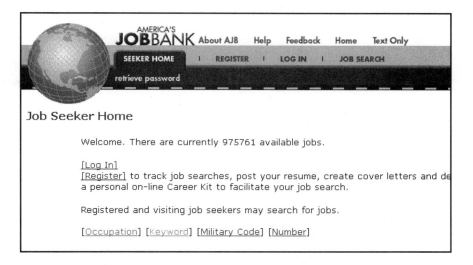

Figure 3.9

America's Job Bank Keyword Search page.

You can also post your resume at America's Job Bank. First, you register on a fill-in-the-blank online form, where you provide such basic information as your name, address, and phone number. You then choose your own username and password, which you'll use in subsequent searches.

After you have completed your registration, you can begin entering your resume into AJB's Resume Builder form. When you submit it, your resume will be posted to America's Talent Bank, the sister service to America's Job Bank. You can modify your resume anytime. Resumes stay active for sixty days, but you also have the option of extending your active period at will. Only employers who have registered with America's Job Bank and have been issued a password can access your resume.

As a registered user, you are able to conduct custom job searches by saving your specific search patterns so that you can call them up for subsequent searches. You can also create cover letters to accompany your electronic resume. You can use AJB's online form, or you can incorporate your own cover letter into the form.

Canada's Job Bank

`jb-ge.hrdc-drhc.gc.ca/index.html`

The Canadian equivalent of America's Job Bank is Job Bank on the Internet, an electronic listing of jobs, work, or business opportunities phoned in to Human Resource Centres of Canada by employers around the country. It is available at no cost to employers and job seekers.

CareerPath.com

`www.careerpath.com`

CareerPath.com was co-founded in October 1995 by six major newspapers: the *Boston Globe,* the *Chicago Tribune,* the *Los Angeles Times,* the *New York Times,* the *San Jose Mercury News,* and the *Washington Post.* The five parent companies of these newspapers—Knight-Ridder, Inc.; New York Times Co.; Times Mirror Co.; Tribune Co.; and The Washington Post Co.—financially backed CareerPath.com with an additional investment from Cox Interactive Media, Gannett Co., and Hearst Corp.

CareerPath.com's job listings come from the help-wanted ads of over eighty U.S. newspapers and from the Web sites of employers. There is no charge to job seekers. You can search the newspaper jobs database by geography, newspaper, job type, and keyword. You can search the employers' listing database by geography, employer, job type, and keyword.

If you register with the site, you can specify and store search criteria and complete a career profile that contains more information than appears in a traditional resume. Employers cannot see personal information identifying the job seeker until you review the job description and authorize CareerPath.com to forward the complete resume for consideration.

HotJobs.com

`www.hotjobs.com`

HotJobs.com, Ltd., was founded by Richard Johnson in 1997 and is head-quartered in New York. In 1995 Mr. Johnson created New Media Labs, a research and development firm, which developed the technology that enabled fourteen million Columbia House mail-order members to shop online. He oversaw the development of one of the first interactive job boards, which was used in-house by his firm's recruiters to manage their accounts on a real-time basis. By February 1996 the Web site was launched as a separate company, and HotJobs.com was established as the world's first truly interactive job board where companies could post job openings directly onto the World Wide Web.

HotJobs.com publishes a list of its member companies that can see the job seeker's resume. This makes it possible for the job seeker to control which of these companies can view the resume. HotJobs.com features a Personal Search Agent that finds the jobs you want and e-mails them directly to you.

HotJobs.com also features four forums, or message boards, that allow you to interact with fellow job seekers and HotJobs.com staff. The forums are titled Job Seekers, Salary & Compensation, Technical Support for Job Seekers, and Consulting.

Monster.com
www.monster.com

Monster.com, formerly the Monster Board, is a large, user-friendly online recruiting service that was established in October 1994 as the 455th registered site on the World Wide Web. For an earlier edition of this book, Mary spoke with Thom Guertin, who was then Associate Creative Director of Monster.com.

He told us that Monster.com was the brainchild of Jeff Taylor, who is now the Executive Vice President of Interactive Services for TMP Worldwide, Inc. Taylor was looking for another way to expand the recruiting reach of corporations and shorten their hiring cycle. Monster.com started as a big idea and turned into a "monster idea" in no time flat. Monster.com tries to make the job search/hiring process less stressful and more fun for all involved. The friendly user interface, bold graphics, and unique name serve as differentiators online. Their in-house mantra is "functional, fast, and fun."

Monster.com became a premier career site on the World Wide Web. It is absolutely free to job seekers. Candidates can search and apply online for nearly 230,000 jobs in minutes. They can also submit their resumes to an international database, research potential employers, and read up on the latest career trends at no cost.

All Monster.com memberships for employers include the privilege of posting jobs in real-time, access to over one million resumes in the Monster.com database, candidate prescreening, and having a corporate profile posted on the site. Nonmembers can post jobs for viewing by Monster.com's five million–plus monthly visitors at a cost of $225 for one job for a sixty-day posting.

Figure 3.10 shows Monster.com's home page. If you select Search Jobs, you'll see a page that allows you to search by location, job category, and keyword (see figure 3.11).

Figure 3.10

Monster.com's home page.

Figure 3.11

You can select location and category, and search by keyword.

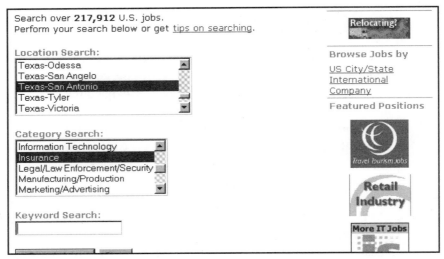

Our search using San Antonio, Texas for location and Insurance for category located three jobs. You are presented with a list of these jobs and can see the complete job description with application information by clicking on the position in which you're interested.

Figure 3.12

The list of jobs that our search found.

monster Search Jobs

| SEARCH JOBS | STORE RESUME | RESEARCH COMPANIES | MY MONSTER | VISIT OUR ZONES | JOIN CHAT | FOR EMPLOYERS |

All Jobs ▾   [Subsearch]

[New Search]

Jobs 1 to 3 of 3

Date	Location	Job Title	Company
Jun 3	US-TX-San Antonio	Agency Development Representative	Nationwide Insurance
May 27	US-TX-San Antonio	Cost estimator/Analyst	Environmental Staffing
May 4	US-TX-San Antonio	Sr. Life Health Underwriter	USAA

Search Jobs | Store Resume | Research Companies | My Monster | Zones | Chat | For Employers

Help | Privacy Commitment | Terms of Use | About Monster.com | Contact Us

Figure 3.13

More detailed information about one of the jobs.

US-TX-San Antonio-Agency Development Representative

Nationwide Insurance is a Fortune 200 company that's the 4th largest auto insurer in the U.S. If you're looking for an employer who rewards and encour forward thinking and motivation, we're the company for you. We are currently seeking enthusiastic candidates to join our team in San Antonio.

In this role, you will solicit appointments for agents, inform prospects of products, gather client information and provide customer service and office clerical support for agents. Qualifications include 2 years of related offic experience and high school studies. Bilingual English/Spanish, and sales ski are preferred. College students are encouraged to apply.

We offer a competitive salary, benefits, and unlimited earnings potential.

Please send your resume, with salary requirements, to:

Nationwide Insurance
Attn: Jay Moyer
8415 Datapoint Rd.

JobOptions
www.joboptions.com/

JobOptions is a premier online recruiting service that has been around a long time. In fact, it was the first online job and employment site, originally established as Adnet in 1990. The company was later known as E-Span, a service we profiled in earlier editions of this book. In 1998, E-Span was acquired by Gund Business Investments, who hired Michael Forrest, a seasoned veteran of online recruiting, as president. Forrest changed the name of the company to JobOptions and began a series of enhancements and changes that made JobOptions one of the easiest and most successful services on the Web. Today, JobOptions has more than 6,000 employers and 151,000 resumes in its database. Those employers post thousands of job openings.

Mary spoke with Michael Forrest about JobOptions and how it helps job seekers.

Mary: How is JobOptions different from other sites?

Michael: JobOptions is the only major site that offers a true Resume Builder...one that not only builds a professional resume from scratch (with a single-click choice of three formats) for online viewing, but also formats the resulting resume for printing and e-mail. And, we're the only major site to offer Real Resume Privacy. JobOptions also offers the deepest career planning content, with 2,019 links to proprietary and public information updated monthly to remove broken links and assure up-to-date information.

Mary: Explain how Real Resume Privacy protects the job seeker.

Michael: When the Privacy Option is invoked, the employer can conduct keyword searches of a private resume, except for the confidential parts. An employer then only views a profile that summarizes qualifications and specifies length of experience by industry; type of work sought (e.g., full-time, part-time, contract, telecommuting); level of experience (e.g., professional, managerial, senior management); education; skill sets; willingness to relocate; location (area code and state); and citizenship status. Upon finding a profile of interest, the employer sends a Private Job Announcement to the candidate via e-mail through JobOptions. If the candidate is interested in the position/company upon reading the e-mail, she or he can forward his or her resume by simply replying to the e-mail; if not, she or he simply deletes the e-mail.

Mary: How does your service work for passive job seekers?

Michael: JobOptions was designed, first and foremost, for the passive job seeker. Its Job Alert function employs Real Push Technology to e-mail postings of actual jobs to candidates that match their respective interests. Other sites merely send announcements, asking users to return to the site to view newly posted jobs that match their interests.

The JobOptions Resume Builder not only helps the candidates pull together a first-class resume for online viewing, print, and e-mail, but a resume that is easily "updatable." When you open your resume, it is presented to you on a separate page to be printed out cleanly.

JobOptions Resume Privacy function was designed with the passive job seeker in mind...to be the ultimate job and career networking tool that keeps the candidate in play, and assures privacy by keeping his or her name, contact information, and employer[s] names confidential.

Mary: What do you most want job seekers to know about your service?

Michael: Online job hunting is clearly an up-and-coming way of finding a job, and as a market leader, JobOptions ought to be one of those top-tier sites that they use [in their] efforts to find employment. But JobOptions, uniquely, is designed with total career management in mind...not just job hunting. We clearly have the best-of-class resume building features and allow for one-click formatting, e-mailing, and printing...all easily updated or edited whenever there's a need. But it's the unique Real Resume Privacy feature that allows candidates to "keep their hats in the ring" when new opportunities arise, even when not actively sought out, that is perhaps the most exciting.

Other Notable Job Banks

Here are a few more job banks that have become popular:

Careerfile

`careerfile.com`

Careerfile offers a unique service to job seekers and employers. Job seekers register a profile. Employers search the profiles for free and can request the complete resume for a small fee.

CareerMart

`www.careermart.com`

CareerMart is a service of BSA Advertising, the world's largest privately held, multioffice recruitment advertising agency.

CareerMosaic

`www.careermosaic.com`

CareerMosaic is a longstanding Internet employment site sponsored by Bernard Hodes Advertising. The CareerMosaic International Gateway provides links to CareerMosaic sites in ASEAN (the Association of South East Asian Nations—Singapore, Malaysia, Thailand, Brunei, and Indonesia), Australia, Canada, France, Hong Kong, Japan, Korea, New Zealand, Quebec, and the U.K. CareerMosaic also has industry-specific boards for accounting and finance, electronic engineering, health care, human resources, insurance, government, and marketing.

JobNET
www.JobNET.com

JobNET is an extensive online job service based in Exton, Pennsylvania. It has been around for a long time, appearing in July 1992 as a local DOS-based bulletin board system known as Online Opportunities. Today, it is the Philadelphia area's leading online recruitment service.

Executive Director Ward Christman says there are some 50,000 resumes in JobNET's database at any given time. There is no charge to job seekers for browsing jobs. You can either search jobs in JobNET's local area—Philadelphia, New Jersey, or Delaware—or you can search jobs around the world through links to other job-search sites. Figures 3.14 and 3.5 give you a look at their site.

Figure 3.14

JobNET's home page.

We clicked on Search Jobs and entered the keyword "retail manager" for jobs in the Pennsylvania, New Jersey, and Delaware area.

Figure 3.15

JobNET's Job Search page.

We were presented with the results page shown in figure 3.16.

Figure 3.16

JobNET's Search Results screen.

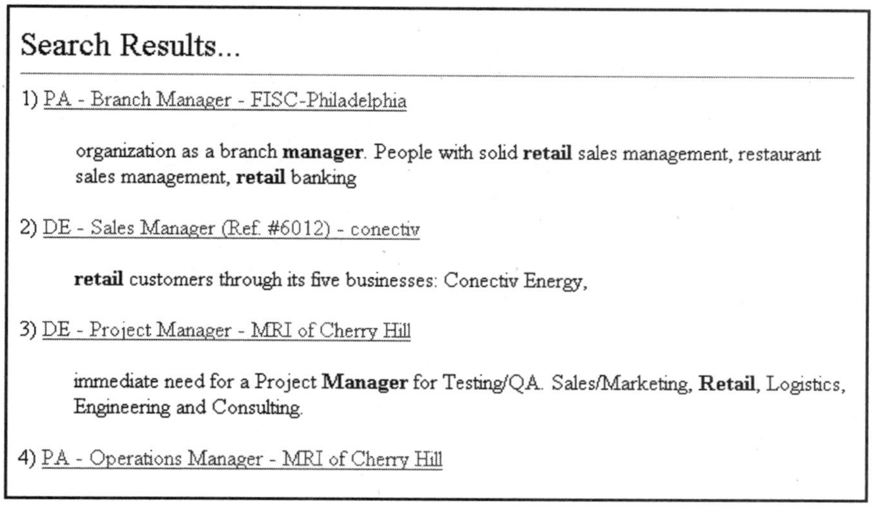

> ### Search Results...
>
> 1) PA - Branch Manager - FISC-Philadelphia
>
>   organization as a branch **manager**. People with solid **retail** sales management, restaurant sales management, **retail** banking
>
> 2) DE - Sales Manager (Ref. #6012) - conectiv
>
>   **retail** customers through its five businesses: Conectiv Energy,
>
> 3) DE - Project Manager - MRI of Cherry Hill
>
>   immediate need for a Project **Manager** for Testing/QA. Sales/Marketing, **Retail**, Logistics, Engineering and Consulting.
>
> 4) PA - Operations Manager - MRI of Cherry Hill

If you click on Hot Links to Hot Companies, you are taken to a list of major companies with job postings (see figure 3.17).

Figure 3.17

A partial list of JobNET employers.

Contract and Consulting Firms	Corporate Employers
Accountants on Call Ⓙ	Accu-Sort Systems Ⓙ Ⓡ
Accounting Solutions (Division of Placers) Ⓙ	Advanta Mortgage Ⓙ Ⓡ
Apex Financial Search Ⓙ	AIG Life Insurance Ⓙ Ⓡ
Bradley Burns, Inc. Ⓙ Ⓡ	AIG Marketing Ⓙ
CAP Gemini America Ⓙ	AJILON Ⓙ
CDI Corporation Ⓙ	Alfa Laval Separation Ⓙ Ⓡ
Centrell Group	American Express Financial Advisors Ⓙ
ChrisLan, Inc. Ⓙ	AnswerThink Consulting Group Ⓙ
CMIS Ⓙ	Assessment Systems, Inc. Ⓙ
Computer Horizons Ⓙ	ASTM Ⓙ
Computer Professionals, Inc. Ⓙ	Atlantic Employees Federal Credit Union Ⓙ
Contemporary Staffing Solutions Ⓙ	Atlas Communications Ⓙ
Davis Advertising Ⓙ	B & G Manufacturing Ⓙ
Decision Associates	BetzDearborn Ⓙ Ⓡ

Just click on the "J" button next to the company, and you will be presented with the current jobs available at that particular company (see figure 3.18).

Figure 3.18 *A list of job postings from Advanta Mortgage.*	**Search Results...** 1) PA - SENIOR INTERACTIVE/ WEB DESIGNER - ADVANTA CORPORATION 2) NY - Account Executive/Wholesale - Advanta Mortgage Corp. 3) NY - Account Executive/Wholesale - Advanta Mortgage Corp. 4) PA - Account Executive/Wholesale - Advanta Mortgage Corp. 5) FL - Account Executive/Wholesale - Advanta Mortgage Corp. 6) MD - Account Executive/Wholesale - Advanta Mortgage Corp. 7) NC - Account Executive/Wholesale - Advanta Mortgage Corp.

Jobs.com
www.jobs.com

Dallas-based Jobs.com was launched in 1992 and is one of the largest locally focused sites on the Internet. Jobs.com is used by some 2,000 companies nationwide.

In the summer of 1999, CBS Corp. announced plans to buy a 38 percent stake in Jobs.com in exchange for $62 million in advertising for five years. This makes it a site to watch for growth.

JOBTRAK
www.jobtrak.com

JOBTRAK is available to students and alumni of over 400 colleges and universities nationwide. It is used by over 10,000 college students and recent graduates, and over 170,000 employers.

The job vacancies are specifically targeted to college students and recent graduates. You can search JOBTRAK by keywords. It also provides skill-assessment tools, resume-writing tips, interviewing techniques, and salary-negotiation advice.

The site is free to users, but they must identify their college or university and enter a password. You must get that password from your college or university placement office or alumni office.

For more information on JOBTRAK, see chapter 11, "Advice for College Students."

Transition Assistance Online (TAO)
`taonline.com`

Owned by DI-USA, Inc. and Army Times Publishing Company (Gannett), TAO aids separating U.S. military service members and veterans in finding employment in the civilian sector and federal government, and helps companies find and hire these individuals. The site includes a resume database, job postings, company profiles, and job-hunting and resume-writing advice.

Even More Databases

The number of job and resume databases continues to grow. In the following list, we've provided even more you might want to review. Remember how quickly things can change on the Internet. More databases will appear; some will change their address; and others may disappear.

Find this database:	At this location:
+JOBS Canada	www.canada.plusjobs.com/
4Work	www.4work.com/
Accounting & Finance Jobs (CareerMosaic)	www.accountingjobs.com/
AJR (American Journalism Review)	www.ajr.newslink.org/ newjoblink.html
AmericanJobs.com (hi-tech)	www.americanjobs.com/
America's Employers	www.americasemployers.com
America's TV Job Network	www.tvjobnet.com
Asia.Net (bilingual English and Japanese, Chinese, and Korean)	www.asia-net.com/
Avalanche of Jobs (writers, editors, copywriters)	www.sunoasis.com/
Aviation Employee Placement Service	www.aeps.com/aeps/aepshm.html
Bankjobs.com	www.bankjobs.com/
Best Jobs U.S.A.	www.bestjobsusa.com/
The Business Job Finder	www.cob.ohio-state.edu/fin/ jobslist.htm
Byron Employment Australia	www.employment.byron.com.au/
Canadian Resume Centre	canres.com/
Career Avenue	careeravenue.com/
The Career Builder Network	careerbuilder.com/
CareerBuzz.com	careerbuzz.com/
CareerCast	www.careercast.com/
CareerCity (professional and technical jobs)	www.careercity.com/
Career.com (HEART Advertising Network, Inc.)	www.career.com/
CareerExchange	www.careerexchange.com/
Career Exposure	careerexposure.com/index2.html

(continues)

(continued)

Find this database:	At this location:
CareerMagazine	www.careermag.com/
Careers.com	www.careers.com/
CareerShop.com	www.careershop.com/
CareerSite.com	www.careersite.com/
CareerSpan	www.careerspan.com/
CareerWeb (professional, technical, and managerial)	www.careerweb.com/
Carolinas CareerWeb	carolinas.careerweb.com/
Cell Press Job Bank (biological sciences)	jobs.cell.com/
Chicagolands Virtual Job Resource (hi-tech)	staffsolutions.com/
The Chronicle of Higher Education (faculty and administrators)	chronicle.com/jobs/
Classified Ads from JOM (Minerals, Metals, & Materials Society)	www.tms.org/pubs/journals/JOM/classifieds.html
Classifieds2000 (Excite)	www.classifieds.2000.com/
College Grad Job Hunter	www.collegegrad.com/
Colorado Online Job Connection	www.jobsincolorado.com/
Commonwealth Jobsearch (hi-tech in Canada)	www.corpinfohub.com/cjs.htm
Communication Arts magazine	www.commarts.com/career/
ComputerJobs.com	www.computerjobs.com/
Computer People (IT jobs in Australia)	cpg.com.au/people/index.htm
Contract Employment Weekly Online (engineering, IT/IS, and technical)	www.ceweekly.wa.com/
ContractJobs.com (computer contractors, technical consultants, and engineering freelancers)	www.ContractJobs.com/
Corporate Gray Online (career transition for military personnel)	www.greentogray.com/
Developers.net (software developers)	www.deverlopers1.net/
dice.com (computer professionals)	dice.com/
Digital City (AOL)	www.digitalcity.com/
Direct Marketing World Job Center	www.dmworld.com/jobcenter/jobs.html
DiversiLink Employment Web Site (Society of Hispanic Professional Engineers)	www.diversilink.com/
Don Fitzpatrick Associates (television)	tvspy.com/
Education JobSite (K–12 teachers and administrators)	www.edjobsite.com/
EE Times Career Center (Career Mosaic) (electronic engineering)	www.careermosaic.com/cm/eet/
Employment Opportunities in Australia	www.employment.com.au/
EngineeringJobs.Com	www.engineeringjobs.com/
Engineerjobs.com	www.engineerjobs.com/

Find this database:	At this location:
Entry Level Job Seeker Assistant	`members.aol.com/Dylander/jobhome.html`
Environmental Career Opportunities	`www.ecojobs.com/`
Environmental Careers World	`environmental-jobs.com/jobs.html`
Environmental Jobs and Careers	`www.ejobs.org/`
Federal Jobs Central (U.S.)	`www.fedjobs.com/`
Federal Jobs Digest (U.S.)	`www.jobsfed.com/`
Financialjobs.com	`www.financialjobs.com/`
Florida Jobs Online	`www.florida-jobs-online.com/`
Foodservice.com	`foodservice.com/employment.htm`
Future Access Employment Guide	`futureaccess.com/`
GETAJOB	`www.getajob.com/`
HeadHunter.Net	`www.HeadHunter.NET/`
HealthCareerWeb	`www.healthcareerweb.com/`
HealthOpps (CareerMosaic)	`www.healthopps.com/`
Health Search USA (physicians)	`www.healthsearchusa.com/`
Help Wanted USA	`www.iccweb.com`
Heuristics Search, Inc. (computer staffing)	`www.heuristicsearch.com/`
Hospitality Careers.net	`www.hospitalitycareers.net/jobslist.htm`
The Hospitality Job Forum	`orbit.unh.edu/jobforum/`
HospitalityNET	`www.hospitalitynet.org/`
HR Job Opportunities (Career Mosaic)	`www.hrplaza.com/hrcareercenter/hrjobs.html`
Infoworks (computer jobs)	`www.it123.com/`
The Insurance Career Center (CareerMosaic)	`www.connectyou.com/talent/`
The Internet Job Locator	`www.joblocator.com/jobs/`
The Internet Job Source	`www.statejobs.com/`
The Irish Jobs Page	`www.exp.ie/`
JobBank USA	`www.jobbankusa.com/`
The Job Connection	`www.jobconnection.com/`
JobDirect.com (college students and recent graduates)	`www.jobdirect.com/`
jobEngine (computer industry)	`www.jobEngine.com/`
The JobExchange (newspaper ads)	`www.jobexchange.com/`
Jobfind.com	`www.jobfind.com/`
Job Link U.S.A.	`joblink-usa.com/`
JobNet (engineers)	`www.jobnet.org/`
The Job Resource (recent college graduates)	`www.thejobresource.com/`
Job Search for Engineers	`www.interec.net/jobsearch/`
JobServe (IT jobs in the U.K.)	`www.jobserve.com/`
Jobs in Government	`www.jobsingovernment.com/`

(continues)

(continued)

Find this database:	At this location:
JobSite (Europe)	www.jobsite.co.uk/
Jobsite.Com (real estate, construction, real estate finance, and A/E industries)	www.jobsite.com/
Jobs Online	www.jobs-online.com/
Jobs Online	www.jobs-online.net/
JobsJobsJobs	jobsjobsjobs.com/
JobStar Los Angeles	jobstar.org/socal/index.htm
JobStar Sacramento	jobstar.org/sacto/index.htm
JobStar San Diego	jobstar.org/sd/index.htm
JobStar San Francisco	jobstar.org/nocal/index.htm
JobWeb (National Association of Colleges and Employers)	www.jobweb.org/
Jobworld (U.K.)	www.jobworld.co.uk
JobsNorthwest (Washington, Oregon, Montana, Idaho, and British Columbia)	www.jobsnorthwest.com/
The LatPro Professional Network (English, Spanish, and Portuguese)	www.latpro.com/
LawMatch (legal professionals)	www.lawmatch.com/
Lycos Classifieds (Select Employment)	www.lycos.com/classifieds/
MarketingJobs.com (sales, marketing, and advertising)	www.marketingjobs.com/
MedZilla	www.medzilla.com/
Minorities' Job Bank	www.minorities-jb.com/
Monster Healthcare	www.medsearch.com/
MSBET Career Central (Microsoft and Black Entertainment Television)	findajob.msbet.com/
Nando Classifieds (McClatchy newspapers' classified ads)	www.nandotimes.com/mcclatchy/classads/
National Association of Broadcasters	www.nab.org/
The National Diversity Newspaper Job Bank	www.newsjobs.com/
National Federation of Paralegal Associations	www.paralegals.org/
National NurseSearch	www.nursesearch.net/
NationJob Network	www.nationjob.com/
Net-Temps	www.net-temps.com/
Ohio Careers Resource Center	www.ohiocareers.com/
Online Sports Career Center (sports and recreation industries)	www.onlinesports.com/pages/CareerCenter.html
ORAsearch (Oracle professionals)	www.orasearch.com/
Passport Access (technical jobs)	www.passportaccess.com/
Pencom Career Center	www.pencomsi.com/careerhome.html
People Bank (London based)	www.peoplebank.com/
Planet Resume (technology)	www.planetresume.com/
Public Relations Student Society of America	www.prssa.org/

Find this database:	At this location:
Public Sector Jobs (CareerMosaic)	www.publicsectorjobs.com/cm/public/
PursuitNet Online	www.pursuit.com/jobs
Recruiters Online Network	www.ipa.com/ or www.recruitersonline.com/
Reed Online (U.K.)	www.reed.co.uk/
Sales & Marketing Management Career Center (CareerMosaic)	www.careermosaic.com/cm/smm/
Saludos Hispanos	www.saludos.com/
Science Professional Network (American Association for the Advancement of Science)	www.sciencemag.org/
The Seamless Legal Job Center	seamless.com/jobs/
SEEK (Australia)	www.seek.com.au/
SelectJOBS (computer professionals)	www.selectjobs.com/
Showbizjobs	www.showbizjobs.com/
Singapore Job Bank	www.jobbank.com.sg/
SpaceCareers	www.spacelinks.com/SpaceCareers/Welcome.html
TCM's HR Careers (training and development)	www.tcm.com/hr-careers/career/
Teacher Jobs (K–12 teachers and administrators)	www.teacherjobs.com
Teachers@Work	www.teachersatwork.com/
TechJobBank	www.techjobbank.com/
Texas A&M University Department of Wildlife and Fisheries	wfscnet.tamu.edu/jobs.htm
Today's Careers (Seattle and Portland)	www.todays-careers.com/
TrainingSuperSite (training and HR)	www.trainingsupersite.com/
Transition Assistance Online (military and veterans)	www.taonline.com/
USAJobs (U.S. federal government vacancies)	www.usajobs.opm.gov/
Virtual Job Fair (high-tech careers)	www.VJF.com/
Virtually Hired (Chicago)	www.virtuallyhired.com/
Western New York Jobs (Buffalo & Rochester)	www.wnyjobs.com/
The World Wide Web Employment Office	www.toa-services.net/annex.html
Yahoo! Classifieds (Select Employment for job listings)	www.yahoo.com/

Finding Even More Job Banks

As we've warned you, job banks can change their names and URLs, new ones will be developed, and some may close. No list can keep up with all those changes. There is one way you can find out about new lists. That is by visiting what are called *meta-lists* on the Internet. Meta-lists are sites that list other sites and allow you to link directly from them to the other sites. Some of the job-bank meta-lists also contain valuable job-search information.

Here are some that we have found useful:

The Riley Guide
www.dbm.com/jobguide/

www.rileyguide.com

> The Riley Guide to Employment Opportunities and Job Resources on the Internet has been online since February 1994. Originally compiled by Margaret Riley while a librarian at Worcester Polytechnic Institute, The Riley Guide is now hosted by the outplacement consulting firm Drake Beam Morin.

> Because The Riley Guide is constantly updated and revised, it is a valuable Internet job-search guide.

JobSource Network.com
www.jobsourcenetwork.com/

> JobSource Network.com is a job and career directory with links to thousands of U.S. and international job sites.

JobHunt
www.job-hunt.org/classified.shtml

> JobHunt is a meta-list of online job search resources and services.

The Entire List of Employment Resources on the Internet
members.iquest.net/~swlodin/jobs/all.html

> This site has over 500 links to job sites.

The Australian Resume Server
www.herenow.com.au/Jobseeker/index.html

> The Australian Resume Server has a more complete list of Australian Employment Internet sites.

SEB Computer Services
www.cybertap.com/sebservices/employ.htm

> SEB Computer Services provides a site listing links to Canadian Internet employment sites.

EscapeArtist
www.escapeartist.com/jobs/overseas.htm

> EscapeArtist, "a Web site for the borderless world," has a page devoted to jobs around the world. It also has links to other job boards across the globe.

Searching the Job Banks

With so many job banks available on the Internet, it was only a matter of time before search engines just for the job bank sites were developed.

The Job-Search-Engine at **www.job-search-engine.com/** allows you to search up to ten job sites by keyword and location. The Job-Search-Engine allows you to select from the following job banks:

Best Jobs USA
CareerCity
CareerMagazine
CareerMosaic
HeadHunter.NET
JobBank USA
JobOptions
JobWeb
Monster.com
NationJob Network
Net-Temps
Recruiters Online Network
Yahoo! Classifieds
ZDNet's jobEngine

Clnet SEARCH.COM is located at **search.cnet.com/**. Click on Employment. This Clnet site allows you to search the following job banks:

Accountemps
Alternative Resources Corporation Job Search
America's Job Bank
CareerBuilder.com
Career City and Career City Newsgroup Search
CareerMagazine
Career Mosaic and Career Mosaic Usenet Search
CareerPath
CareerWeb Job Match
Chronicle of Higher Education Job Openings
Community Career Center (nonprofits)
Coolware Classifieds Electronic Job Guide
Computer Jobs Store
Computerwork.com
Help Wanted—USA
Hot Jobs
JobCenter Employment Services
JobOptions
Jobs Across America

JobWeb
Law Journal Listings
Monster and Monster Job Newsgroups
NationJob Network
Net-Temps
Newsclassifieds Employment Search (Australia)
RHI Consulting Job Search
Talent Scout

You should have no doubt now that the place to look for a job is on the World Wide Web job boards. Let us remind you again that a site's URL may change and a site might go out of business. We've done our best to make this list accurate. If you can't find a site mentioned in this chapter, just move on to another—there are now hundreds to search through.

And there is another place on the Internet to search for jobs. In the next chapter you'll read about newsgroups, a place on the Internet where employers can post job openings at no cost.

Chapter 4

Usenet Newsgroups

U senet newsgroups were on the Internet even before there was a World Wide Web. Usenet is a worldwide conferencing system, and newsgroups are discussion groups. No one person or organization controls Usenet, so it is a huge cooperative anarchy; but among the thousands of discussion groups are some jewels for job seekers and employers. Newsgroups are not as important in the job search as World Wide Web resume banks, but they remain useful—particularly for job searches that are limited to one city or state.

What Are Newsgroups and How Do I Use Them?

Don't let the word "newsgroup" mislead you. What is referred to as "news" is not current events, but instead what we might more appropriately call *postings.*

Think of a newsgroup as the electronic equivalent of a bulletin board in your local grocery store or on your college campus. Let's say your dog is missing. You can post a message about your dog on a bulletin board for people to read as they pass by. If someone has seen your dog, that person can copy down your telephone number and call you to report where your dog may be. Another person with a dog of the same breed can leave you a message to tell you about some available puppies. And because bulletin boards are visible to anyone who passes by, another person may write graffiti all over your message.

Newsgroups function in the same way that bulletin boards do, and they are a bargain in your job search because there are no charges for reading, placing, or responding to a posting—other than, of course, the regular cost of your Internet service provider.

Online Forums—Another Type of Newsgroup

Commercial Internet service providers may give you access to their own version of newsgroups, called *forums*. America Online has an area devoted to the concerns of job seekers. It is called Real Life. Contained within this area is a message board feature from which job seekers may obtain advice and opinions from other job seekers and employers. One forum is called "Getting the Pink Slip" and deals with the frustrations and concerns of laid-off workers. Another is called "Coping with Job Loss."

CompuServe also has a support service for job seekers. It's called "Career Management Forum." Here you access workshops on such things as networking and interviewing strategies. One forum, called "Job Search Depression," enables members to vent their feelings about the process of searching for work. In a forum called "Support and Success," job seekers share job-hunting tips and offer support and encouragement to each other. They also post their success stories when they land jobs.

Accessing the Newsgroups

Today there are about 30,000 Usenet newsgroups. Some of the newsgroups are serious discussions on serious topics; others are just for fun; still others are frank, explicit discussions of adult topics; and some you may find offensive.

You may access Usenet newsgroups directly through your Internet service provider or by using Dejanews on the World Wide Web. Some of the job data banks also offer you access to the job-related newsgroups.

Using Your Internet Service Provider to Access Newsgroups

If you have access through your Internet service provider, you still may not have access to all the thousands of newsgroups. Some Internet service providers block offensive ones or provide access to only a portion of all those that are available.

AOL provides access to newsgroups with a click on the globe icon. Select newsgroups from the drop-down box. There is a "Netiquette" section that explains proper behavior in newsgroups, a listing of newly added newsgroups, and a glossary of newsgroup terms. You may build your own file of preferred newsgroups and add to it as you choose. AOL can also filter junk postings. Select Preferences and choose the Junk Posting option.

To access Usenet newsgroups on some Internet service providers, you may need newsreader software. If you use Microsoft Internet Explorer or Netscape Communicator, you already have everything you need.

With Internet Explorer 4.0, begin at a Web page and click on the Mail button in the toolbar. Then select Read News. This opens Outlook Express, which is Internet Explorer's newsgroup program. The first time you use it, you will be prompted to provide your name, e-mail address, and the name of your Internet service provider's mail server. Outlook Express will then list the names of all the newsgroups available on your Internet service provider's news server.

Newsgroups are identified in a `word.word` or `word.word.word` format. The words may be abbreviated, as in the following example: `biz.jobs.offered`. This is a popular newsgroup for listing business jobs.

Outlook Express then asks which groups you want to subscribe to. Subscribe means something different here than it does with online mailing lists. It doesn't mean putting your name on a list to receive messages in your e-mail. Instead, it is a command to the newsreader to automatically check messages in the newsgroups you designate each time you open the software.

Netscape Communicator's newsreader is called Collabra. Begin at a Web page and select Collabra Discussion Groups from the Communicator menu. After Collabra loads, you select Preferences from the Edit menu and then click on Groups Server under Mail and Groups. In the Groups Server field, type the name of your Internet service provider's news server and then click Okay. Back in the main Collabra program, click on the Subscribe button in the toolbar. Collabra then starts downloading newsgroup names from the news server. Collabra groups newsgroups by the word they start with. To download the newsgroup names from a particular grouping, click on the grouping. When you find a newsgroup in the list that interests you, select it and click on the Subscribe button.

More advanced users will be interested in shareware newsreader programs available on the Internet. Some of the more popular shareware newsreaders for Windows are Free Agent, Gravity, and TIFNY. Macintosh users have Newswatcher, MT-Newswatcher, and Nuntius.

If you have no experience with newsgroups, one place to begin is the newsgroup

`news.announce.newusers`

which provides articles on how to best use newsgroups.

Using the World Wide Web to Access Newsgroups

The easiest way to access newsgroups is to use Dejanews on the World Wide Web at:

`www.dejanews.com`

Dejanews is a search engine dedicated to newsgroups. You search the newsgroups by typing in search words in the field provided. The postings that Dejanews returns to you are from any newsgroup. Thus, if you selected "jobs" and entered "Ohio" in the Dejanews search engine, you would be presented with a list of over 1,600 postings from newsgroups such as `mi.jobs, chi.jobs, misc.jobs, akr.jobs, cmh.jobs, alt.jobs,` and others.

Using the Job Banks to Access Newsgroups

Another easy way to search through newsgroup job postings is to go to a job bank on the World Wide Web that provides access to the newsgroups. Some of the job banks can search through some of the job-related newsgroups by keyword. Read through the screens carefully: You may have to select Search Newsgroups or go to a separate part of the search screen designated "Usenet Search."

For example, CareerMosaic offers keyword searches of some 60,000 job postings. CareerMosaic's index is rebuilt every twenty-four hours and deletes postings after seven days. The newsgroups included in CareerMosaic's index are shown in bold in table 4.1 later in this chapter. You can find CareerMosaic on the World Wide Web at:

`www.careermosaic.com`

Another easy way we've found is the CareerCast site at:

`www.careercast.com/`

This site features a search engine that makes it possible to search over seventy Usenet sites at once.

The Help-Wanted.Network offers a search engine for newsgroups at:

`www.Help-Wanted.net/`

Finally, CareerSpan features a search engine that searches the individual sites you designate. CareerSpan is located at:

`www.careerspan.com/`

Reading Newsgroup Postings

In the newsgroups, you'll see the postings identified by their subject (or title) line. The postings look like e-mail messages. They can be as recent as five minutes old or as dated as several months old.

The return address of the person who posted the announcement will be shown differently depending on your reader. The return address may be in the upper-left corner in two lines, such as the following example:

```
fjandt

(at igc.apc.org)
```

To respond to that person by return e-mail, you use the following address:

```
fjandt@igc.apc.org
```

Job Posting Newsgroups

Some of the newsgroups with job listings predominantly contain computer-related job openings. If you go to one of those newsgroups and if you're not looking for one of those positions, you'll just have to look through a lot of job listings for people with computer skills before you find a job opening that's more appropriate for you.

Just as the Internet is dynamic and ever changing, so are the newsgroups. Some become inactive; many new ones will be added. In table 4.1, we've identified from the many thousands of newsgroups the major job-related ones.

You'll notice that there are general, national newsgroups as well as some more specialized ones. National newsgroups include **misc.jobs.contract** for applicants looking for contract work and **misc.jobs.offered**, a site containing a variety of offerings. Most of the newsgroups that list jobs are specialized for a particular city, state, country, occupation, or employer; for example, **seattle.jobs.offered** is for jobs in the Seattle area and **vegas.jobs** is for finding opportunities in Las Vegas.

67

TABLE 4.1

Usenet newsgroups with job announcements*

ab.jobs	**alt.building.jobs**
alt.jobs	alt.jobs
alt.jobs.offer	alt.jobs.overs
at.jobs	**atl.jobs**
au.jobs	aus.ads.jobs
aus.jobs	**austin.jobs**
az.jobs	ba.jobs.agency
ba.jobs.contract	ba.jobs.contract.agency
ba.jobs.contract.direct	**ba.jobs.direct**
ba.jobs.misc	**ba.jobs.offered**
balt.jobs	**bc.jobs**
bermuda.jobs.offered	bionet.jobs
bionet.jobs.offered	**biz.jobs.offered**
can.jobs	**chi.jobs**
cit.jobs	**cmh.jobs**
co.jobs	comp.databases.oracle.marketplace
comp.jobs	comp.jobs.offered
conn.jobs.offered	**dc.jobs**
de.markt.jobs	**dfw.jobs**
dod.jobs	eunet.jobs
euro.jobs	**fl.jobs**
fr.jobs.offres	**hepnet.jobs**
houston.jobs.offered	**hsv.jobs**
il.jobs.misc	**il.jobs.offered**
in.jobs	**israel.jobs.offered**
ithaca.jobs	**kw.jobs**
la.jobs	**li.jobs**
lou.lft.jobs	**mi.jobs**
milw.jobs	**misc.jobs**
misc.jobs.contract	misc.jobs.fiel
misc.jobs.misc	**misc.jobs.offered**
misc.jobs.offered.entry	mn.jobs
nb.jobs	**ne.jobs**
ne.jobs.contract	**nj.jobs**
nm.jobs	ny.jobs
nyc.jobs	**nyc.jobs.contract**
nyc.jobs.misc	**nyc.jobs.offered**
nv.jobs	**oh.jobs**
ont.jobs	**ott.jobs**
pa.jobs.offered	**pdaxs.jobs.clerical**
pdaxs.jobs.computers	**pdaxs.jobs.construction**
pdaxs.jobs.engineering	**pdaxs.jobs.management**
pdaxs.jobs.sales	**pdaxs.jobs.secretary**
pdaxs.jobs.temporary	**pgh.jobs.offered**
phl.jobs.offered	**qc.jobs**
sat.jobs	scot.jobs
sdnet.jobs	**seattle.jobs.offered**
stl.jobs	**stl.jobs.offered**
tnn.jobs	**tor.jobs**
triangle.jobs	**tx.jobs**
ucb.cs.jobs	ucb.jobs
uk.jobs	**uk.jobs.contract**
uk.jobs.offered	**us.jobs.contract**
us.jobs.offered	ut.jobs
va.jobs	**vegas.jobs**
za.ads.jobs	

Newsgroups printed in bold can be searched at the CareerMosaic World Wide Web site.

Sample Job Postings

Here are some job postings we've taken from various newsgroups. Look at the examples carefully. Read the complete job announcement for instructions for applying. Some will specify an e-mail address to which you can send applications; others request that resumes be faxed or mailed.

Some newsgroup readers may have a reply function, which enables the reader to send a reply to the whole group or just to the original poster. If you reply to the whole group, your message will be public, for anyone to read as a reply. If you reply to the original poster, your e-mail message goes only to the poster.

Figure 4.1

A job posting from tx.jobs.

```
Topic 5794 TX, San Antonio / RF Design Engineer

hri tx.jobs 12:58 AM Jan 20, 1999

(at cyberport.net) (From News system)

POSITION ID: HR1210TXS-U

POSITION TITLE: RF Design Engineer (cellular)

LOCATIONS: Salt Lake City, UT; Phoenix, AZ; Houston,
TX;Dallas, TX; San Antonio, TX; New Orleans, LA;
Atlanta, GA; Pleasonton, CA

COMPENSATION: $50,000 - $60,000 + bonuses + full
benefits + full relocation.

REQUIREMENTS:

An EE degree with 2+ years experience in wireless
and/or cellular telecommunications. 1+ years of
experience with one or more of the following: IS136
(TDMA), IS95 (CDMA), GSM or PCS (see definitions
below).

DUTIES/RESPONSIBILITIES:

Perform RF planning, designing and optimization
engineering for a PCS provider in a new market area.
Participate in the new cell site launch, build out
and expansion of this company's products in new
service coverage territory(s).
```

(continues)

(continued)

INDUSTRY: Telecom/Wireless & Telecommunications

FUNCTION: Design/Product Development

KEYWORDS: Cellular, engineer, wireless, network, design, planning, electrical, site, spectrum, Electrical Engineering, radio frequency, CDMA, TDMA, GSM, PCS.

DURATION: Direct Hire

* CDMA (Code-Division Multiple Access) is one of the three wireless telephone transmission technologies.

* TDMA (Time Division Multiple Access) is another of the three wireless telephone transmission technologies.

* GSM (Global System for Mobile communication) is a digital mobile telephone system that is widely used in Europe and other parts of the world.

* PCS (Personal Communications Services) is a wireless phone service somewhat similar to cellular telephone service.

IMPORTANT: Do not apply unless you are confident that you are qualified and want the above position and that you have one of the following: U.S. Citizenship, Green Card or current H1B.

Contact:

George Hawes, Recruitment Specialist

Hawes Resources International

P. O. Box 5

Somers, MT 59932

Phone: (406) 857-2196

Fax: (406) 857-2241

Email: hri@cyberport.net

URL: http://www.cyberport.net/hri/

All resumes are confidential (not posted on-line or submitted without your authorization). All inquiries are confidential. Employers pay our fee. Please include your email address on your faxed resumes.

The professionals at Hawes Resources International
are recruiting specialists for permanent and contract
staffing. Hawes Resources International is a full
service provider of Human Resource solutions, spe-
cializing in the areas of WIRELESS TELECOMMUNICATIONS
and CELLULAR. HRI works with professionals in the
fields of RF engineering, design, planning, testing,
marketing and sales. HRI also recruits for candidates
with experience in GSM, PCS, CDMA, TDMA, 5ESS, etc.

With our affiliation and leverage in the recruiting
industry, we can offer you the best selection of high
quality job opportunities, whether permanent or
contract.

An Equal Opportunity Employer

Authors' Comments: *Note that the posting states that you should include your e-mail address on a faxed resume. This job announcement was posted by a recruiting firm—as are most newsgroup job announcements.*

Figure 4.2

A posting from **oh.jobs.**

Topic 2464 USA-OH-Animal Lab Technician - Hist

newsgrp oh.jobs 11:44 PM Jan 20, 1999

(at careermag.com) (From News system)

Title: Animal Lab Technician-Histology Microtomy

City: Columbus

State: Ohio

Country: USA

Skills Required: Animal Lab Necroscopy

Type: Contract

Job ID Number: 43081/CM/243002871

Job Description:

(continues)

(continued)

USA-OH-Animal Lab Technician-Histology Microtomy-
43081/CM/243002871

Pay Rate: $10.00/HOURLY - $15.00/HOURLY. Animal Lab
Technician, Critical Skills & Knowledge-Necroscopy,
tissue trimming, embedding, microtomy, standard (H&E)
staining, special staining, manual and automated
coverslipping, quality control and data archiving.
Key Tasks-Operate and perform maintenance of
histology equipment. Properly detect macroscopic
changes when performing necroscopy or trim, and
accurately orient and identify tissues
microscopically when working in microtomy or QC. Keep
required logs and records logs, as indicated in
applicable SOPs.

Email your resume to JOBS@TECHNICAL.MANPOWER.COM

Or submit your resume to:

http://www.careermag.com/db/
cmag_resume_count_main?job_id=310336&client=10027

email=JOBS@TECHNICAL.MANPOWER.COM&table=job_inc

formatted as a text file, or fax your scanner-quality
resume to

(414) 906-6188 or mail it to Manpower Technical,
Resumes, 5301 North Ironwood Road, Milwaukee,
Wisconsin 53217.

Posted through Career Magazine's employer service at
http://www.careermag.com" TARGET="_top

See our Employer Profile in Career Magazine at:
http://www.careermag.com/

Authors' Comments: *This announcement was posted by a
recruiting firm through Career Magazine's World Wide Web
site. Note the four methods of applying. This is an example of
when you should probably use a text-scannable resume. See
chapter 7 for information on how to prepare a scannable
resume.*

Figure 4.3

A posting from `nyc.jobs.misc`.

```
Topic 430 NY, New York / HR Director

(at jobs-net.net) (From News system)

Please reply to recruiter listed below. Do not reply
to quickpost@jobs-net.net

POSITION ID: 115

DATE POSTED: 1/12/99

DURATION: Direct Hire

POSITION TITLE: HR Director (Sales performance
executive)

INDUSTRY: Financial Services

SECONDARY INDUSTRY:

FUNCTION: Human Resources

SECONDARY FUNCTION:

LOCATION: NY

GENERAL AREA: New York-New York

RELOCATION: no

KEYWORDS: Human Resources, Director, Management,
Staffing, Training, Compensation

YEARS EXPERIENCE: 8

EDUCATION: 4 yr Degree

TRAVEL: 0%

CITIZENSHIP: US Citizenship

COMPENSATION: $90 K-$100 K

COMMENTS:

INSTRUCTIONS: fax or email resume (attach as Word
document)

REQUIREMENTS:

7-10 years HR experience (in a sales organization
preferred)
```

(continues)

(continued)

Bachelor's degree (MBA desired but not necessary)

Proven track record of success in implementing policies and procedures that improve employee satisfaction

Experience interacting with senior executives

Experience in financial services organization is preferred

Excellent communication and influencing skills

Leadership skills & team orientation

Computer technology proficient

DUTIES/RESPONSIBILITIES:

Leveraging the investments, processes, and resources of National Human Resources with national sales and marketing organization

Staffing

Performance management

Compensation

Career planning

Education & training

CONTACT:

Management Recruiters Of Chicago—Far West

Marc Chaifetz

564 S. Washington St., Suite 203

Naperville, IL 60540

Tel: 630-305-0200

Fax: 630-305-0273

E-MAIL ID: 630-305-0200@ron.ipa.com

URL: http://www.ipa.com/eoffice/630-305-0200.html

Recruiters OnLine Network—free resume submittal to thousands of recruiters. Huge free jobs database.

Go to http://www.recruitersonline.com/ or email info@recruitersonline.com

Authors' Comments: Note that if you apply by e-mail, you are directed to attach your resume as a Word document. Do not assume that all employers can open attachments. (See chapter 7 for more information about working with attachments.) This job announcement was posted by Recruiters OnLine Network, a large, free job database. You can post your resume there at no cost.

Figure 4.4

A posting from `tor.jobs`.

```
Toronto—Senior Graphics Designer

Author: Steve Hope <shope@reach-management.com>

Date: 1999/01/20

Forum: tor.jobs

http://www.reach-management.com/

SENIOR GRAPHICS DESIGNER: Toronto

Dynamic, creative, hip, leading edge designer for
Toronto based New Media company with clients in
Canada; Europe; Asia; USA.

Excels in the design, illustration & animation (3D) of
CD-ROM Titles & WWW Sites. Proven ability to lead
others on large scale projects. Expertise must include:
Director, Illustrator, PhotoShop, Painter, Avid etc.

TELEPHONE INQUIRIES:

STEVE HOPE, "HEADHUNTER", REACH MANAGEMENT CONSULTANTS
INC.

20 Bay Street, Suite 1205, Toronto, Ont., M5J 2N8
CANADA

TEL: (416) 927-0723 FAX: (416) 927-0724

PLEASE SEND PLAIN TEXT RESUMES TO: shope@reach-
management.com

For Browsers with direct links:

<a href=mailto:shope@reach-management.com>E-mail me at
this link</a>

Or visit our website for more jobs at:

<a href=http://www.reach-management.com>www.reach-
management.com</a>
```

> **Authors' Comments:** *Note the "Headhunter" designation in the contact section. This posting was placed by a recruiter, and we viewed it at Dejanews on the World Wide Web. One advantage of viewing newsgroups on the World Wide Web is that you can use the links to submit your resume directly or go to the recruiter's homepage.*

Figure 4.5

A posting from `misc.jobs.offered.`

```
Path:
server31.careermosaic.com!hodes.com!ix.netcom.com!netnews
.com!howland.erols.net!newsfeed.fast.net!uunet!in1.uu.net!not-
for-mail

From: nospam@net-temps.com (Source Services San
Francisco)

Newsgroups:
misc.jobs.offered,alt.jobs,biz.jobs.offered,comp.jobs.offered

Subject: US-CA-Sf Bay-IN-HOUSE REAL ESTATE

Date: 18 Jan 1999 18:37:17 GMT

Organization: Source Services San Francisco

Lines: 36

Expires: +7days

Message-ID: <77vv0t$pkv$2825@news0-alterdial.uu.net>

Reply-To: astemps@net-temps.com

NNTP-Posting-Host: ww1.net-temps.com

Xref: server31.careermosaic.com
misc.jobs.offered:4711984 alt.jobs:1895969
biz.jobs.offered:1317430

**** IMPORTANT PLEASE REPLY TO THIS EMAIL ADDRESS ****

astemps@net-temps.com or mailto:astemps@net-temps.com

Job Title: IN-HOUSE REAL ESTATE
```

Job Description:

Dynamic and growing Bay Area based corporation seeks a real estate attorney for its in-house real estate department to focus on commercial leasing work.

Required:

Excellent credentials essential.

Location: CA Sf Bay

Duration: Direct Placement

Pay Rate: Open

IMPORTANT:

PLEASE REFERENCE "Net-TempsCBJOIN" in Subject line on all replies.

Source Services San Francisco

425 California Street, Ste. 1200

San Francisco, CA 94104

Contact: Source Services San Francisco

415-434-2410

Email mailto:astemps@net-temps.com

FAX to 415-296-9843

Visit our Web Site at http://www.net-temps.com/ astemps

Posted by Net-Temps Inc.

Search Thousands of Jobs at Net-Temps:

Home Page: http://www.net-temps.com

Authors' Comments: We viewed this posting at the CareerMosaic World Wide Web site. Note the asterisks at the reply-to e-mail address instructions. You must e-mail replies as indicated. No hard information is provided for requirements. You should send a very detailed resume.

Resume Newsgroups

In some of the newsgroups, you'll notice that people have posted their own job-wanted announcements and their resumes. The Internet has many newsgroups that are dedicated to posting resumes. In table 4.2, we've identified the major newsgroups devoted to resumes.

Most of the resume newsgroups serve a defined geographical area or a specific industry. If you live in one of the geographical regions listed in table 4.2 or if you want to work in a particular location, use the newsgroup that is listed.

TABLE 4.2

Usenet newsgroups for posting resumes.

General/worldwide—appropriate for most resumes

```
misc.jobs.resumes
```

Regional/industry:

alt.medical.sales.jobs.resumes	atl.resumes
ba.jobs.resumes	bionet.jobs.wanted
fl.jobs.resumes	houston.jobs.wanted
il.jobs.resumes	israel.jobs.resumes
nyc.jobs.wanted	pa.jobs.wanted
pdaxs.jobs.resumes	pdaxs.jobs.wanted
pgh.jobs.wanted	phl.jobs.wanted
qc.jobs.wanted	sdnet.jobs.wanted
seattle.jobs.wanted	stl.jobs.resumes
uk.jobs.wanted	

Sample Resume Postings

Here are some resume postings we've taken off various newsgroups. We include them here so that you can see what they look like and understand some of the problems associated with them. Our comments appear at the end of each resume.

Figure 4.6

A resume from **misc.jobs.resumes**.

```
Sat, 23 Jan 1999 09:00:16 misc.jobs.resumes Thread
168 of 249

Lines 91 Resume: TECHNICAL, DOCUMENTATION SPECIALIST
No responses

JobBankUSA@data.jobbankusa.com 24hoursupport.com

[RESUME ANNOUNCEMENT]
```

Info:

ResumeId: 1000080016

Position: TECHNICAL, DOCUMENTATION SPECIALIST

City/State/Zip: DORAVILLE, GA 30340

Location: GA

Relocate: Y

Years Exp: 5/10

Salary: 36,000

Salary Type: YR

Position Type: P

Resume:

Objective: A challenging position with an organization that could benefit from my Engineering, Electronics, Industrial/Position Management and drafting experience and training, offering advancement opportunities based on accomplishment.

Summary of Qualifications:

Profile Experienced in both digital and analog circuitry.

Extensive interaction with various electromechanical devices experienced with numerous types of system test equipment.

Able to direct test programs to ensure conformity of equipment and systems to requirements.

Ability to articulate ideas; strong communication and research skills.

Experienced in the programming and setup of numerical control machines.

Enjoy taking initiative; challenge acceptance with increasing levels of responsibility.

Education

Jackson State University—Jackson, Mississippi

B.S. in Industrial Technology, 1988

(continues)

(continued)

Relevant course work completed:

Basic and Intermediate Electronics Air Navigation

Electronic Drafting Digital Logic I-II

Industrial Management Manufacturing Process

1st Line Supervisor Electronic Lab I-II

Employment History

September 1995-Present Engineering Support Specialist

MICROMERTICIS INSTRUMENT CORPORATION—Norcross, Georgia

Entering new drawing in the computer, changing REV level. Keeping the status of over 2,000 new drawing, etc. Also CAD drafting, creating drawings, also making changes on current drawings that, due to a process known as Engineering chance notice, CAD key, training in the company. 7.5 CAD key, introduction to CAD key, ISO 9000, Certified 1994. MSDS training (hazardous material) ESD training.

July 94-95 Documentation Control Specialist

MICROMERTICS INSTRUMENTS CORPORATION—NORCROSS, GEORGIA

Entering new drawing in the computer, Changing REV level. Keeping the status of over 2,000 drawing, etc.

July 90-93 Mechanical Assembler & Wire Harnesser

MICROMERTICS INSTRUMENTS CORPORATION—NORCROSS, GEORGIA

Assembled Laboratory equipment using blueprints and electrical drawings. Inspected parts for defects. Performed tests on assemblies, which require a vacuum or pressure to check for leaks and/or structure defects.

December 89-July 90 Mechanical Assembler & Moving Coordinator

SIEMENS ENERGY AND AUTOMATION—ROSWELL, GEORGIA

Assembled DC drivers following specific details of blueprints. Responsible also for technical drafting, changing blueprints with a process known as ECN. Coordinated the move of the company from Roswell to Forsyth County.

1983-1986 Construction Worker

FLEETWOOD MOBILE HOMES—LEXINGTON, MISSISSIPPI

Built mobile homes on an assembly line using blueprints. Responsible for the side and interior walls. An average of 15 homes was produced each day.

REFERENCES Available upon request.

This candidate is posted anonymously by <http://www.jobbankusa.com/>

In order to view contact information for this candidate or view similar resumes please contact JobBank USA.

JobBank USA

Recognized by employers, recruiters, and job candidates as one of the Internet's leading employment information providers since 1995.

Services available from JobBank USA:

*Unlimited resume searches (full contact information available to Members)

*Unlimited employment advertising

*Free distribution to Newsgroups, Yahoo & more

*Banner advertising

For prices and information please visit our membership information page at http://www.jobbankusa.com/searform.html

Authors' Comments: This job candidate posted this resume through JobBank USA. This enables the candidate to remain anonymous. A potential employer must make contact through JobBank USA. There are some grammar and punctuation errors, and the resume is not neatly formatted. You should construct text resumes carefully. See chapter 7 for information on how to do this.

Figure 4.7

A resume from `pa.jobs.wanted`.

Topic 20 VirtualResume * Bilingual, internet

janegoddard pa.jobs.wanted 11:05 PM Jan 19, 1999

(at Solutions-Team.com) (From News system)

SEARCH THE RESUMES OF THOUSANDS OF SKILLED CANDIDATES AT

VirtualResume <http://www.virtualresume.com>

Name: Jane Goddard

Phone: 215 628-2929 W 610 584-2462 H

E-mail: janegoddard@Solutions-Team.com
janegoddard@mailexcite.com

Location: Fishers IN USA

JANE COLLINS-GODDARD

22330 Mission Drive

Fishers, Indiana 46032

(317) 555-1212 (work)

(317) 555-1212 (home)

janegoddard@excite.com

EDUCATION

INDIANA UNIVERSITY J.D. December 1997

INDIANA UNIVERSITY-PURDUE UNIVERSITY—INDIANAPOLIS

Honors: 1997 Harvey Brown International Law Moot Court Team, 1997 Appellate Moot Court Board, IULS Excellence for the Future Award for Comparative Commercial Law

Activities: Phi Alpha Delta Law Fraternity International (a service fraternity); Student Bar Association

INDIANA UNIVERSITY SCHOOL OF LAW Diploma, Summer 1996

INSTITUTE ON INTERNATIONAL AND COMPARATIVE LAW

Diploma, Summer 1997

London, England

Paris, France

Diploma received for completion of four courses in International Business Transactions, Public International Law, European Community Law and International Civil Litigation in American Courts as well as for two internships with a barrister and a solicitor.

Honors: Highest grade in International Business Transactions

UNIVERSITY OF EVANSVILLE B.A. May, 1994

Evansville, IN

GPA: 3.52 Major: Psychology

Honors: Cum Laude, Psi Chi (Psychology Honor Society)

Conferences: Subliminal Perception (presented at the Ohio Valley Psychological Conference in 1994), Pictures and Foreign Language Learning (presented at the Ohio Valley Psychological Conference in 1993), Colors and Reading Speed (presented at the Ohio Valley Psychological Conference in 1992).

Activities: Student Council Committee on Faculty-Student Relations; Resident Adviser 1993-1994.

LEGAL EXPERIENCE

121 STONE BUILDINGS BARRISTER CHAMBERS July/August 1997

London, England

Intern. Attended conferences with solicitors and hearings at the Royal Courts of Justice and the Old Bailey. Researched issues pertaining to "Carecraft" briefs, covenants in restraint of trade, Mareva motions and insurance claims. Assisted in preparing trial bundles.

LEACH AND ROWLANDS SOLICITORS June 1997

London, England

(continues)

(continued)

Intern. Attended client interviews, hearings at the Coroner's Court, the Royal Courts of Justice and County Courts. Researched issues pertaining to communications law, customs and excise, software licensing and evidentiary privileges.

NON-LEGAL EXPERIENCE

ONLINE CONSULTATIONS. January 1998-present

Indianapolis, IN June-August 1990

Secretary. Maintained office files, prepared payroll, typed, greeted clients and answered phones.

SKILLS

Fluent in French (matrisse convenable); proficient in Word Perfect (5.1, 5.2 for Windows, 7.0 for Windows), Microsoft Word (6.0, 97 and Word for Windows); computerized legal research including Westlaw, Lexis-Nexis and Internet research; manual legal research including state and federal reporters, CCH reporters, Halisbury's Statutes, Halisbury's Laws.

REFERENCES

Professor John A. Jones	Professor Louis Ralph
Indiana University	Indiana University
1500 South Senate Street	1500 South Senate Street
Indianapolis, IN 46203	Indianapolis, IN 46203
(317) 555-1212	(317) 555-1212

VirtualResume <http://www.virtualresume.com>

mailto: info@virtualresume.com

*Free BASIC resume posting

*Free guest access to our resume database

*Customized USENET resume distribution

CAREERspan <http://www.careerspan.com>

mailto: info@careerspan.com

voice 718-398-3210 fax 718-398-3293

M-Fri 9-7 (EST)

> **Authors' Comments:** *This resume was posted through Virtual Resume. It was not formatted carefully. Note the problem with indenting. This job seeker posted reference contact information to the newsgroup. You should never list reference information on your traditional resume, let alone an electronic resume that can be read by millions of people. However, the content is interesting and well described.*

Preparing Your Resume for Newsgroups

Getting your resume ready for a newsgroup posting is easy as long as you use a little creativity. Because so many resumes are on the Internet today, you have to make sure that yours stands out. The next two sections give you some advice about preparing your resume for the newsgroups.

The Subject Line

Remember that newsgroup postings are identified by their subject (or title) line. An employer decides which postings to read by their subject lines. Too many applicants throw an opportunity away by entering overused or mundane words for the subject line, such as "Resume" or "Resume for Registered Nurse." When an employer scans hundreds of resumes listed by subject line, the catchy ones get looked at first:

HIGHLY SKILLED, DEDICATED, COMPASSIONATE REGISTERED NURSE

Don't decide simply to throw out a few words that are related to your particular field. This approach is just not wise. You want to somehow distinguish yourself from the rest of the throng and at the same time give the employer a reason to want to read your resume instead of all the others in the newsgroup.

You can use a few creative ideas with the subject line to catch a prospective employer's attention. For example, put your subject in capital letters or surround it with asterisks. Use angle brackets (> <) as arrows pointing to your subject line. Put spaces and backslash marks between titles or terms. Use adjectives. Be bold! Use attention-getting words such as *talented, innovative, ambitious,* and *creative*. Each of the following subject lines uses these ideas to catch an employer's attention:

WRITER / MANAGER / ANALYST / V. QUALIFIED / CURIOUS

TALENTED, GIFTED, AMBITIOUS COMPUTER SCIENTIST

===========TOP SALES POSITION WANTED===========

*****>>>>>CREATIVE FREELANCE PHOTOGRAPHER<<<<<*****

INNOVATIVE P.R. PROFESSIONAL>>>>PROVEN TRACK RECORD

Compare the innovative subject lines with these more common ones:

entry-level psych research position

Systems/software

Management

proj. 1dr/rdbms/client-server/imaging

A creative subject line grabs the employer's attention and invites the individual to look at your resume. Use the subject line with flair! Become a standout in that endless field of boring one-liners. You'll get noticed. But be careful—nothing too funny, and never off-color.

Date

Newsgroups are public, which means that anyone—a resume data bank, for example—can copy your resume from the newsgroup. This access can be both an advantage and a disadvantage. When you're a job seeker, you may want your resume in as many places as possible to increase the probability that an employer will find you. On the other hand, your resume could appear in several data banks long after your circumstances have changed.

We recommend that you add the line "Last Updated on *date*" to a resume posted in a newsgroup. This one line ensures that an employer knows whether your resume is current.

ASCII (or Plain) Text

You submit your resumes to newsgroups via e-mail. Every e-mail program supports the ASCII (American Standard Code for Information Interchange) format. ASCII text is straight text; in other words, it has no indents, no centering, **no bold text**, no underlines, *no italics*, no color, no tables, no graphics, no pictures—just text.

Even with these limitations, you can easily prepare an attractive resume for posting in newsgroups by following these guidelines:

✔ Build your resume in your word processor.

✔ Because you can't use tabs or the centerline feature, space everything as you type it and then save the file.

✔ If you don't use spacing, everything will be left-aligned when you cut and paste it into your e-mail message.

✔ Because you can't use bold text or italics, use uppercase and line breaks effectively.

✔ Double-check to make sure that no line wraps around to the next line.

✔ Typographical errors and misspellings are deadly in a resume. Remember to do a spell check. Save your resume as a text (ASCII) file.

✔ When you're ready to post your resume to a newsgroup, cut and paste it directly into the body of your e-mail message.

✔ Check your work by sending a copy to your own e-mail address first.

Submitting Your Resume

You can post your resume in newsgroups at no cost. Follow the directions provided by your Internet service provider or by your newsreader software.

Even if you don't have access to these newsgroups, you can still post your resume there by using one of the resume data banks, which will post your resume in newsgroups when you submit it to them. By using newsgroups, you are getting your resume out where others can see it, even if you can't see it yourself. The following list includes some of the resume banks that provide this service.

HeadHunter.Net
www.HeadHunter.NET/

Resumes from all career fields are posted to newsgroups and other Internet sites.

JobCenter
www.jobcenter.com

Resumes from all career fields are posted to your choice of the Usenet newsgroups once every other week.

MedZilla
www.medzilla.com

Abstracts of health care resumes are posted without identifying information. MedZilla also serves as the contact to protect the job seeker's identity.

VirtualResume
virtualresume.com

Resumes from all career fields are posted and appear under the job seeker's own name and e-mail address.

Because of the volume of resumes posted to newsgroups, your resume may be purged in less than a week. In an active, popular resume newsgroup, you may need to consider reposting your resume when it is no longer available on the newsgroup or when you change your resume. Be sure to check your resume posting to make sure it is available in the newsgroup and that it looks as it did in your word processor.

Posting your resume in a newsgroup is called a *passive posting* because you never know who—if anyone—has read your resume. You never know when it is read, where it is read, or why it is read. With a passive posting, all you can do is wait to be contacted. If you do post your resume to a newsgroup, bear this limitation in mind. Make frequent visits and don't allow your resume to languish there forever.

Posting your resume in a newsgroup costs nothing and takes very little time; however, this kind of posting is not as likely to result in an offer of employment as the more active methods that are made possible by job and resume data banks. Newsgroups are not as important in the job search as the World Wide Web resume banks are today, but they remain useful—particularly for job searches that are limited to one city or state.

Chapter 5

Career Resources on the Internet

Today's job seekers and employers alike are in need of timely and accurate information on the labor market and careers. Job-search professionals stress that one of job seekers' most critical needs is to have access to factual information and the skills to use that information.

You may feel there is just too much information available and that you couldn't possibly deal with all of it. The characters in James Joyce's famous novel, *Ulysses* (1922), are constantly sending letters, wiring telegrams, even writing messages in the sand on the beach. Joyce was foreseeing a picture of life as "sending, carrying, and receiving information." Today, we would say that the job-search process is the same.

In his book *The Road Ahead* (Viking, 1995), Microsoft cofounder Bill Gates defined information as the "reduction of uncertainty." Many years earlier, the linguist and novelist Walker Percy observed in *The Message in the Bottle* (Farrar, Straus and Giroux, 1975) that information is not all of equal value. Percy asks us to imagine a man who finds himself a castaway on an island. Walking the beach each morning, he comes upon bottles washed up by the ocean waves. Each bottle contains a message. Percy examines the differences between knowledge and information and defines information as that communication which has a bearing on the person's predicament. A message that says "A ship passes east of this island once a month" is valuable information to the castaway. But a message that says "Chicago is on Lake Michigan" is of no use to him. What is information to one person may be just noise to another.

Percy was foreseeing the Internet, where it is possible to miss seeing information in a sea of knowledge. There is so much material available that it's easy to get lost or to be distracted by the trivial and overlook what you really need. Increasingly, user-oriented Web agents continually perform automatic searches of the entire World Wide Web for only the information the user specifies.

For example, the *Los Angeles Times* Web Site at `www.latimes.com` offers Hunter, the golden news retriever who fetches the most recent stories in the areas you've specified. For example, I've told Hunter to watch for stories about the Internet. In late May, 1996, I signed onto the *Los Angeles Times* Web Site and clicked on Hunter and on my interest area of Internet stories. The first story Hunter brought me was "Number of Job Listings on the Net Rising." The first sentence read "up to 95% of all major newspapers' classified job listings now available on the Internet." By the way, I had read the *Los Angeles Times* that morning and hadn't seen that story!

A Practical Example

Let's say you have a $45,000-a-year job in Indianapolis. You post your resume in resume banks and study vacancies posted in job banks. You find several jobs that interest you and apply electronically. Eventually, you get two job offers—one in San Francisco paying $60,000 and one in Salt Lake City paying $55,000. Assuming that all other factors are equal for you, which job should you take? On the face of it, the one in San Francisco paying $60,000 seems like a better deal, right?

If you were using the resources on the Internet, you'd be able to determine that the job in Salt Lake City paying $55,000 was the better offer. How? You'd know to go to the Homefair.com site at

`www.homefair.com`

and use their Salary Calculator. The Salary Calculator would tell you that if you make $45,000 in Indianapolis, as a homeowner you would need to make $76,952 in San Francisco and $50,907 in Salt Lake City to compensate for the different costs of living in different areas.

This is just one simple example of how the Internet is a valuable library for the job seeker. In chapter 1, "Introducing the Internet," we described the Internet as a very large library. This library has valuable information for the job seeker and for the employer.

Learning from the Competition

Let's review ways to use the information in resume databases and job databases you now know how to access.

Others' resumes are valuable information. So valuable, in fact, that before the Internet, some job seekers would place fictitious newspaper advertisements for a position they themselves were looking for. Their ads contained no employer information and asked applicants to mail their resumes to a post office box. Of course, these applications were never acknowledged. People placed the ads merely to get copies of their competitors' resumes and then carefully studied them. This unethical and expensive tactic made it possible for those who placed the ads to rewrite their own resumes so that they would stand out from the others.

You can learn a great deal about how to present yourself in a resume by studying how others present themselves in theirs. On the Internet, you can honestly and freely review the resumes of others.

In the same way, job databases are valuable information. The search engines make it easy to search the job databases by job title. That lets you see those—and only those—job announcements. If you follow this job-search strategy on the Internet, you'll probably find a position like your last one. That's okay sometimes, but at other times you may want to expand your job search. Carefully studying vacancy announcements may encourage you to change your employment objective to stress the skills that employers are looking for today.

General Career Information

There's much more out there. You just need to know what's there and how to use it. We've listed below some sites that include some particularly useful job-search information.

Canadian Career Page
www.canadiancareers.com/

The Canadian Career Page has Canadian career news as well as Canadian job postings.

Canadian Jobs Catalogue
www.kenevacorp.mb.ca/

The Canadian Jobs Catalogue is a Canadian-only site with job listings, resumes, and links to thousands of job-search resources, career development sites, and job interview sites.

CareerMagazine Online
www.careermag.com/

CareerMagazine Online is not only a job and resume bank, it is a major source of articles on job search and the working world as well.

College Grad Job Hunter
www.collegegrad.com/

> College Grad Job Hunter has information on job postings, resumes and cover letters, and interview and negotiations specifically targeted for college students. It also has the complete text of Brian Krueger's book, *College Grad Job Hunter,* online.

Gonyea Guide to Online Career & Employment Sites
www.onlinecareerguide.com/

> Gonyea Guide to Online Career & Employment Sites has a collection of links from Adult/Continuing Education Programs to Workplace Violence.

Internet Sites for Job Seekers and Employers
www.cco.purdue.edu/Student/jobsites.htm

> Internet Sites for Job Seekers and Employers, maintained by Purdue University Placement Services, is a very large list of job resources on the Internet. It is well organized and highly recommended.

JOBWEB
ww.jobweb.org/

> JOBWEB, provided by the National Association of Colleges and Employers, contains an extensive listing of links on job-search information and career services resources.

The Riley Guide
www.rileyguide.com

> The Riley Guide to Employment Opportunities and Job Resources on the Internet is maintained by Margaret Riley.

Yahoo! Careers
careers.yahoo.com/

> Finally, the Yahoo! Careers site brings together links to the best on the Web.

Researching Employers

> Frequently referred to as "doing homework," researching the employer is an often-overlooked step that's crucial to a successful job search. You can do employer research through formal or informal means, on the Web, or at your local public library.

Well-Known Sites for Employer Information
EDGAR
www.sec.gov/edgarhp.htm

> Public companies must file regular disclosure statements with the Securities and Exchange Commission. Although there are places you can buy this

information, SEC reports are free. Most public companies post their own SEC report on their Web sites.

EDGAR, the Electronic Data Gathering, Analysis, and Retrieval system, contains the publicly available filings submitted to the SEC since January 1994.

Various different types of documents are filed with the SEC and available through EDGAR. A public company's annual report, or 10-K, which is filed within ninety days of the end of its fiscal year, describes the company's overall direction and contains financial data and information on research projects in development and other plans. From a company's prospectus, which is filed when the company issues new securities, you might be able to learn potential risks that lie ahead in the marketplace. From a company's proxy statement, you will learn its executives' salaries and stock holdings, special contracts, and information on pending legal proceedings. And 13D and 14D-1 filings show when more than 5 percent of a class of the firm's shares are changing hands.

The downside to all this is that only about 2 percent of companies are public. You'll have to look elsewhere for information on the 98 percent that are private.

Hoover's Online
www.hoovers.com/

Hoover's Online contains "company capsules" on every U.S. company traded on a major stock exchange, as well as some 2,000 private companies. The capsules contain recent reports, brief financial data, and links to each company's Web site. You can search the information at Hoover's by company name and ticker symbol.

Forbes 500 Largest Private Companies
www.forbes.com/tool/toolbox/private500/

Forbes 500 Largest Private Companies includes a brief company description, number of employees, sales rank, and a link to the company's Web site.

Companies Online
www.companiesonline.com/

Companies Online, a joint project of Lycos and Dun & Bradstreet, includes many private companies.

"Best Companies" Lists

You can also find some information on various "best companies" lists.

Fortune magazine's 100 Best Companies to Work for in America is located at

`cgi.pathfinder.com/fortune/bestcompanies/index.html`

Fortune magazine's ranking of the most admired companies is located at

`pathfinder.com/fortune/mostadmired/index.html`

Women's Wire's list of the best companies in the U.S. for women, based on salary, benefits, and opportunities for advancement, is located at

`www.womenswire.com/work/work.html`

Working Woman magazine's list of the top 500 women-owned companies is located at

`www.workingwomanmag.com/`

The Hispanic Business 500 directory is located at

`www.hispanstar.com/ht/players/getpdf-500.asp`

U.S. Government Sites

In our earlier books we identified some federal government sites with job and career information. Since that time, we've seen the Department of Labor become the major source of job and career information, as well as the major job and resume bank, on the Internet.

Your first stop should be the U.S. Department of Labor Employment and Training Administration site at

`www.doleta.gov/`

Figure 5.1	
The ETA home page at **www.doleta.gov/.**	

At the site, look for America's One-Stop Career Center System. Here you'll find links to several valuable sites for job seekers, including:

✔ America's Job and Talent Bank (see chapter 3, "Getting Job Information from Corporate Sites and Job Boards").

✔ America's Career InfoNet, a comprehensive source of occupational and economic information to help you make informed career decisions. Here you can learn what are the fastest-growing occupations and the occupations with the most openings.

✔ America's Learning eXchange, a database connecting people to training and education.

✔ ALMIS DataBase System, America's Labor Market Information System, is a database of labor market and occupational information.

✔ Links to each state's One-Stop Web Sites.

✔ General Info for Job Seekers takes you to a job-search strategies page with helpful information for using the Internet in your job search.

✔ General Info for Job Seekers can also take you to several databases on career exploration.

✔ General Info for Job Seekers can also take you to the O*NET, where you can find out what you can do with your background and degree.

O*NET, the Occupational Information Network, is a database of occupation information that you can obtain for free and run on your PC. It replaces the *Dictionary of Occupational Titles* (DOT), a reference book that was developed sixty years ago. O*NET describes over 1,100 occupations by skill requirements. O*NET 98 is available on CD-ROM, diskettes, and Internet download.

The database identifies and describes information about occupations, worker skills, and training requirements. You can use the O*NET to ensure that you are using the common language for occupational information on your resume. Using recognized job titles is critical today because, as we have seen, employers are searching resume databases by occupational keywords.

Other useful U.S. government sites include:

✔ The Bureau of Labor Statistics, located at **stats.bls.gov**. At this site you'll find state, area, and nationwide labor market information.

✔ The U.S. Census Bureau, located at **www.census.gov**. This site offers a wealth of information, including data about jobs, income, housing, recreation, and more, which can be viewed on a national, state, or county level. There are tables about employment in the fastest growing and declining occupations, population estimates and projections, migration, journey to work, and educational attainment demographic information.

Canadian Government Sites

JOB BANK on the Internet is an electronic listing of jobs and work or business opportunities phoned in to Human Resource Centres of Canada by employers around the country. It is located at

    jb-ge.hrdc-drhc.gc.ca/

There you'll find a link to Labor Market Information for detailed information on local labour markets in Canada's provinces and territories.

You'll also find a link to WorkSearch, a comprehensive guide to exploring careers and looking for work.

Figure 5.2

WorkSearch's site map.

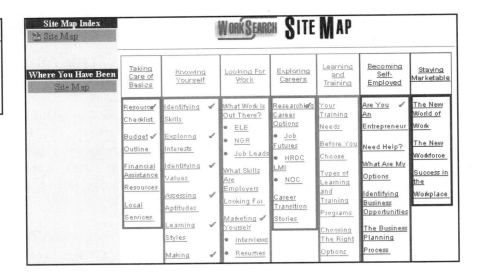

Relocation Information

In addition to career information, the Internet is an excellent way to research cities where you'd consider relocating for a new job.

MapQuest
www.movequest.com/

MapQuest provides online maps, travel guides, and driving directions.

citysearch.com

`www.citysearch.com/`

> Citysearch.com provides information on major cities in Australia, Canada, Scandinavia, and the United States.

Excite

`www.city.net/`

> The city guides on Excite provide extensive information.

Avatar's Consumer's Guide to Moving & Storage

`www.avatar-moving.com`

> A comprehensive collection of articles about planning a move.

Homefair.com

`www.homefair.com/index.html`

> Homefair.com provides calculators to help you estimate moving costs.

National Public School Locator

`nces.ed.gov/ccdweb/school/school.as`

> The National Public School Locator provides a searchable database that gives basic information about schools.

Chapter 6

Cautions: Job Search and Privacy Issues on the Web

In chapter 1, "Introducing the Internet," you read some of the success stories job seekers shared with us. In this chapter we want to share some of the horror stories they told us so that you'll be able to avoid those problems. We want to prepare you for the Internet job search so that *you* won't be sending us any horror stories.

The pitfalls we're about to share with you span many different areas. We begin with the horror stories of job seekers and employers on the Net. Next we cover privacy and security, the loss of which can lead to consequences ranging from minor inconvenience to a loss of significant amounts of money—even your entire livelihood. We also talk about "spamming," and about ways to avoid exposing your kids to some of the more prurient content on the Internet.

Horror Stories

We posted messages to several employment newsgroups and asked people to share their success and horror stories about Internet job hunting. The response was overwhelming. People contacted us from all over the world.

Some job seekers had complaints about what they experienced in their Internet job search. They were happy to tell their stories to help others avoid, or at least recognize, similar pitfalls. Here are their stories:

Applicants Don't Follow Instructions

The president of a publishing company whose name is similar to that of a film company wrote to tell about a misguided and irritating applicant.

The applicant, who had confused the publisher for the film company, began bombarding their site with his resume every other week. At the same time, he was sending a mass mailing to every other domain he could think of. The president of the company wrote to tell the job seeker of his mistake, and told him that his sloppiness in marketing himself precluded the company from considering him.

Instead of being grateful, the applicant started making "profane and vociferous comments" toward the president. Big mistake! The president forwarded these comments to every company on the man's mailing list. So much for his chances of landing a job with any of those companies.

Another employer complained of applicants who ignored the requirement that they be U.S. citizens to apply. The conclusion he drew was that the Internet makes it too easy to send out canned resumes to many employers at once, without paying attention to the specific requirements and instructions. In some of the resumes, the number of mistakes made him believe the applicants didn't even have access to a good word processor.

Employers Don't Follow Instructions

One student who was a senior in college wrote to complain about employers who ignored the fact that he was still in school and wanted him to start right away. I suppose there are worse problems to have!

Work-at-Home Scams

A woman wrote to tell of her bad experience with a company that promised her big bucks to work at home. For $24.95, the company would send her a list of companies that were looking for people to work at home. The company's Web site looked completely legitimate to her: They had success stories on the site, complete with pictures. So she mailed them her check.

Of course, she never heard from them. When she went back to their Web site, it had disappeared. Messages sent to their e-mail address came back to her. This story turns out okay, though, because she was able to put a stop-payment on the check. But many, many people out there have not been so lucky. Be wary of any Internet job prospect that sounds too good to be true.

Other Scams

One person wrote about responding to an Internet posting for human resources professionals. He received an enthusiastic response, and was asked for his address. He received a videotape in the mail. He expected something regarding the recruiting position; instead the tape was about a weight-loss scheme. And now that "they" have his address, he's been getting weekly junk mail about the scheme.

More Unscrupulous Activity

One reader wrote to tell of his Internet pet peeves:

First, some companies have asked him "interview" questions about technical problems. These questions turned out to be their attempt to get free consulting advice, and the companies had no intention of hiring anyone.

He has noted that some headhunters ask questions about when you got your degree, in a way of subtly determining who is over 40, and then excluding them from consideration.

Finally, the reader mentions some companies who continue to interview applicants, even after the job is filled. This is their way around the company quotas regarding the number of people who must be interviewed for each position, but it wastes a lot of people's time and gives them false hopes.

Headhunter Woes

One reader wrote about headhunters who lie and say they have more jobs available than they do. He noted that these people are more interested in getting a commission than helping anyone.

Another wrote about being inundated by calls from headhunters. "They call all day, and even nights and weekends," he said.

What We Learned

In all the horror stories we received, two major problems are most commonly mentioned: multilevel marketing postings and headhunters.

We've received several horror story messages containing a single word: the name of an organization or company. We cannot reproduce those here, obviously, but we can tell you that there are several companies that try to recruit people to their multilevel marketing or pyramid-type businesses.

> *Tip:* Read the announcement carefully; then research the company thoroughly. Understand exactly what you're getting into. Perhaps some people have been successful in multilevel marketing ventures; we believe many more have not.

There is widespread dissatisfaction with opportunistic headhunters. Also known as "independent recruiters" or "executive search consultants," headhunters are hired by companies to find job seekers who match the company's specific requirements, usually for higher-level jobs. Headhunters relieve the company from searching through resumes. Legitimate headhunters are paid by the employer, either on a retained basis for filling a certain number of positions or on a contingent basis when the search is completed. Some headhunters get up to 25 percent of the candidate's starting salary.

If your resume is on the Internet, you might be contacted by a headhunter. You can find them on the Internet using search engines with the words "headhunter" and your industry or city.

Legitimate headhunters accept only candidates they believe they can place. Some people say they are contacted by headhunters and then never hear from them again. Others feel that headhunters will say or do anything, true or not, to get a client placed. In reality, headhunters have to pay the most attention to the people they have the best chance of placing, since they make their money from companies only after a successful placement. The reputable ones will let you know up front if they decide not to continue spending time trying to place you.

> *Tip:* Use only reputable firms. Get referrals from contacts in your industry. Consider a headhunter to be just one of your job-search strategies—not your only one.

Online Privacy in Your Job Search

Michael Forrest, president of JobOptions, is a strong advocate of privacy in the online job search. He warns that there are three things that potentially can befall unwary job seekers:

> First, people are really getting fired for searching major companies while still employed. Many companies have agents hunting for employees' resumes out there. Second, if you're in the high-demand areas, you get hounded by recruiters at all hours of the night. And lastly, your personal security can be compromised by failing to guard your privacy.

We advise you to consider his warning. There very likely is information about you in computer data banks right now. Every economic transaction that you participate in—a check, a credit card, a telephone call—creates a record that can be connected to you. An increasing number of employers do check out job applicants' records with information search companies.

Here's the true story of Bronti Wayne Kelly, as reported by David Kalish in 1997 for the Associated Press:

In 1990 Bronti Kelly worked as a salesman in the Robinson-May department store in Riverside, California. In May of that year his wallet containing $4, his driver's license, Social Security card, and military I.D. was stolen. He reported the theft to the police.

Seven months later the personnel office at Robinson-May notified him he was terminated because he had been caught shoplifting by security guards in another Robinson's. Even though Kelly was able to get a letter from his commanding Air Force officer saying he was on duty as a reservist when the crime occurred, he was fired anyway.

Kelly had years of experience in sales so he expected no problems in finding another job. He applied at department stores throughout southern California but was rejected hundreds of times. When he did get a job, he was fired within days.

For the next two years he lived on his $700 a month salary as a mechanic at his local Air Force base. When his reserve duty ended, Kelly had no job. He filed for bankruptcy. He was evicted from his apartment and stayed with friends until he wore out his welcome. He applied for food stamps and welfare but was rejected because he had no residence.

Kelly finally was hired by another department store in August 1994, but the day before his first day of work he was told his services weren't needed. He demanded to know why. The store's personnel manager told him to contact Stores Protective Association. SPA collects and exchanges information about the employees of its more than 100 retail chain members. Most of the employers who had rejected Kelly were members of SPA.

Kelly wrote to SPA, and finally in January 1995, discovered that the SPA had been reporting the false shoplifting offense from four years earlier.

Could the same thing happen to you? Could some computer data bank hold misinformation about you? You might think the answer is to avoid appearing in any computer data bank, but you're already there.

Consumers' Union in San Francisco found that half of the credit bureau reports surveyed in 1991 contained errors, about 20 percent of which were big enough to prevent an individual from buying a home or a car.

The Detroit-based human resources firm, Aon Consulting, reports that about 95 percent of U.S. corporations surveyed said they now conduct a background check of some sort on applicants. In addition to checking previous employment and references, many companies now check driving and credit histories, criminal records, and lawsuits applicants have filed or had filed against them.

Under the Fair Credit Reporting Act passed in 1982 and broadened in 1997, employers are required to get a job applicant's authorization for a background check and to notify the applicant if something is found that could cost her the job. The employer is required to furnish the name, address, and telephone number of the consumer reporting agency that furnished the report and tell the applicant how to receive a free copy of that report. The intent of the law is to make it possible for the job applicant to correct any inaccuracies in the report and to explain anything that may have been found. We're sure many employers comply with the law; some people also believe many don't.

If you're curious as to what a prospective employer could find out about you on the Internet, you can check yourself. Remember that a prospective employer may check and discover information about another person with the same name as you. You need to know that such a thing is possible. The first place to start is a search engine. Go to:

    www.altavista.com

and type your name in quotation marks. Without the quotation marks, the search engine searches for each name in your full name separately; for example, if you enter Mary Nemnich without quotation marks, the search engine returns information on all Marys, and all Nemnichs, but if you enter "Mary Nemnich," the search engine returns information on Mary Nemnich only.

It's also wise to check your credit reports. You can get more information about this online at one of the following sites:

    www.equifax.com

    www.experian.com

    www.tuc.com

If you want to check more in depth, there are dozens of online investigative services, including the following:

    www.1800ussearch.com

    www.knowx.com

These services offer to "find out what others can find out about you" for a small fee. Their reports typically include your address; phone numbers; names and phone numbers of your neighbors; driver's license information; list of assets, including property, automobiles, boats, and planes; lawsuits; and corporate affiliations.

Misinformation Can Be Duplicated

You may discover that a data bank contains misinformation about you. Misinformation, though, is not the major problem. The major problem is how that misinformation can be repeated in multiple data banks.

Bronti Kelly discovered that an inaccurate black mark left on a person's profile can be duplicated again and again without the victim's knowledge. When Kelly contacted the Los Angeles Police Department for help in clearing up the misinformation in the SPA's records, he discovered the Los Angeles Police Department's records showed he'd been arrested five years earlier, not only for shoplifting, but for burglary and arson as well.

How did this happen? Whoever stole or found Kelly's wallet years earlier— or someone who later acquired it—used Kelly's identity with authorities when arrested for shoplifting and other crimes. To clear up this misinformation, Kelly submitted his fingerprints to prove he wasn't the man who had been arrested. The Los Angeles Police gave Kelly a "Certificate of Clearance," which states that Kelly wasn't the person arrested. The police department, however, does not delete the original information. Police officials say they need the charges on record in case the impostor is arrested for other crimes.

After correcting his records with SPA and the Los Angeles Police Department, Kelly was still rejected from another fifty jobs. His story came to the attention of the Associated Press, which in August 1997 hired an information search company to conduct a computer search of Kelly's background. Using only Kelly's name and Social Security number, the search company reported that Kelly had been arrested for arson, theft, and disturbing the peace. The search company didn't create the misinformation; it simply reported what it found in various computer data banks.

After eight years of unsuccessful job search, Kelly sued the May Company for failing to correct the erroneous information. He was awarded $73,000. It has even been suggested that because there's no way for Kelly to know where the misinformation about him now exists, the best course of action for him is to change his name.

Recommended Precautions

After reading about Bronti Kelly, you may be worried. Should you be? We think you should be cautious:

Periodically check your "cyber profile" and attempt to correct errors. This may take time, so it's not something you'll want to be doing during a job search. Be aware of what potential employers can learn about you from data banks.

Be cautious about putting personal information in your online resume. Posting a resume with an address, telephone number, or even return e-mail address puts the job seeker at risk of receiving junk e-mail or, worse, being approached by con artists who use information from the resume to gain trust and take advantage of the job seeker at a vulnerable time. The greatest risks are those of being stalked and of risking identity theft. Perpetrators can actually use resume information to apply for new identification papers and then use these papers to open credit card accounts or commit other crimes.

You want a prospective employer to be able to reach you easily, and you want a reasonable degree of privacy. Some resume data banks offer you the protection of removing your identifying information from your resume. An employer is able to contact you only through the resume data bank.

E-Mail Security

Can you assume that your e-mail is secure? What about e-mail sent from your current employer?

Some employers monitor employee e-mail. In a 1996 court case, *Smyth v. Pillsbury Co.,* the United States District Court for the Eastern District of Pennsylvania held that a private-sector at-will employee has no right to privacy of the contents of e-mail sent over the employer's e-mail system. Although the decision has been criticized as flawed, it is simply prudent to assume that e-mail sent from your desk at work can be monitored.

What about e-mail sent from your personal computer in the privacy of your own home? Internet e-mail relies on a transmission protocol called *packet switching*. This means that an e-mail message is transmitted through several small packets or discrete digital units. When the digital packets reach their destination, they are reassembled into the original e-mail message. Even so, it is possible, although not easy, to intercept an e-mail message while it is in transmission. It is prudent to assume that no e-mail is private.

Encryption is one way to make e-mail private. Phil Zimmermann developed the electronic privacy program PGP (Pretty Good Privacy). When encrypted, e-mail looks like a meaningless jumble of random characters. PGP encrypts your e-mail so that nobody but the intended person can read it. It is claimed that even the most sophisticated forms of analysis have not yet been able to read encrypted PGP mail. PGP can be downloaded from the Internet.

Anonymous remailers are another way to ensure privacy. A remailer receives your e-mail message (plain text or PGP-encrypted) and sends it to the person or newsgroup you want to receive it. In the process, the remailer removes any information in the e-mail header that might point back to you. It is also possible for the recipient to reply without being able to determine your address. Why would any law-abiding person have a legitimate reason to use anonymous remailers? Some people seeking employment on the Internet feel they might jeopardize their present job if their employer had any evidence of their job search.

Posting to any bulletin board or participating in a chat room using your actual e-mail address can get you on a spam list. So there are even more reasons for a law-abiding person to practice prudence when communicating with someone he doesn't know. There are also cross-reference search utilities where you can enter an e-mail address and find someone's mailing address and phone number. These are all good reasons to practice "safe Internetting."

Lists of remailers are available on the Internet, but you should exercise caution. Some are legitimate; others are not. The experts recommend using what are called Cypherpunk or Mixmaster programs that route your messages through several anonymous remailers. Some are free; others charge a small fee.

Unwanted E-Mail

It seems reasonable to assume that the least risky personal information to use in your Internet job search is your e-mail address. It is reasonable to ask, then, if you use your e-mail address, will it be put on mailing lists and will you start receiving unwanted and annoying junk e-mail? This unsolicited e-mail is popularly known as *spam*. Just being on the Internet for any purpose makes you a target for spam.

Many e-mail programs have settings to block spam. If you are using America Online (AOL), go to keyword "Mail Controls" and choose from several options for blocking some or all incoming e-mail. Some companies make software to block spam, but these programs are not yet totally reliable.

Because much spam is fraudulent or offensive, AOL has established an aggressive program. AOL has developed technologies to identify junk e-mail and block it before it gets to subscribers' mailboxes. It blocks millions of pieces of junk e-mail each day. AOL has taken individuals and companies to court for sending junk e-mail and is working with state and federal lawmakers to develop new laws to address junk e-mail practices. Different Internet service providers deal with spam in different ways. Consult your ISP for its own policies and procedures.

We know it's tempting to reply to a spam with a message asking to be removed from their mailing list. Unfortunately, by replying, you confirm that your e-mail address is legitimate; that can result in even more spam. AOL and other Internet service providers recommend reporting it. The best response to unwanted junk e-mail is to use your Delete key.

Unwanted Web Sites

In almost every training seminar we do on the Internet job search, someone will ask about protecting family members from offensive Web sites. Offensive Web sites can appear on your screen without you looking for them. One legitimate URL we have in the past published for a job data bank is now a site offering sexually explicit materials. The job data bank closed. We don't know how its URL became that of an adult site. Unfortunately, someone looking for that particular job data bank today will see an adult site. The concern is legitimate.

Although the screening is not perfect, the following sites offer some protection:

Cyber Patrol	`www.cyberpatrol.com/`
CYBERsitter	`www.solidoak.com/`
Net Nanny	`www.netnanny.com/netnanny/`
SurfWatch	`www1.surfwatch.com/`

For More Information

Most people believe privacy is more important than unregulated access to public records; but as you've read, information about you is already in data banks. If this issue concerns you, you can subscribe to the biweekly newsletter of the nonprofit Electronic Privacy Information Center at

`www.epic.org`

which will keep you up-to-date on privacy and the Internet.

Chapter 7

Preparing Your Electronic Resume

What would you do if you received some 50 to 100 letters per week? Let's say that you already know the general ideas covered in each letter and that only the details vary. How likely would you be to pore over every single one of them? Wouldn't you be more likely to just skim through them to find the one that looked most interesting and give that letter your full attention first? This scenario adequately describes the weekly task of most human resource professionals: going through many resumes, looking for the one that stands out.

In the labor market of the Information Age, the flood of resumes threatens to bury most human resource managers. Thanks to the Internet, there is another source of resumes assailing personnel administrators: the electronic resume. Resume data banks, newsgroups, and e-mail have added to the crush of paper resumes waiting in their in baskets. Human resource managers look for the most expedient way to get through the "stack" to find the people they want to talk to. This chapter is devoted to getting you into the "keep" pile.

In general, the rules for writing a winning traditional paper resume apply to electronic resumes, but some special problems arise when you translate your resume to the electronic medium. These problems require your close attention. In the following pages, you will learn how to adapt the rules of paper resumes to the electronic medium. Tips on how to make paper resumes attractive and professional will be applied to electronic ones, too.

You will probably prepare two types of electronic resumes: scannable and HTML. Because the rules for preparing these two types of resumes differ markedly, this chapter first focuses on what to include in any electronic resume and then gives the specific rules for preparing scannable and e-mail resumes. HTML resumes are discussed in chapter 8.

The Audience

When you prepare your electronic resume, a primary thing to keep in mind is the audience—who will read your resume. Of course, you want the readers to be employers; but remember, the Internet is public—anyone could possibly read your resume.

When using e-mail to transmit your resume, always keep in mind that it is not secure. You have no control, for example, over where and to whom your recipient forwards your message. As we have discussed, privacy online is important. For example, you wouldn't want your resume sent to your current employer, or your personal data to be sold to a mailing list.

Technically, it is possible that other people could read your mail on its way from your computer to the recipient's. Users concerned with e-mail privacy can use programs to encrypt their messages. The two most widely used protocols are S/MIME from RSA Data Security and OpenPGP from Pretty Good Privacy. If you encrypt a message with one protocol, the recipient must decrypt your message using a package that relies on the same protocol. You can, however, use PGP with any e-mail program. Anonymous remailers, which remove your address from your e-mail messages, also are available.

> **Note:** For more information on specific e-mail privacy programs, type "privacy programs e-mail" or a similar combination of keywords at any search engine.

Now, let's look at the basics of preparing an electronic resume.

Building Your Resume

Any word processing program can be used to create, edit, and update your resume. Unlike the old days of the typewriter, today you can—and should—easily make changes to adapt your resume to each job. Some word processing programs come with templates to help you create a resume. Microsoft Word, for example, offers a resume "wizard." You decide on a style and the information you want included and how you want it organized. The resume wizard offers several different headings that you can put in any order or customize by adding your own headings. The program presents you with a "fill-in-the-blanks" template to enter the information. You can use the same program to compose cover letters and follow-up letters, and send the resume and cover letter to someone by e-mail or fax, provided that your computer supports these services. WordPerfect offers three resume templates from which to choose: contemporary, cosmopolitan, and traditional. For help creating resumes in WordPerfect specifically, see *Using WordPerfect in Your Job Search*, by David F. Noble (JIST Works, Inc., 1995).

Resume Software

Software packages are available to walk you through the creation of your resume. They are similar to the resume templates in Word, in that they are based on a fill-in-the-blanks format. However, they include more comprehensive features. Here are some resume programs:

You're Hired!

This resume software walks you through the process of writing a resume by giving you formatting choices and providing sample statements and technical words from which to choose. You're Hired! uses an easy-to-use toolbox for making selections. It also includes cover letter formats, and it even helps you manage your job-search contacts.

Professional Web Resume

This software is an "all-in-one Web job search and career management tool." It provides you with the capability to build and publish your Web resume and submit it instantly to online career boards and recruiter networks. The program contains resume templates, a contact manager, word processor compatibility, and resume and cover-letter samples from professional writers.

WinWay Resume V6.0 Win95/98/NT by WinWay Corp

WinWay includes resume and letter-writing features and a job-search database. The AutoWriter feature automatically writes your resume with job-specific phrases and computer-scannable keywords. The package also includes video career counseling and video simulated interviews. WinWay Resume V6.0 requires a 486 or higher processor, 12 MB of free disk space, and a CD-ROM drive. It also includes a Windows 3.1 version in the 95/98 package.

Job Hunt Manager for Mac

For Macintosh users, there is Job Hunt Manager for Mac. It's a FileMaker Pro template by Chet Bottone. This template can help you organize your job search and set up mailing and calling campaigns. It has a contact manager and enables you to schedule appointments and interviews, log calls, and track when and where you send resumes, letters, and faxes. It contains templates for cover letters and fax sheets. You can also use the program to print envelopes and labels.

These are just a few of the many resume software packages available to you. You can order them online, at computer stores, or through bookstores. However, with some thought and care and the right word processor, you can create the perfect electronic resume yourself without the expense of purchasing a special software program. We recommend that you complete your own resume and don't consider using a resume service, as these companies get paid to make you look good on paper. You want to represent yourself fairly and honestly. Besides, most employers can spot resumes that have been prepared by third-party services and don't necessarily trust that all the information contained in them is accurate.

In the next section, we will discuss how to create an attractive and readable resume.

Resume ABCs

Three basic factors should serve as guiding principles for resume preparation. We call them the ABCs of resume preparation. Simply put, a resume should be **a**ttractive, **b**rief, and **c**lear.

The first factor, *attractiveness*, captures a prospective employer's attention and invites the employer to read on. The second factor, *brevity*, keeps the employer interested enough to finish reading. The third, *clarity*, enables the employer to conclude whether you have the skills, education, and talent required for the available position. In the next sections, we examine all three factors and apply them to the electronic resume.

Making Your Resume Attractive

This section discusses the many factors that go into creating an attractive resume. Of utmost importance is making sure it is in a format that is readable to online recipients. We also discuss font and paragraph formatting, as well as choice of paper for presentation resumes.

Text-Only and Rich-Text Format

Before we begin to look at the how-to's of preparing your electronic resume, we need to take a look at a principal difference between traditional presentation resumes and electronic resumes: text files.

In order to e-mail a resume to an employer or post a resume on an employer's site on the World Wide Web, it is necessary to save the resume in a text-only file. Text-only saves text without its formatting. It converts all page breaks, section breaks, and new-line characters to paragraph marks.

Because text-only documents do not retain special formatting, it is difficult to make your e-mail resume attractive. When the resume arrives on the employer's screen, it is no longer formatted. Instead, it is totally left-aligned and not at all attractive.

Accordingly, when you type your resume to be saved as a text-only file, you can't use the "center line" feature, special fonts, boldfacing, italics, etc. So, when you send it to an employer, it will not look as professional as a properly formatted resume. See chapter 8, "Preparing an HTML Resume," for more on special resume formatting.

Rich-text format (RTF) saves all formatting. It converts formatting to instructions that other Microsoft programs can read and interpret. However, RTF may not be usable to some employers because of the tools they use. One employer even requested that resumes be saved in ASCII (American Standard Code for Information Interchange) format. He wrote, "I appreciate e-mail, but please use plain ASCII text, not HTML-ized e-mail or rich-text format. I use a lot of UNIX tools and the formatting only gets in the way. Lately I've gotten e-mail I can't even read because it is in some odd format apparently promoted by Microsoft. I am a Linux user." ASCII is a text-only format that allows any employer to view your e-mailed resume, regardless of the computer platform they use.

The bottom line for preparing and saving a resume for online use is this: Resumes for posting to an employer's online resume template or for scanning into an employer's database **must** be prepared as text-only documents.

Now, let's look at how to arrange your electronic resume to give it an attractive "lie" and make it more readable.

The "Lie" of the Resume

One of the aspects of formatting is called the "lie" of the resume. By this, we don't mean that you should stretch the truth of your background! The "lie" of a resume refers to its arrangement on the page, or for our purposes, the screen. This is also known as the "white space" rule: the more white space that shows through the text, the more readable the resume is. Of course, with electronic resumes, the white space becomes blue screen (or black, or green, or...), but the idea is the same.

This arrangement is key in getting an employer to read your resume. If a resume is too wordy, covered with print, and has very little screen showing through, the employer might deem it too time-consuming to read. Consider again that this person has many more such resumes to plow through. The best resumes are spare, with good spacing between the body of the resume and the headings, and with generous margins.

Headings

The easiest kind of resume to read has headings on the left, separated by at least five spaces from the body of the resume. Employers like this style of resume because this format is easy to scan for information. For example, if an employer is looking specifically for an applicant's educational background, it is simple to glance at the side headings for "Education" and quickly locate the desired information. Employers appreciate this kind of format in electronic resumes as well.

In some resumes, the headings are centered above the appropriate sections. In paper resumes, which should usually be no more than a page in length, space is at a premium. Without a fair amount of spacing—say at least two expensive lines—between headings and sections, centered headings are more difficult to find and thus more frustrating to employers. (These are people you haven't even met yet. Now is certainly not a good time to frustrate them.) With electronic resumes, space is not such a crucial factor; however, it still requires a bit more looking on the part of the employer to find the needed heading if it is centered above the section. It is preferable to set your headings off to the left of the body of the resume. If you do choose to center your headings, be sure to allow good spacing—say, two spaces—between the heading and the body of your resume.

On paper resumes, headings should be in boldface type to make them easier to read. With a variety of fonts available through word processors, the headings can also be in a different size or style than the body. The idea is to make the heading stand out. You don't have the luxury of fonts in text-only documents, so the best way to make your headings eye-catching is to put them in all caps.

Choosing Fonts

Another choice for constructing an attractive resume is fonts. Your word processor gives you the choice of several fonts, including **Helvetica**, Garamond, and Avant Garde. With a presentation resume, you may choose the fonts to make your resume interesting and good looking. We caution you not to go crazy with different fonts, though, or your resume could wind up with a "ransom note" appearance.

With electronic resumes, however, all these appearance factors are eliminated. The "paper" is all the same—a computer screen. Additionally, as a rule, no special fonts or inks are available to you. This is especially true with scannable resumes. Thus, you need to concentrate on those aspects of appearance that you *can* control.

> **Note:** If you are submitting your resume to a company that uses resume scanners, you need to make your resume as basic as possible. For more information, see the section titled, "Preparing Your Resume for Scanning," later in this chapter.

Choosing Paper

One of the most apparent indicators of attractiveness in a traditional paper (or presentation) resume is the paper itself. You should give time and thought to selecting paper that is the proper weight and shade. The same is true for choosing a color of ink that complements your paper choice. Your word processing program enables you to select different colored fonts. You can print your resume using your choice of ink, provided that you have a color printer. For example, a resume printed with burgundy ink on dove (pale gray) paper makes a more distinctive impression than regular black type on white bond paper. Navy ink on pale blue parchment is elegant and crisp. Some new papers are available that contain artistic borders on one or more sides. Ecru paper, bordered in mahogany marble with brown ink, would surely stand out in a crowd of black-on-whites.

As long as you choose a heavy enough paper and suitable font styles, black-on-white resumes are still the business standard.

Making Your Resume Brief

All employers have had the unpleasant experience of wading through a resume that is several pages long. On presentation resumes, this is simply inexcusable. The general rule is that a resume should not exceed one or two pages in length, with one-page resumes being preferable. Longer resumes are not only daunting to read, but are also considered pretentious by most employers. How to fit all of their experience on one concise page is troubling to many job seekers. This is an area in which the electronic resume has some advantages over the paper resume.

Employers are accustomed to paging through several screens or scrolling down while reading e-mail. This is quite different from shuffling a sheaf of papers mailed by a job seeker. A full page of type will not fit on a single computer screen. Thus, a resume that fills several screens is not considered breaking the "one page" rule. You have a bit more latitude in the computer medium, although even here you need to be careful. A resume that rambles on for six or seven screens will be as annoying to an employer as a paper resume that goes on for three or four pages.

Craig Bussey, a longtime human resources professional, adds, "A resume is like a teaser for a movie. You're not supposed to show the whole movie. The idea with a resume is to get an interview. If you give too much information, there's no reason to do one."

So, you still need to edit your experience. Here are some tips:

✔ **Prioritize your experience.** Limit your job experiences to those that are most important or relevant to the job for which you are applying. Rank them in order, from most to least important. Focus on those skills that you know will be most significant to the prospective employer.

✔ **Use bullets.** Full sentences take employers longer to read. It's much more expedient to use short statements that summarize your experience and place them in a bulleted list. For example, consider the following excerpt from an auto mechanic's resume:

I have repaired and rebuilt all types of cars, both foreign and domestic. I can do all phases of auto repair from simple tune-ups to complete engine rebuilds. I have all of my own tools, including both standard and metric. I have all kinds of manuals and my own rollaway. I have had lots of experience in repairing Nissan and Toyota models. I am certified for headlight adjustment and smog inspections and repair.

This job description is wordy and also breaks another rule of proper resume etiquette: It uses personal pronouns. Bullets, along with the elimination of personal pronouns, make the message easier and faster to read:

■ Full service on all makes and models, foreign and domestic, tune-up to rebuild

■ Complete set of tools, standard/metric; manuals; rollaway

■ Nissan and Toyota specialist, including electronic systems

■ Smog and headlamp certified

When you're preparing a paper resume, bullets usually take less space than full paragraphs. Additionally, the look is cleaner and allows for more white space.

> *Note:* Bullets present problems for scannable resumes. See the section on scannable resumes later in this chapter for tips on getting around this problem.

Limit the scope of previous jobs. There are two factors to consider when you're deciding which previous employment to include in your resume. First, resumes should never go back more than ten years. Depending on your field, some experience is stale after a mere five years. Employers are simply not interested in ancient history. (Of course, the exception here is if you have had the same job for the past ten years.) Second, you should include only work history that is relevant to the position for which you are applying. If you are an administrative office assistant, for example, your experience as a house painter during college is simply not relevant to the employer. It is helpful if you title your work history section "Significant Experience," rather than "Experience." This lets the employer know that you plan to concentrate only on those things in your background that relate directly to the desired position.

Never list references on your resume. Unless you are specifically asked by the employer to provide references, do not list them on your resume. Generally, references are checked only when the employer is interested in hiring you. To add them to an unsolicited resume not only wastes valuable space, but also unnecessarily invades the privacy of your friends and business associates.

Choose judiciously, write frugally, edit ruthlessly. Keep it brief!

Making Your Resume Clear

Have you ever known someone who tries to build you a clock whenever you ask him or her what time it is? The person ends up giving you so much useless information that you practically forget what it was you asked for in the first place. This is a common problem in resume writing. Employers want you to tell them in the clearest, most comprehendable terms what it is you did and exactly what job you want. Too many job seekers end up getting bogged down in jargon, acronyms, or vague and inappropriate language. Here are some suggestions on how to clarify your information.

Avoiding Jargon

Jargon is in-house, job-related language that people use as a sort of "shorthand" to describe different duties, activities, or responsibilities at work. Bureaucracies, the military, and government are especially good at using jargon, but all companies and professions use it to a certain extent. Some positions or job-related activities occur in various industries but are called by different names. Thus, the jargon used to describe them can vary widely.

Consider this example. A person who checks product quality can be known as a quality control technician, a quality assurance evaluator, a production checker, a quality tech, a process control supervisor, a line inspector, or a quality examiner (just to name a few!). Imagine the confusion when you describe yourself as a PCS (production control supervisor) to an employer who uses QCTs (quality control technicians). Just because your former company knew what a PCS was, doesn't mean your future company will.

Even something as mundane as an interoffice memo can become confusing when referred to in company jargon. Memos are known variously as "buck slips," "sheets," even "snowflakes"! Some companies refer to quality control inspections as "surveillance," even though most people associate surveillance with law enforcement.

Applicants who have served a lengthy period of time in the military have a particularly hard time freeing their resumes of jargon. When, for example, they want to reflect time spent in a temporary assignment, former military personnel often refer to it as "TDY." This acronym stands for temporary duty. When they are moved permanently, they call it "PCS" (permanent change of station). To an employer firmly rooted in the civilian world of employment, it is gobbledygook to read "PCS to Guam" followed by a job description on a resume. These applicants often have difficulty translating military language to civilian terms as well. For instance, people in the business world don't "command" or "lead." They "supervise" or "manage."

> *Note:* Former and current military personnel can find special help in preparing their resumes through an online service called Transition Assistance Online. This site gives tips on how to translate military terms into civilian language. Go to **www.taonline.com.**

It is absolutely essential that you communicate clearly on a resume. After you write your job descriptions, have two people who are completely unfamiliar with your profession read them. If they encounter something they don't understand, you have most likely fallen into a jargon trap. Is there another term to describe the word you used? Perhaps it can be explained rather than named. Find a way around it. Confused employers everywhere will thank you.

Using Professional Language

Keep the language of your resume crisp and professional, but allow your own sense of style to show through. Job seekers frequently believe that resumes should be like the job application, only without lines on the page. The result is a lackluster, dry recitation of facts, with no hint of the applicant as a person. The fact is that a resume is meant to be much more than a work history. The primary function of a resume should be to capture the employer's attention. It is often the first picture an employer has of an applicant. Consider how you want it to represent you.

When preparing an electronic resume, you want to strike a balance between language that is too rigid and language that is inappropriately informal. Apply the basic rules of proper grammar and spelling. Avoid slang and familiarity. Describe your duties in professional, understandable language, but choose language that is more colorful when describing personal and professional strengths. The busy personnel manager who must read a multitude of e-mail resumes will appreciate it.

Resume Formats

Before writing your resume, you must select the format you want to follow. There are three basic resume formats. These are chronological, functional, and combination. The following sections describe each of these formats.

The Chronological Format

The chronological format puts your work history into a time-based sequence—the period of time that you held each position. This resume format allows you to emphasize your past work history. In a chronological resume, you arrange your work experience by date, starting with the most recent job and working backward. This format works best when you have had continuous experience in one field and are applying for a new job in that same field. To construct this type of resume, list the dates of employment in the left column, separated by several spaces from the body of the resume. Provide details for each job by listing the company, position title, and job description. Jobs are listed in reverse order, beginning with the most recent position and working backward through your previous jobs.

Employers prefer the chronological format because it is easy to see where and when you attained the skills you say you possess.

The Functional Format

The functional format focuses on your skills and abilities without putting them into any time frame. It is arranged by grouping your experiences and abilities under one or more broad skill categories, or "functions." Place these categories in the order of their importance to your objective, rather than by the dates when you attained them. For instance, if you want to select three basic "functions" of a business resume, these might be "Management," "Finance," and "Accounting." You would use each of these functions as a heading and then detail all the skills, knowledge, and abilities you have in each major area. These broad functional paragraphs are followed by a brief employment history, showing places, titles, and dates.

The Combination Format

The combination resume combines elements of the chronological and functional resumes. It generally begins with a functional section, where the applicant lists several areas in which she has expertise. This is followed by a brief chronology—a chronological listing of places where the applicant has worked, including dates of employment. Often, the chronology also contains skills and brief descriptions.

Next we'll examine the proper order for organizing the material in an electronic resume.

Organizing Your Resume

When you create a paper resume, you arrange the information in a certain order. In a chronological resume, the contact heading typically goes first: name, address, and phone numbers. Next comes the position objective. This is where you tell the employer in specific terms what you are looking for. In some resumes this is followed by a summary paragraph, in which you briefly describe your experience.

Experience and education sections follow. These two headings can switch places, depending on what you have to offer. For example, if you recently received your degree in engineering, that is your most valuable asset and should go first. If you have fifteen years of experience as an engineer as well as a degree, however, you should lead off with your experience. The areas following experience and education can also vary. Some common optional headings are "Military Service," "Publications," "Community Service," "Activities," "Specialized Training," and "Awards and Honors."

Most resumes conclude with "References furnished upon request." This last line is not really necessary because most employers assume that permission to contact references will be given at the appropriate time. You might want to save that space for something more important.

This standard paper format must be manipulated a bit for electronic resumes. Remember that with an e-mail resume, the first few lines on the employer's computer screen may be taken up with the e-mail header: your return address, date/time, and so forth. If you begin the resume itself with your name, address, and phone number, that may be all the employer sees on page one. This is not a strong incentive to read on. The employer might also just see your heading plus a fragment of what comes next, which doesn't create a professional first impression.

If you are reluctant to put your full address, at least indicate your city and state and your e-mail address in the contact information space. In the event that you are e-mailing your resume, put only your name and job title at the top of the resume as a heading rather than waste that first screen with header and address. Following the heading, you should write a summary.

With only about twenty lines to work with on the first screen, it is imperative that you make a strong, favorable impression in those first few lines. Therefore, we suggest that you lead off with a summary paragraph immediately following your name and job title. Include your most outstanding skills, abilities, and qualities. Make the employer want to page to the next screen! This summary paragraph sets up the rest of the resume in much the same way that a lead paragraph in a news story previews the report and invites the reader to read on. It also saves the employer some time. The summary paragraph should contain some of the main keywords that describe your skills. Thus, the first part of your resume will look something like this:

```
J.B. Seeker

Public Relations Specialist

SUMMARY: Talented Public Relations Practitioner
with more than 15 years of experience and a proven
track record in community and media relations.
Excellent writing skills. Facility with desktop
publishing, including PageMaker (7.0), Quark, and
Microsoft Publisher. Familiar with Microsoft Word
and Windows 98. Motivational speaker. Adept at
press relations and creative advertising. MA in
Communication Studies, PR emphasis.
```

This opening can be followed by a traditional resume, beginning with your contact information, then your employment history. You'll see a complete sample of a properly formatted electronic resume later in this chapter.

Preparing Your Resume for Keyword Searches

To get the most out of online resume services, your resume must contain certain words that employers are likely to enter as keywords when they are searching through a resume database. This is an important part of getting your resume read by automatic resume tracking systems. To get your resume read by a resume tracking service, it must first be scanned into the system. After that, it is read for keywords that the employer specifies. In this section, we show you how to use keywords in your resume so that it gets the maximum number of "hits," or selections, by employers.

How can employers deal with all the resumes they receive, much less all those posted on the Internet? Resumes on the World Wide Web are searched by keywords. You need to write a resume that is rich in words that describe your skills, knowledge, and abilities.

Keyword searches are done with sophisticated technology known as *extraction engines,* which can recognize hundreds of thousands of words. Some recognize millions of resume terms! Make your electronic resume as keyword-intensive as possible, and chances are good that you will receive a "hit."

The hub of the extraction engine is its *knowledge base.* This is the vocabulary of employment-related terms that the engine uses when doing skill extraction from your resume. The engine performs skill extraction on every section of your resume. This process is very thorough; the engine reads and categorizes every possible keyword. The extraction engine looks for synonyms and similarities. It can even recognize terms when they are misspelled (although we urge you to spell check, double spell check, and have a third reader check for misspellings)!

Consider the job titles you use to describe your past positions. The same job often can have several different titles. Think about a secretary, for example. This position could also be called office clerk, office assistant, administrative assistant, file clerk, or typist—even coordinator. An extraction engine will search your entire resume for synonyms for the keywords the employer has specified.

Our recommendation is to use your actual job title at the beginning of the job listing, and then use other synonyms in your job description. That way, you have a better chance of matching the particular keywords the employer has chosen to search for.

Give careful attention to all the words you use in your resume. It wasn't too many years ago that job seekers were advised to use active words, verbs such as *developed* and *implemented.* This is no longer the case. Employers don't do keyword searches on verbs alone; they do keyword searches for specific skills. Keyword searches are more likely to be done on nouns such as *finance* and *electrical engineer.* Personal traits and attitudes—dependable, leadership, high energy—are also potential keywords.

If you don't use the words employers use for keyword searches, your resume may never be seen by human eyes! How do you know which words to use? One way is to study current job listings for the popular keywords. A good place to find job descriptions with ideas for keywords is the O*NET, a listing of job titles, descriptions, and needed skills that's available in book form from JIST and online at `www.doleta.gov/programs/onet/onet_hp.htm`.

You should use keywords in your resume to make it more "scanner friendly"—that is, to ensure that it is selected when examined by a resume scanner. Scannable resumes are the most keyword-intensive resumes.

The following section will explain about scanners and the special considerations they present to online job seekers.

Preparing Your Resume for Scanning

In simplest terms, a scanner is a device that takes a "picture" of your resume so that it can be put into a computer. A scanner uses a moving beam of light to capture an image of your resume. It then digitizes the image so that it can be stored on a computer. Essentially, it puts what you have written on paper into a form that is usable by a computer. Scanning creates an electronic representation of your resume.

Many companies, such as AT&T, Ford Motor Company, Hewlett-Packard, and Texas Instruments, now use software that makes it possible for them to turn the resumes they receive into a database that they can search by keywords. Since 1991, Hewlett-Packard has been using software that can handle the more than 300,000 resumes the company receives yearly.

Let's say you've prepared a resume you're proud of: You had it prepared in an unusual, attention-getting typeface, used selective underlining to emphasize your skills, and had 500 copies printed on a special colored paper. You're ready to use the World Wide Web to find job vacancies, but you'd really rather mail your prefect resume to prospective employers. When the company receives your resume, they are likely to scan it into a computerized database. Your unusual typeface, underlining, and colored paper may not scan accurately.

You should print your resume on white paper in a popular font such as Times, Helvetica, Arial, or Courier, which scan the most accurately. You should also use a font that is 12 points or larger, because scanners have a difficult time reading smaller type. Don't use italics, because scanners often have trouble reading them, as well. Be careful also not to fold or crease your paper resume, because some scanners can't read into the fold.

Some companies give specific instructions about submitting a resume that is suitable for scanning. For example, The Good Guys is a retailer of audio, video, personal computer, and personal electronics merchandise. Their Web site contains an area for recruitment. They post the following message at their site:

Thanks for your interest in The Good Guys. You can E-Mail your resume using this response form, or do it yourself directly to: jobs@thegoodguys.com (no attachments please). (Fax and Mail instructions are also given.)

In order to make every word of your resume searchable by our recruiters, please submit your resume on white or light colored paper, with a 12-point font. Avoid using graphics, bullets, bold type, italics, or underlined characters.

Online Resume Templates

Many company Web sites and resume databases now use resume templates to simplify the process of resume scanning. These templates provide a fill-in-the-blank system of capturing your resume data. The good thing about using a template is that resumes entered into online templates are guaranteed to be scannable. Some sites allow you to cut and paste your resume directly from your word processor into their site. *Remember: In order to paste your resume into an online template, it must be in ASCII or plain text form, so that it can be scanned!*

Scannable Resume Tips from Restrac

Restrac is a desktop software solution that is used to index jobs and resumes electronically. Corporate recruiters can use the Restrac system to do a keyword search through thousands of jobs and resumes. Restrac's service assists companies in scanning resumes, identifying candidates, managing documents, and reporting results. The main focus of the business, however, is to help companies create and manage a resume pool.

Restrac offers these tips for preparing a scannable resume:

✔ Do use white paper.

✔ Do provide a typed or laser-quality original document.

✔ Do print on one side only.

✔ Do use fonts that are 12 to 14 points in size.

✔ Do use standard fonts such as Arial, Futura, Optima, Universe, Times, Palatino, or Courier.

✔ Do use a structured resume format—these scan very well.

✔ Do include:

  ■ Name, address, phone number, fax number, and e-mail address—each on separate lines

- Objective

- Experience

- Work history

- Positions held

- Summary of qualifications, skills, and accomplishments

- Education

- Certifications

✔ Do use terms specific to your industry.

✔ Do spell out any acronyms.

✔ Do use words that describe your experience in a concise and accurate manner.

✔ Do list specific skills and increase your use of keywords.

✔ Do use more than one page if you need to.

✔ Do not use colored or dark papers.

✔ Do not send photocopies if you can avoid it.

✔ Do not fold or staple your materials.

✔ Do not use italics, underlining, shadows, or reversed type.

✔ Do not use bullets.

✔ Do not use lines (vertical or horizontal), borders, boxes, or graphics.

✔ Do not use vague or excessive descriptions of your experience.

The Summary Section

A word of caution about the resume summary: Although the summary paragraph on a resume is the first thing the scanner will encounter, it is not the only part of the resume that will be searched for keywords. Remember that a scanner passes the entire length of the document from top to bottom. The extraction engine will pull out your skills no matter where your keywords appear. Therefore, although it's important that the summary contain keywords, you should realize that, once your resume is scanned and

sent to an employer, it will still be read by a human being. Thus, your summary paragraph should be written as a cohesive, organized statement, not just a collection of disjointed words.

"The automated resume system is really only a tool and doesn't replace the human thought process," says HR Specialist Craig Bussey. "[Applicants] are better off structuring some type of summary statement that includes as many key terms as it can, yet still makes sense. Remember that if I like the resume, I'm going to print it and take it to the hiring manager. I am not going to "re-do" a resume. It has to look right and make sense when it arrives at my screen."

Applicant-Tracking Software

Hundreds of companies use applicant-tracking software. This type of software makes it possible for companies to manage the huge numbers of resumes they receive each year and to track candidates and employees alike. These programs contain millions of terms for specific skills typically linked to a general profession title. The advantage of using applicant-tracking software is that employers (with shrinking human resources budgets) are able to manage increasing numbers of job applicants.

The advantage to the job seeker is that the employer will be doing keyword searches through all the resumes submitted, not just those submitted for a particular vacancy. So you'll automatically be considered for all the vacancies the employer has—possibly including some you didn't know about but would still be interested in.

Many resume-posting sites use applicant-tracking systems. The resume-posting site Monster.com offers companies with Restrac software the capability to download resumes directly into their databases. The federal government uses Resumix software to manage its resume pool.

An Electronic Resume Template

Now, let's look at a complete sample of an electronic resume format. Note that asterisks are used for bullets. Asterisks are okay to use as bullets because they are characters on the keyboard rather than inserted symbols. Also note that all spacing, centering, and indenting are done with hard returns, not with centerline or tab features.

Figure 7.1

Electronic resume format.

```
                               Name

                             Job Title

Summary:                 *  Strong, short opening paragraph,
                            summarizing your best
                            skills/strengths

                         *  Identify your profession

                         *  Highlight four or five of your job
                            strengths. Think in terms of
                            keywords (nouns, rather than verbs)

                         *  Entice the employer to read on

                             Name

                         E-mail address

                   Phone (H) Phone (msg)

(NOTE: You may include your street address if you want. We
left it out due to privacy concerns.)

POSITION OBJECTIVE: State a specific goal. Gives the
                    resume direction.

SIGNIFICANT
EXPERIENCE:          List jobs that support the Position
                     Objective.

(Dates go here)      Position title

                     Name and location of
                     company

                     *  Put each job description in "bullet"
                        form to save space.

                     *  Work in reverse order.

                     *  List the most important duties.

                     *  Do not use personal pronouns.

EDUCATION:           Name and location of
                     college/university

                     Type of degree and major

                     Honors, if appropriate.
```

(continues)

(continued)

                          Certain applicable coursework, if
                          required.

Optional headings:

MILITARY SERVICE: Branch. Dates. Rank/job.

SPECIALIZED
TRAINING: Job-related, not covered in education
                          section.

PUBLICATIONS   Name of publication. Title. Date.

HONORS/AWARDS   Job-related awards are most helpful
                          here.

PERSONAL STATEMENT: * List personal qualities that reflect
                            fitness for employment.

                          * Make an assertive statement of your
                            job-related strengths.

REFERENCES: Saying "References will be submitted on
                          request" is optional. Employers assume
                          references will be supplied. Never list
                          reference information (names, addresses,
                          etc.) on the resume, however.

Name

E-Mail Address

The following sample puts information into the above format to give you an idea of how to arrange an electronic resume. This has been prepared and formatted in ASCII for transmission via e-mail. It will also work for the World Wide Web, where you might consider adding a graphic. Remember, though, that scanner-friendly resumes do not include graphics, special fonts, or pictures. Asterisks appear on a keyboard and are scannable.

Figure 7.2

Sample electronic resume.

```
J.B. Seeker

Public Relations Specialist

***************************

SUMMARY: Talented Public Relations Practitioner with more
than 15 years of experience and a proven track record in
community and media relations. Excellent writing skills.
Facility with desktop publishing, including PageMaker,
Quark, and Microsoft Publisher. Familiar with Microsoft Word
and Windows 95. Motivational speaker. Adept at press
relations and creative advertising. MA in Communication
Studies, PR emphasis.

J. B. Seeker

jseeker@igc.apc.org

(909) 555-4285

OBJECTIVE: Challenging position as Public Relations director
for a progressive company with an eye on the future.

SIGNIFICANT EXPERIENCE:

1987-Present: PUBLIC RELATIONS MANAGER

The Westbrook Group, Palm Springs, CA

* Managed staff of PR and advertising professionals,
developing PR program that increased visibility and
acceptance of company programs.

* Directed advertising department. Wrote and edited copy,
designed advertising campaigns.

* Interfaced with television, radio, and print media,
building strong contacts and positive relations.

* Represented company as featured speaker and ambassador at
various community and charitable functions.

1983-87: PUBLIC RELATIONS REPRESENTATIVE

Eagle Manufacturing, San Francisco, CA

* Designed successful PR campaigns for company products and
services.

* Acted as media liaison. Official spokesperson during labor
crisis.

* Promoted good will as company representative through
community contacts.

* Developed in-house training programs.

* Designed company brochure and point-of-purchase materials.

EDUCATION: Master of Arts, Public Relations

University of San Francisco

Bachelor of Arts, Communication Studies

University of California, San Diego

PERSONAL STATEMENT: Creative and innovative. Cutting-edge
approach to public relations.

Energetic and loyal company advocate with a healthy
understanding of the bottom line.
```

Some Actual Sample Resumes

Now that you have the basic tools for creating an electronic resume, let's look at some actual samples from the World Wide Web. (We have fictionalized them.) Each of the styles—chronological, functional, and combination—are represented here. For even more examples of online resumes, see our other book, *Cyberspace Resume Kit.*

Note: For a scannable resume, remember to use asterisks for bullets, and caps rather than bold for headings.

Figure 7.3 is a chronological resume. The summary paragraph is headed "Profile," and the applicant has used centered headings. Experience is listed first, because it is the strongest offering. Personal attributes are listed in the profile section and within job descriptions. The resume is prepared in Courier font, from a 12-point size to a 14-point size.

Figure 7.3

Sample chronological resume.

Elaine Simmons
1900 Idea Avenue
Denver, CO 00000
555-555-5555

PROFILE
Results Oriented Executive with 15 years experience in sales, marketing, product management with expertise in many aspects of network-based services: Internet /Intranet strategic planning and implementation and interactive voice-response technology. Trouble-shooter who can recommend state-of-the-art technology solutions and identify new market opportunities in the field of network communication and e-commerce.

- Generate practical solutions applied to complex business communication problems based on a solid reputation for creative, innovative project management
- Effect a positive impact on the corporate bottom line by supporting companies through technical and strategic marketing changes
- Three years sales and marketing experience in financial services industry addressing automated and interactive business applications: brokerage, investment banking and international banking

PROFESSIONAL EXPERIENCE

19XX-Present
    Senior Marketing Brand Manager for Internet Services.
Computer Systems Company, Northern City, CA

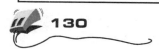

- Standardize value-added bundling of Internet/Intranet service
- Position company with industry analysts and customers through Extranets and Internet solutions
- Liaison with technical competency group to roll out training programs to sales teams

19XX-19XX

Communications Company, Eastern City, NY
Product / Marketing Manager:
Create, develop and manage company's Internet Directory

- Market research and market sensing resulted in identification of 25 high-end accounts with potential to host 4830 Web sites
- Project Manager leading teams to develop and deliver multi-web bundled solution, responsible for growing 75% of forecast results in multiple sales channels.
- Strong team player, shared technical knowledge and Internet expertise with marketing team integral to research and assessment of competitive web pages, legacy systems and database integration
- Targeted financial services community for Internet directory links

19XX-19XX

Another Communication Company in New York

Sales Account Executive
Managed sales territory as Account Executive driving sales of high end accounts in financial services: brokerage, investment banking and mortgage companies and retail and professional service companies

- Earned branch recognition for 150% quota attainment
- Noted for retention management of client relationships, with highest base retention exceeding quota objectives month after month:

EDUCATION
MBA Western University, Graduate School of Business. Marketing, 19XX
MLS Eastern University, Library and Information Science
BA Eastern State College, Major in English and Education

Affiliations:

A National Marketing Association
A City Chamber of Commerce

Sample 7.4 is a functional resume. The summary paragraph is listed as "Key Qualifications." This resume leads off with education, followed by job experience. The headings are uppercase and in a larger font. Personal attributes are listed under key qualifications. The resume is scannable, prepared in Arial 12-point font, with no special formatting.

Figure 7.4

Sample functional resume.

Emily Wood
0000 Some Street
Some City, Texas 00000
Phone: (555) 555-5555

OBJECTIVE

A challenging and creative senior position in the sales industry.

KEY QUALIFICATIONS

- Expert sales professional with over 12 years hands-on experience.
- Demonstrated ability to work effectively with clients.
- Excellent communication skills, both written and verbal.
- Life, Health and Variable Annuity Insurance License.
- Life Underwriting Training Council
- Computer literate - can quickly learn new software.
- Successful and proven ability to close sales.
- An experienced team player, bringing enthusiasm and energy into group efforts.
- Consistently make significant contributions to corporate goals for business growth and profit.

EDUCATION

Some University
Some City, Some State
Bachelor of Business Administration (19XX)
- Finance

BUSINESS EXPERIENCE

Sales and New Account Development
- Conceived, developed, produced and executed advertising campaigns and promotional activities that resulted in a significant increase in new accounts.
- Conducted financial planning seminars; located prospective clients by making formal presentations to groups and individuals.
- Provided continual follow-up to potential clients to ensure future sales.

- Consistently successful in exceeding company quota.
- Ranked within the top 5 of a large national sales team.

Client Relations

- Utilized verbal communication and listening abilities to identify clients needs and/or problems.
- Ultimately responsible for customer satisfaction.
- Established contacts in the local Chamber of Commerce.
- Developed loyal client base and increased sales volume through personal attention and consultative selling approach to clients.
- Interacted daily with diverse clients on financial planning.
- Attained strong product knowledge and expanded client base while maintaining excellent client relations.

EMPLOYMENT HISTORY

Some Corporation (19XX - 19XX)
Any Town, TX
Financial Consultant

Another Company (19XX - 19XX)
Medium City, TX
Financial Consultant

A Large Corporation (19XX - 19XX)
Big City, TX
Financial Consultant

PROFESSIONAL AFFILIATIONS

- Well Known Charitable Organization
- Speaker's Bureau
- Fraternal Organization

Sample 7.5 is an example of a combination resume. The summary paragraph is titled "Highlights of Qualifications." This resume does not include a personal paragraph, though we recommend that you include one. It is prepared in Tahoma font, from a 12-point to a 16-point, and contains formatting, such as bullets, that would not be suitable for scanning.

Figure 7.5

Sample combination resume.

Sarah Marx
XXXX Summer Street
Bossier, LA 00000
(555) 555-5555

Objective: Sales/Marketing Position

Highlights of Qualifications

• Over 15 years professional experience with the public.
• Personable and persuasive in communicating creatively with thousands of customers from all cultures and economic levels.
• Proven skill in persevering to solve customers problems.
• Self-motivated and confident in making independent decisions.
• Very well organized and able to meet deadlines.

Relevant Experience

Sales & Marketing

• Made direct presentations to retail store owners and buyers, marketing Christmas ornaments and gift items imported from the Philippines.
• Co-hosted sales seminars for potential real estate partnership investors.
• Oriented customers by answering questions regarding project details.
• Followed up by phone to verify their commitment to invest in the partnership.
• Canvassed by cold calling for contributions to a nonprofit organization.
• Consistently surpassed sales quotas in retail clothing and housewares departments.
• Persuaded 2500 citizens to sign a petition in support of placing a community improvement initiative on the ballot.

Organization & Customer Service

•Resolved wide range of customer problems, applying diplomacy and assertiveness to delivery delays, fee and budget problems, property management decisions, airline emergencies and in-flight problems, and culture/communication barriers.
•Organized the logistics of speaking engagements and investment seminars: location - catering - seating - literature - speakers - travel.
•Maintained extensive financial records regarding individual and corporate clients.
•Successfully collected thousands of dollars in overdue or unbilled fees by thoroughly auditing billing records and persevering in telephone collection follow-ups.

Employment History

19XX – Present
Office Manager/Bookkeeper Accounting Firm, Orlando, FL
Managed financial records; general ledger; handled collections; billing and receivables
19XX – XX
Office Manager/Bookkeeper. Investment Company. Orlando, FL
Receivables, payables, payroll; made travel arrangements; budget planning
19XX - XX
Self-Employed, Nonprofit organization, Author/Lecturer
Made presentations, organized seminars; canvassed contributors by phone; marketed services area-wide to customers

Education
B.A., Communication Studies – Excellent University, Miami, Florida

---

Note: If these resumes were e-mailed, only the name and job title would display at the top, with the full contact heading following the summary paragraph. (See the J.B. Seeker sample earlier in this chapter.)

The Online Curriculum Vitae

One other type of resume we felt you should be aware of is the Curriculum Vitae (CV). A Curriculum Vitae, also known simply as a "Vita," is the preferred format for those in education or science. In Canada and Europe,

a resume is referred to as a CV, and you will often come across company sites in other countries that request that you forward a CV for the job. In those cases, the term is used interchangeably with "resume." International CVs often contain personal information, such as date and place of birth, that would never be included in a U.S. resume.

Academic and scientific CVs typically are very lengthy; they chronicle not only the work history and educational background of the candidate, but all research projects, publications, academic awards, presentations, and teaching history as well. If the candidate has served internships and residencies, these are included. Any post-doctoral studies are represented. Affiliations in professional societies are listed, as well as memberships on boards.

It is not unusual for a CV to be six, eight, or even more pages when printed. In figure 7.6, we have included a format for a CV so that you can see how they are laid out.

Figure 7.6

Curriculum Vitae format.

Your Name and Title
Office Address
(Include your department, office phone number and e-mail address)

Education
(Follow the same pattern for listing your education as in a chronological resume.)

Honors and/or Awards
List by year, then award, in chronological order. Spell out award, do not use acronyms

Publications
These should be listed under separate categories:
Papers
Books
Text Books
Theses
Works in Progress
Journal Articles
Book Chapters
Monographs

Conference Presentations
List by date, in chronological order. List title of seminar or conference and give a one-sentence summation of what was presented.

Work Experience

Teaching Experience

Internships and Residencies (if applicable)

Post-Doctoral Training (if applicable)

Professional Affiliations

References
Unlike other resume formats, CVs contain the reference contact information on the resume itself.

To view a CV template and a sample Curriculum Vitae, take a look at COMPURECRUIT's Web site for international recruitment: `www.ca.compurecruit.com/`.

Figure 7.7

An online CV template.

Please, fill in the form below:

*fields with a star are optional

Domain Name:
(Domain name you would like your CV to be accessed under).

`http://www.` `.cv-online.net`
(Valid characters are "a-z", "0-9", "-" or "_".)

User Code

Password
(It will be asked for later if you want to update your Resume)

Language
Please, tell us the language you are using to write the information.

English

Advert Title
(i.e. Windows Programmer)

(Say what type of job you are looking for, skills, experience, etc.)

Description
(360 characters max. 9-10 lines aprox.)

Sectors
(use CTRL+mouse)

Admin./Clerical
Agric./Construction
Art/Design/Media
Education/Training
Engineering

(continues)

 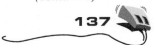

(continued)

Town/Province/Country of Residence

If you want to choose foreign countries, please visit our international edition.

Would like to work in
(Choose ten max., use CTRL+mouse)

Canada
Canada/Alberta
Canada/British Columbia
Canada/Manitoba
Canada/New Brunswick

Details*

Type   Any

Date Available

Availability to Travel/Relocate

E-Mail

Personal Information:

- The following fields are optional.

Name and Surname*

Age*

Telephone*

Fax*

Web Site*   http://

Photo*   http://
(Type here the internet address where you keep your photograph. The size must be 150x180 pixels)

*fields with a star are optional

Type or paste here your Resume*:

- **Maximum allowed is 120 (two sheets of 60) lines and 75 characters per line. Extra lines/characters will be cut out.**
- Do not include margins, they will appear automatically.
- To show bold text use the symbols ?b**bold**!b between the text.
- For *italic* and <u>underlined</u> use ?i!i and ?u!u.
- Press here to see an example of Resume.

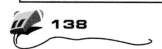

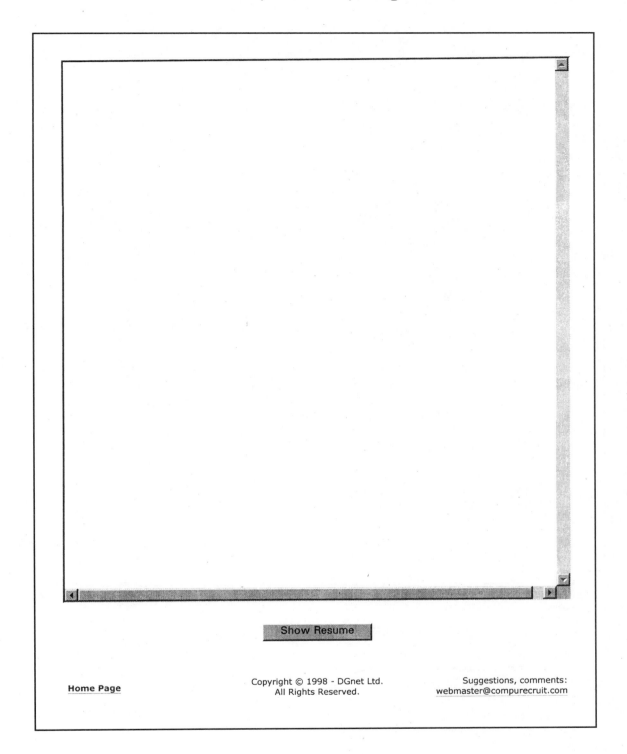

Show Resume

Look at this sample of a completed online Canadian CV.

Figure 7.8

A sample CV.

Profile

Internet Analyst/Programmer
Computer Science graduate is looking for permanent position as internet analyst/programmer. More than 3 years experience on internet technologies. Main skills: HTML, Java, SQL, TCP/IP, JavaScript, Unix, etc.

Date:	3 October
Sectors:	I.T.& Telecomm..
Residence:	London/United Kingdom
Available:	Immediately
Travel/Relocate:	100% travel, relocation only within Europe.
Type:	Full-Time
Would like to work in:	Western Europe, United Kingdom, Spain.
Name:	John Smith
Age:	24
E-Mail:	jsmith@bogusmail.com
Tel.:	+44 171 1234567
Fax:	+44 171 7654321
WWW:	www.myweb.com

Curriculum Vitae

```
John Smith Tel: +44 (0)171 1234567
London, United Kingdom E-mail: jsmith@bogusmail.com
----------------------------------------------------------------------

Personal Information
Date of Birth: 30 April 1974, in London; Status: Single;
Nationality: British; Clean driving licence.

Education
University of London Madrid, Spain
Bsc Computer Science Sept.92 to Jun.96
First class honours.

Experience
Fake Computer Systems Ltd. London, United Kingdom
· Intranet Information Systems Manager Feb.98 to Present
Leading projects for the development of intranet information systems
for sport events (Pan-American Games 1998, Olympic Games 2000).
```

· Internet Programming Department Manager Jul.96 to Jan.98
Leading projects for the development of web sites for several sport or-
ganisations (www.fakeltd.com), information systems for sport events
(Ryder Cup 1997) and helping in the improvement of existing web sites
developing specific communications applications (AAF Circuit 1997-98,
Ryder Cup 1997).

· Internet Programmer (part time) Nov.95 to Jun.96
Internet programmer. Development of Sport Web Sites(Spain Cyclist Tour,
Sierra Nevada Ski Championship 1996, Golf Tournaments, see http:\\www.
fakeltd.com) and information systems with intranet architecture (Europe
Football Cup 96).

Knowledge Engineering Institute - Neural Networks Division
University of London London, UK
· Research Collaborator Jul.95 to Sept.95
Helped in research and development of expert system for credit card
fraud detection.

School of Informatics - University of London London, UK
· Computer Room Assistant (part time) Jan.95 to Jun.95
Network administration and software package installation.

Knowledge Engineering Institute - University of London London, UK
· Multimedia Programmer July 94
Worked with "Authorware" in multimedia project.

Technical Summary
·Development, installation and support of internet/intranet systems.
·Protocols TCP/IP, FTP, SMTP, TELNET, HTTP, Ethernet networks.
·Microsoft SQL Server, Windows 95 and Windows NT.
·Internet/intranet database access tools (CGI, Active Server Pages, IBM
Net Data).
·C++, Java, HTML, Visual Basic, JavaScript, Visual Basic Script.
·Working knowledge OS/2 Warp and UNIX (Aix, Solaris 2.x, Linux, Lynx).
·Basic knowledge of SmallTalk, Pascal, Lisp, FORTRAN y Basic.

Languages
English: mother tongue.
Spanish: fluent. *Test of Spanish as a Foreign Language (TOSFL)* taken in
November 95 with a final score of 650 over 667.

At the Harvard School of Public Health Web site, you will find instructions
for preparing a CV. Access their Web site at

www.hsph.harvard.edu

and type "Curriculum Vitae" at their search engine.

Chapter 8

Preparing an HTML Resume for the Web

HTML (**Hypertext Markup Language**) makes it possible for you to take advantage of all the World Wide Web has to offer—photos, sound, video, links to other Web sites, and even more advanced features—in your resume.

Why Have an HTML Resume?

HTML gives you more control over the content and form of your resume. One benefit of an HTML resume is the flexibility you have in presentation. Just in the text itself you can use bold, italics, underlining, and various font sizes. You can include tables and graphics as well as shading and color.

An HTML resume can increase your exposure on the Web. If your resume is in one resume data bank, potential employers must go to that site to find you. With an HTML resume that is indexed in the major Internet search engines, employers can find your resume by searching for your keywords.

With an HTML resume, you'll have your own unique Internet address, or URL, which you can include in correspondence and on your business card. The URL directs people to your home page. This online presence demonstrates to employers your awareness of technology. It may be the little extra touch that puts you ahead of the competition.

Developing a Web Resume

Today anyone can have an HTML resume. The purpose of this chapter is first to help you decide whether you should have one. If you decide you do want one, you should know that there are various ways that it can be done—

from building one using a simple fill-in-the blanks format to creating one yourself. To help you make these decisions, we'll first describe what should and shouldn't be included in an HTML resume, the layout of an HTML resume, and how you can build a simple resume using HTML and put it on the Web.

A Web resume can include text, links, images, and even video and sound.

Text

The first step in developing a Web resume is to create the text. Start with your print resume. If it isn't already divided into sections, create headings, which will make it easier for readers to find the specific information they're looking for.

Links

Consider adding links, which allow the reader to click on an image or highlighted text, thereby displaying another page with more information on the subject. If you limit the number of links you use, and make sure they're appropriate, employers will find them helpful. Here are some ideas:

✔ **E-mail address:** This is a fast, no-hassle way for the employer to get to you directly. The employer just clicks on your e-mail address, and a box pops up from which he or she can send you a message, without even having to type your address. We highly recommend including a link to your e-mail address in your resume.

✔ **References:** Include e-mail links to former professors, supervisors, or others the employer can contact to verify your employment history. This is another link we highly recommend, but only *after* you have gotten permission from the people you want to use as references.

✔ **Publications:** If you've been mentioned favorably on a Web site, consider a link to that site. If you have been published, consider a link to a review of your work. The same would apply to designs, compositions, and artwork.

✔ **Notable people and organizations:** If you have worked for or with someone who is a known public figure, link to an informational site about that person. Consider carefully, though, an employer's reactions to political and religiously affiliated people.

✔ **Colleges and universities:** Boola-boola and all that networking stuff— your school ties can help you land a job. But remember that some college and university sites may also have other graduates' resumes. You don't want to lead a potential employer to other candidates!

✔ **Scholastic societies:** Phi Beta Kappa, Phi Kappa Phi, and so on.

✔ **Awards:** If you mention an award you have received, an employer might be interested in learning more about it.

✔ **Multiple languages:** If you are seeking work in another country and you speak the language, prepare a separate resume in that language and then put a link to it in the English-language resume. We noted several resumes in other languages. There was one in German that looked appealing, but, although Fred has some facility with the language, we couldn't translate fully. A link to an English version would have been helpful. Remember that the Web is international. Write for that audience.

Remember to keep links to a minimum. We wouldn't recommend more than one or two at the most. Keep the employer interested in your resume: It should be the destination, not a link to take the employer away from you.

Using links to other sites might not always be in your best interest. Although you can add links to the university you attended and to your former employers, remember that links take the reader away from your resume. The employer may get sidetracked and never return! It's also possible that you might include links that the employer finds offensive or not in line with the interests of the company. For example, if you are sending a resume to UPS (United Parcel Service) and you plug in a link to the home page of your former employer, which happens to be Federal Express, it might not sit well with the UPS representative reading your resume.

Don't include a link to your personal home page, particularly if it includes those photos of you at last year's New Year's Eve party, trivia about your dog, and your poetry. Your personal home page may not be the side of you that you want a potential employer to see. Most home pages are much more informal than would be appropriate to show a prospective employer.

Images

Use images with care. If you choose to use an image on your resume, make sure it is simple, tasteful, appropriate, and really necessary. Include only images that actually serve a purpose. Unnecessary images make your resume look cluttered and disorganized.

Be alert to how long it takes a viewer to load your page. You don't want to "lock" an employer on your page, waiting and waiting for your page to finish loading. Remember that small images transfer more quickly than larger images. And the fewer images your page has, the faster it will load. Most employers use the Internet during normal business hours and many use modems instead of a T1 line. If a resume takes longer than 10 to 15 seconds to load over a modem, they will stop and go on to the next one.

Keep images tasteful and appropriate. Bullets are a good use of graphics in a resume. You want everything about your resume to appear professional. Remember, too, that not all artwork is in the public domain. Don't put a cartoon on your resume that is protected by copyright. Software packages for building Web pages usually include clip art that is available for public use.

What about your photograph? For many years, job seekers have been warned not to include a photo of themselves on their resumes. The one exception to this rule has been for people in the performing arts, such as actors and singers. The reason for omitting personal photographs is that you don't want to include anything that might prejudice the employer *in any way*. Visual cues are powerful. Decisions may be made about you, rightly or wrongly, based on your facial expression, your mode of dress, even your hairstyle in the picture.

In conventional recruiting, before the advent of the Internet, it was never considered a good idea to take the gamble of putting a photograph on a resume. Then, along comes the World Wide Web, and job seekers now feel duty-bound to take advantage of all its capabilities. The very first thing they think of is to include a photo. Photos of yourself are just not appropriate on a resume. Even in the electronic labor market of today, they can be risky. If the photograph is unprofessional or, as so many are, of poor quality, it can actually harm your chances. Some computer-generated images are so muddy that you can end up looking as if you haven't slept in days. This online resume is the very first impression an employer has of you and your capabilities.

Craig Bussey, formerly human resources head of Hüls America, Inc., a chemical manufacturing company, put it very bluntly: "Putting your picture on a resume is stupid. It will tend to disqualify you because it sends the wrong message. I'm not looking for a 'pretty face,' I'm looking for a skill. What you look like is not a skill."

For this and other reasons, many human resource departments use a text-only WWW browser—all they'll ever see of your photo or other images are graphics icons—symbols that indicate that graphics are present on the page, not the graphics themselves.

If you do use images, provide a text-only version for those readers who turn off the display of images or use browsers that do not display images.

Other Things That Can Be Included

Some people include a *counter.* This allows them to know how many times their resume has been viewed. It has been suggested that if you do include a counter, access the site yourself several times so that the recorded number of visitors advances regularly.

HTML Resume Layout

After you decide what information you want to include on each page, you should plan the layout of the pages. There are three basic types of layouts: linear, hierarchical, and Web.

Linear

Using a linear layout, you organize pages as you would a book or slide show; that is, from page one you move on to page two. Web pages organized in this way provide links that allow readers to move forward and backward.

Hierarchical

In a hierarchical layout, all the pages branch off a main page that usually contains a table of contents. Think of it as being similar to a company's organizational chart. The main page provides the general information, and additional pages provide more specific, detailed information. Web pages organized in this way provide links back to the main page.

Web

The Web layout has no overall structure and is appropriate for pages that do not need to be read in any specific order. Web pages organized in this way provide links back to the main page or to a map to help readers find the elements they want. To visualize this kind of organization, think of a spider's web.

An Introduction to HTML

After you decide on the content and layout of your resume, you must convert the text to HTML, which is the language used to display information on the Web.

To see how HTML creates a Web page, we'll first look at a Web page as it is displayed and then look at the HTML code that was used to create it. Figure 8.1 is a resume for Clark Kent.

Figure 8.1

A resume from the Resumix site.

Clark Kent

Home Address:
1001 Main Street
Apt 321
Metropolis MN 43211-0000

Work Address:
The Daily Planet
Journalism Dept.
100 Planet Ave.
Metropolis MN 43200-0000

Home: 612-555-3221
Work: 612-555-3000
Fax: 612-555-1000

E-mail: ckent@dplanet.com

OBJECTIVE:

A fast-paced job in journalism that expands and builds upon my skills as an experienced reporter.

EMPLOYMENT HISTORY:

Sept. 1990 - Present, Reporter at The Daily Planet

Headline reporting for a major metropolitan newspaper. Responsibilities include in-the-field reporting, writing and editing front page stories, and working closely with other reporters in covering the daily events of the world.

Oct. 1989 - Sept. 1990, Editor at Smallville Gazette

Head Editor and Chief for the Smallville Gazette. Managed a team of four reporters, plus oversight of typesetting and delivery of a newspaper with a subscription of over 600 loyal readers. Also managed fundraising and finances.

June 1988 - Aug. 1989, Delivery Person at Smallville Pizza Plaza

Delivery of hot, fresh, pizza to customers' doorstep. Never delivered a pizza late.

Figure 8.1, continued

July 1982 - June 1988, Smallville Red Cross

First-aid and CPR instruction, swimming and water-safety instruction. Member of the Smallville National Disaster team.

EDUCATION:

B.A. in Journalism, Metropolis University, 1988, GPA: 3.75
H.S. in English, Smallville High School, 1984, GPA: 3.8

ADDITIONAL SKILLS:

In addition to my experience and abilities as a reporter, and background with the Red Cross, I can also leap tall buildings in a single bound, fly faster than a speeding bullet, stronger than a locomotive, have X-ray vision, and super-hearing.

If you view Clark Kent's resume in Netscape, choose View and Document Source. You will see the HTML code that was used to create Clark Kent's resume page. This code is shown in figure 8.2.

Figure 8.2

The HTML code for Clark Kent's resume page.

```
<HTML><HEAD>
<TITLE>Resume of Clark Kent</TITLE>

</HEAD>

<BODY BGCOLOR=#E4E4ff LINK=#0000ff VLINK=#0000ff>

<CENTER><H2>Clark Kent</H2><strong>Home Address:</
strong><BR>1001 Main Street <BR>Apt 321 <BR>Metropolis MN 43211-
0000<P><strong>Work Address:</strong><BR>The Daily Planet
<BR>Journalism Dept. <BR>100 Planet Ave. <BR>Metropolis MN 43200-
0000<P><strong>Home: </strong>612-555-3221 <BR><strong>Work: </
strong>612-555-3000 <BR><strong>Fax: </strong>612-555-1000
<BR><P><strong>E-mail:</strong> ckent@dplanet.com<P></
CENTER><H3>OBJECTIVE:</H3>A fast-paced job in journalism that ex-
pands and builds upon my skills as an experienced reporter.

<P><H3>EMPLOYMENT HISTORY:</H3><DL><DT><strong>Sept. 1990 -
Present, Reporter at The Daily Planet</strong><DD> Headline reporting for a
major metropolitan newspaper. Responsibilities include in-the-field reporting,
writing and editing front page stories, and working closely with other reports in
covering the daily events of the world.


</DL><DL><DT><strong>Oct. 1989 - Sept. 1990, Editor at Smallville Ga-
zette</strong><DD> Head Editor and Chief for the Smallville Gazette. Man-
aged a team of four reporters, plus oversight of typesetting and delivery of a
newspaper with a subscription of over 600 loyal readers. Also managed
fundraising and finances.

</DL><DL><DT><strong>June 1988 - Aug. 1989, Delivery Person at
Smallville Pizza Plaza</strong><DD> Delivery of hot, fresh, pizza to custom-
ers' doorstep. Never delivered a pizza late.

</DL><DL><DT><strong>July 1982 - June 1988, Smallville Red Cross</
strong><DD> First-aid and CPR instruction, swimming and water-safety
instruction.

Member of the Smallville National Disaster team.

</DL><DL><DT><strong></strong></DL><DL><DT><strong></strong></
DL><H3>EDUCATION:</H3>B.A. in Journalism, Metropolis University,
1988, GPA: 3.75<BR>H.S. in English, Smallville High School, 1984, GPA:
3.8<BR><H3>ADDITIONAL SKILLS:</H3>In addition to my experience and
abilities as a reporter, and background with the Red Cross, I can also leap tall
buildings in a single bound, fly faster than a speeding bullet, stronger than a
locomotive, have X-ray vision, and super-hearing.

<P></BODY></HTML>
```

Figure 8.2 shows the text of Clark Kent's resume and the special HTML instructions, called *tags,* which are surrounded by angle brackets (< >). The tags are information about the structure of the document and the font attributes for the words. Web browsers interpret the tags in the document and display the text.

In text editors such as Notepad for Windows and SimpleText for Macintosh, and in word processors such as Microsoft Word and Corel WordPerfect, you must create HTML tags to format the text in the documents you create. You have to know the correct tags and their proper placement.

An alternative to this is an *HTML editor.* An editor program makes creating HTML documents easier. Two HTML editors we recommend are BBEdit and HomeSite, which you can download for evaluation or trial use:

```
web.barebones.com/free/free.html
www1.allaire.com/products/index.cfm
```

When you select pictures or menu commands in an HTML editor, the editor enters the tags into the document for you. You don't have to memorize tags or know how to place them in the document.

Building a Simple Resume in HTML

It's easy to build your own HTML resume. There are only a few things you need to learn. In most word processing programs, what you see on the screen is what you'll see when you print the document. That's not true for HTML documents. HTML documents have four parts:

✔ **Content** is the text that can be read on the Web page—in this case, your resume.

✔ **Tags** shape the way the content is displayed, but the reader can't see them.

✔ **Links** connect one document to another, or one part of a document to another part of the same document.

✔ **In-line media** are any other media, most commonly graphics, that are displayed as part of the document.

Tags

Tags are instructions placed inside angle brackets (< >) and typically occur in pairs—one at the beginning and one at the end of the content they affect.

HTML tags are always the first and last tags in an HTML document. They identify where the document begins and ends:

Beginning of HTML document: `<HTML>`

End of HTML document: `</HTML>`

Note that the last tag is the same as the first, only preceded with a slash.

The head and body tags divide the document into two sections. The *head* contains the title of the document, which is displayed in the user's WWW browser display window. The title is critical. When a user makes a bookmark for this page in his browser, the title becomes the name of the bookmark. More importantly, World Wide Web search engines catalog pages according to their title elements. We recommend that you use your name and the word "resume" for the title; for example, "Fred X's Resume." The *body* contains all of the content—the text, links, and in-line media—that the browser displays.

Here's what we've done so far:

```
<HTML>
<HEAD>
<TITLE>Fred X's Resume</TITLE>
</HEAD>
<BODY>
</BODY>
</HTML>
```

Adding Colors with Tags

Using a background color can enhance your resume's visual appeal—if the color isn't overwhelming. To add color, you simply designate a color in the `<BODY>` tag. Background color is indicated using a six-digit, hexadecimal (123456789ABCDEF) code. In each six-digit code, there are two characters each for red, green, and blue. The higher the number for each primary color, the more of it appears in the final blended color.

Green:	00FF00
Blue:	0000FF
Turquoise:	3333FF

Go to a site such as `www.maran.com/colorchart`, `www.lynda.com/hex.html`, or `www.infi.net/wwwimages/colorindex.html`. Pick a color you like and record its code. Then change the `<BODY>` tag in your

HTML file. For example, if I wanted my resume to have a turquoise background, I would indicate that with this code:

```
<BODY BGCOLOR="333FF">
```

Be careful in choosing your background color. A background that is too dark may obscure parts of your text. We had to squint to read a link on one resume we saw. The background was a dark purple color, and the link—her e-mail address, a vital piece of information!—was almost impossible to see. If you want the background color to be white, be sure to set **BGCOLOR** to white (**FFFFFF**). Some older browsers use gray as the default color if none is specified.

Most pages on the Web display black text. However, you can change the font color in the entire document in the **<BODY>** tag by typing **TEXT="***color code***"** in which *color code* is the hexadecimal code for the text color you want. You can change the font color in only a portion of the text by typing **<FONT COLOR="***color code***"** in front of the text you want to change and **</FONT>** after the text you want to change. Remember, though, that millions of people are color-blind. The most common form of color blindness is the inability to distinguish between red and green, so avoid a combination of text and background in those two colors. Remember, too, that an employer might want to print your resume. Black text on a white background prints best. If you use a color other than black for text, be sure it prints well.

Section Headings

Section headings on a resume, such as "Education," are created with **<H>** tags. There are six levels of headings, with **<H1>** being the largest. Level four is the same size as the main text in the document, but you have no control over the sizing of **<H>** tags as they appear on other people's screens. The actual size depends on the browser being used. You could indicate the heading "Education" on an HTML resume like this:

```
<H3>Education</H3>
```

Inserting Horizontal Spacing

Line breaks (**
**) indicate the start of a new line. For example:

BA, Texas Lutheran University **
**

MA, Stephen F. Austin State University **
**

PhD, Bowling Green State University **
**

Paragraph tags **<P>** tell the browser to skip a line, leaving a blank line after the text.

Preformatted Text

Preformatted text is useful for lining up information, such as that found in tables. Type `<PRE>` in front of the text you want to use. Then use only spaces—not tabs—to line up the columns. Then type `</PRE>` after the text. The Web browser will display the text using exactly the same spacing you used in the HTML document.

Lists

Bulleted lists are typical in resumes, and they're easy to create in HTML. Bulleted lists are referred to as unordered lists or `<UL>`. Look at the simple list below:

■ Increased sales 15%

■ Reduced overhead 10%

To create that same list in HTML, type the following:

```
<UL>
<LI> Increased sales 15% </LI>
<LI> Reduced overhead 10% </LI>
</UL>
```

To change from bullets to numbers, change the `<UL>` and `</UL>` tags to `<OL>` and `</OL>` (OL stands for *ordered list*).

You can also customize your lists by using graphics as bullets. See "Inline Media—Images" below for more information about including graphics on your Web page.

Text Style Tags

Style tags determine the appearance of the content when it is viewed with a browser. The effect of what are called *logical style tags* depends on the settings that a user has selected in the browser; however, the following are standard effects:

Emphasis (italics): `<EM>` `</EM>`
Strong (bold): `<STRONG>` `</STRONG>`
Citation (a monospaced font such as Courier): `<CITE>` `</CITE>`

The user has little or no control over what are called *forced style tags*. Three forced style tags that are often used in resumes are:

Bold: `<B>` `</B>`
Italics: `<I>` `</I>`
Underline: `<U>` `</U>`

Inserting Links

You might want to include a limited number of links in your HTML resume. By selecting a link, readers can immediately view another Web page. This is easily done with what is called an *anchor tag*. The general format for an anchor tag is as follows:

```
<A HREF="URL address">Content</A>
```

<A> indicates an anchor.

HREF stands for *hypertext reference*. This directs the browser to highlight the words in the content area and make them a link. When the user clicks on the content word or words, the browser retrieves the document indicated by the URL or Uniform Resource Locator.

"URL address" is the exact location for the page on the Internet.

Content is the word or words that will be highlighted to indicate the link.

</A> closes the anchor.

Navigational links allow readers to move back and forth through different sections of long Web pages. This avoids making the reader scroll through a long Web page to find different sections. Navigational links are the most common type of link on the Web.

You can get images to use as navigational links at:

```
www.theshockzone.com/
```

You learn how to insert images later in this chapter.

Remember to provide a link to a text-only version of your resume, sans graphics. Some readers use text-only readers.

A Link to Your E-Mail Address

We recommend you always make your e-mail address a link. This kind of link is often referred to as a *mail-to link*. You set up a mail-to link with an address tag. If we wanted a link to Fred's university e-mail address, we would write:

```
<A HREF=mailto:fjandt@csusb.edu>fjandt@csusb.edu</A>
```

When readers select the e-mail link, their e-mail program will start and a new message will open that contains your address in the To: window. This ensures that the message is sent correctly, and saves the reader the trouble of typing it themselves.

However, some employers do not have e-mail capability within their browser. When you use an e-mail link only, a recruiter without e-mail capability cannot just click and go. He must write down your e-mail address, exit the browser, and call up his e-mail program—maybe more trouble than he wants to go through. So be sure to include telephone contact information as well as a link to your e-mail address.

In-Line Media—Images

You can make video and sound media part of your HTML resume, but that's beyond the scope of this brief introduction. Images are the most common form of in-line media on the Web. Images include photos, drawings, and any other pictorial element, such as dividing lines to separate different sections of your resume.

Horizontal Rules

The basic tag for inserting a horizontal rule is

```
<HR>
```

You change thickness by indicating the number of pixels:

`<HR SIZE=3>` is standard thickness.

You can shorten the rule as in:

```
<HR WIDTH="50%">
```

To align the shortened rule on either side of the page, type one of the following:

```
<HR WIDTH="50%" ALIGN=LEFT>
```

or

```
<HR WIDTH="50%" ALIGN RIGHT>
```

GIF Images

The most widely recognized format for in-line images on the Web is *GIF*, which stands for *Graphic Interchange Format*. All graphical browsers recognize, and are able to display, images that are in GIF format. GIF images are limited to 256 colors, the same number that most monitors can display. JPEG and PNG images can have millions of colors and are used for photographs and complex images. When a Web browser reads the page, the image is called up and displayed automatically.

The basic in-line image tag is

```
<IMG SRC="image.format">
```

IMG SRC stands for *image source*. `image.format` is the name of the graphics file you want to include. For example, if a GIF file is named photo1.gif, the in-line image tag would be:

```
<IMG SRC="photo1.gif">
```

When your Web page is read by a browser, the photo is automatically called up and displayed. By default, the text following a graphic is aligned to the bottom of the graphic.

If you want to center the image, type:

```
<CENTER><IMG SRC="photo1.gif"></CENTER>
```

Create a Test Version of Your Page

You can create a test HTML resume in your word processing program. Save the document as a .txt file if your word processor does not offer the option of saving it as an HTML document. The file name must have the extension (the letters after the dot) .htm if you are using Windows, or .html if you are using Unix or a Macintosh computer.

Then you can review your resume in a World Wide Web browser. In Netscape, open the File menu and select the Open File option. In the dialog box, indicate your resume's file name.

Publishing Your Web Resume

There are several easy ways to make your Web resume available on the Internet.

Commercial ISPs

Commercial Internet service providers, such as America Online, offer space on their Web servers where customers can publish their own Web resumes. Many of these Internet service providers offer easy-to-use programs to help you create your Web page.

Web Presence Providers

Dedicated Web presence providers are companies that specialize in storing Web pages. Some offer technical support in setting up and maintaining your Web site. Two of the largest dedicated Web presence providers are pair Networks at **www.pair.com** and Digital Landlords at **www.clever.net**.

If you use providers such as these, you will get your own domain name—for instance, yourname.com. Having your own domain name showcases your work on the Web. At press time, registering a domain name cost $70 for the first two years.

Resume Banks

Some resume banks store HTML versions of resumes.

A+ On-line Resumes converts your resume to HTML and posts it on the World Wide Web with your own URL address. It registers the URL with search engines using name, job type, and resume as keywords. A+ On-line Resumes charges a fee. It is located at:

```
ol-resume.com
```

The Australian Resume Server provides an optional free HTML resume home page. It is located at:

```
www.herenow.com.au/
```

Your Resume Online provides resume Web page design, hosting, and promotion for a fee. It is located at:

```
www.southerncross.net/rz/rz12.htm
```

Free Web Servers

Free Web servers provide free Web pages. Although there is no fee for storing your Web resume there, readers will be presented with sometimes annoying pop-up advertisements across your resume.

GeoCities invented the concept of free personal home pages and has over three million "homesteaders" in theme "neighborhoods." It offers free space, custom Web design software, and an e-mail address. Beginners can use a template, or you can create your page from scratch. GeoCities is located at:

```
www.geocities.com
```

Some other places that store Web pages for free are

Angelfire at **www.angelfire.com**
Cybertown at **www.cybertown.com**
TheGlobe.com at **www.theglobe.com**

One site we recommend is Tripod Resume Builder, located at

```
www.tripod.com/jobs_career/resume/
```

With your free membership you get a free Web site, which you can use to build your own HTML resume; or you can use Tripod's easy templates to create your HTML resume. At the Tripod site, you complete a short questionnaire about your education and work experience, the kinds of jobs you plan to apply for, the type of employer you're looking for, and so on. Based on the information you provide, Tripod suggests one of six formats: chronological, functional, and combination, and a version of each with either work or education listed first. You could then look at the HTML code and use it elsewhere.

Checking Your Web Resume

Although a Web resume may present your skills in a dramatic way, it can also present your mistakes in a more obvious way. Before you use a Web resume in your job search, do the following:

✔ **Check spelling, grammar, and punctuation.** Such errors raise obvious questions for the employer.

✔ **Verify links.** Check any links in your resume Web page to make sure they take the viewer to the intended destination. Because sites occasionally close or move, check the links on a regular basis.

✔ **Test the presentation.** View your pages to see how easily you can browse through them. Check for formatting and layout errors.

✔ **Turn off images.** Some people view Web pages with images turned off or use Web browsers that cannot display images. Verify that your resume still does the job without images.

✔ **Check different Web browsers.** Web pages do not always look the same when viewed with different Web browsers. At a minimum, check your pages with Netscape Navigator and Microsoft Internet Explorer and make sure the pages appear as you planned with both browsers. If you're serious about using your resume on the Web, you need to know what all readers are seeing.

✔ **Check different Web browser display preferences.** In some browsers, the bars at the top of the screen can cover almost 15 percent of the screen. Make sure that, with all of the bars displayed, important information is not hidden.

✔ **Check different resolutions.** The monitor's resolution determines how much information is displayed on the screen. Check the two most popular resolutions: 640 by 480 and 800 by 600.

✔ **Check modem speeds.** Verify the amount of time it takes to download your pages. If they contain too much text or too many images, the pages will take quite a while to open. You don't want an employer to move on because your page takes too long to open.

✔ **Keep information up-to-date.** Visit your resume Web page and update the information as often as necessary to keep your resume current.

Another way to check your Web resume is to use Web Site Garage, located at

`websitegarage.netscape.com`

Web Site Garage does a free diagnostic of browser compatibility, load time, links, spelling, and design.

Publicizing Your Web Address

You might relocate, but your HTML resume can be your permanent address on the Internet, making it possible for employers to find you. With a dedicated Web presence provider, you can choose the address, or domain name, that people enter to access your Web resume. A personalized domain name does not have to change if you switch to another Web presence provider.

The most obvious way to get people to look at your resume Web page is to directly refer an employer there by including the URL on an application. The following sections show a few other ways to get your page noticed.

Adding Your URL to Search Engines

Alternatively, you might choose to have your Web resume address added to the catalogs of various search tools so that when (and if) an employer searches for a specific skill, your resume comes up.

WebStep TOP 100, which is located at

`www.mmgco.com/top100.html`

provides descriptions of the top 100 Internet search tools. You can add your Web resume to those that best fit your audience.

You can submit your Web resume URL address to many search tools at one time using Submit It!, located at:

`www.submit-it.com`

Another way to register your home page with search engines is with The PostMaster submission service, located at:

www.netcreations.com/postmaster

PostMaster provides a free demo, which submits your site to two dozen top search engines, including AltaVista, Open Text, Webcrawler, and Yahoo!

Linking Your Resume with Other Sites

Another way to have employers find you is to link your resume Web page with other sites.

The Entry Level Job Seeker Assistant is for people who have never held a full-time, permanent job in their field or who have less than one year of nonacademic experience. It does not accept resumes; instead, it contains links to your World Wide Web resume. There is no charge. The Entry Level Job Seeker Assistant is located at

members.aol.com/Dylander/jobhome.html

When a search engine robot, such as those used by AltaVista, visits a site, it automatically indexes all linked pages at that site. Note that your HTML resume must be linked from somewhere else in the site in order to be indexed. It is not enough to be located at a site that the robot visits. The search engine automatically indexes your resume so that it will come up in keyword searches.

Sample HTML Resumes

Let's check out some sample HTML resumes from the World Wide Web.

Figure 8.3

HTML resume #1.

Links to each section of resume

Link to his ASCII-version resume

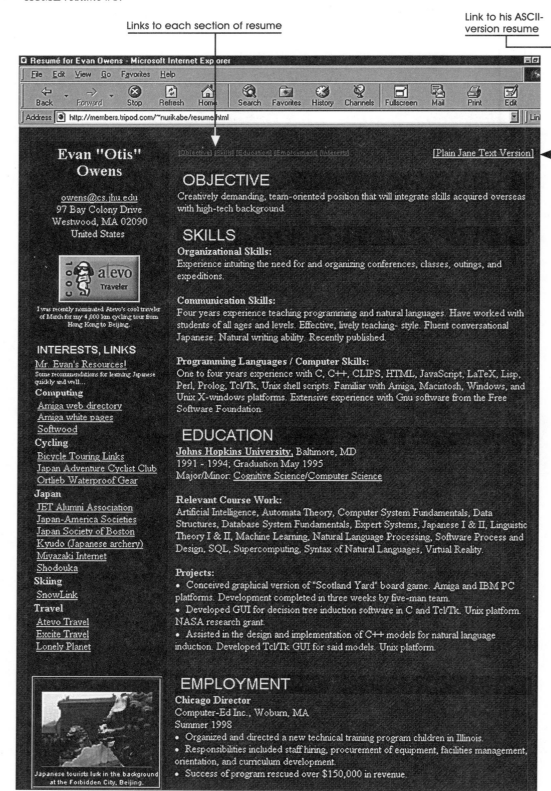

Figure 8.3, continued

Counter

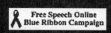

This resumé has been visited 465 times since March 1, 1998.

Graphics Specialist
Colgate Pharmaceuticals, Canton, MA
Winter 1998
• Responsible for design and layout of customized logos using Adobe Illustrator and Photoshop.
• Maintained SAP customer database.
• Prioritized orders to adhere to tight production schedule.
• Coordinated efforts of sales, graphics, and production departments to ensure high quality and timely delivery of products.

Educator in Japan
Japan Exchange and Teaching Programme, Sadowara, Miyazaki, Japan
Summer, 1995 - Summer, 1997
• Hired by Japan's Ministry of Education to work with the Sadowara Board of Education.
• Developed course material.
• Conducted classes in elementary school, middle school, and adult education curricula.
• Periodically served as translator/interpreter.
• Editor of prefecture-wide English-language newsletter.
• Conceived of and organized weekly, prefecture-wide round-table discussions to improve the quality of English education in Miyazaki.

Score Report from the Japanese-Language Proficiency Test

NASA / HST Research Team Member
Medium Deep Survey, Johns Hopkins University, Baltimore, MD
Spring Semester, 1995
• Investigated methods for the classification of galactic morphology in Hubble Space Telescope data. Designed and customized software written in C with supporting Perl scripts.
• Results published as "Using Oblique Decision Trees for the Morphological Classification of Galaxies," Monthly Notices of the Royal Astronomical Society, 281, 153.

Teaching Assistant
Dept. of Computer Science, Johns Hopkins University, Baltimore, MD
Spring Semester, 1993; Spring Semester, 1993; Fall Semester, 1994 Prepared and graded material for multiple courses, including
• Intermediate Programming in C++.
• Organized and conducted additional lectures in all courses.

Educator
Computer-Ed, High-Tech Camp, Newton, MA
Summer, 1993; Summer 1994
• Taught a variety of classes, including Advanced Programming in C++ and Artificial Intelligence Programming in CLIPS.
• Organized extracurricular activities for groups of over 150.
• Director of Counselor Training, 1994.

References furnished upon request

 This page written entirely in hand-coded HTML. No artificial preservatives, flavorings, or colors.

[Objective] [Skills] [Education] [Employment] [Interests]

Figure 8.4

Plain-text version of HTML resume #1.

Link to HTML version

It is a good idea to put all contact information in one place

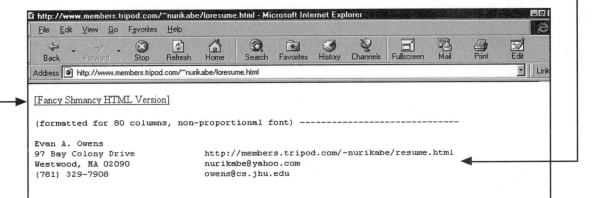

```
http://www.members.tripod.com/~nurikabe/loresume.html - Microsoft Internet Explorer

File  Edit  View  Go  Favorites  Help

 Back   Forward   Stop  Refresh  Home   Search  Favorites  History  Channels  Fullscreen  Mail   Print   Edit

Address  http://www.members.tripod.com/~nurikabe/loresume.html                          Link
```

```
[Fancy Shmancy HTML Version]

(formatted for 80 columns, non-proportional font) -------------------------------

Evan A. Owens
97 Bay Colony Drive              http://members.tripod.com/~nurikabe/resume.html
Westwood, MA 02090               nurikabe@yahoo.com
(781) 329-7908                   owens@cs.jhu.edu



OBJECTIVE

Adventurous candidate seeks creatively demanding, team-oriented position
that will integrate skills acquired overseas with high-tech background.



SKILLS

Managerial/Organizational Skills:
  Experience intuiting the need for and organizing conferences, classes,
  outings, expeditions, and educational programs.

Communication Skills:
  Four years experience teaching programming and natural languages.  Have
  worked with students of all ages and levels.  Effective, lively teaching-
  style.  Natural writing ability.  Recently published.

Programming Languages / Computer Skills:
  One to four years experience with C, C++, CGI, CLIPS, FSF (GNU) Software,
  HTML, Java, LaTeX, Lisp, Perl, Prolog, Tcl/Tk, Unix shell scripts.  Familiar
  with Amiga, Macintosh, Windows, and Unix X-windows platforms.



EDUCATION

Johns Hopkins University, Baltimore, MD  (Bachelor of Arts, May 1995)
  Cognitive Science / Computer Science
  Concentration in Natural Language Processing

Relevant Course Work:
  Artificial Intelligence, Automata Theory, Computer System Fundamentals, Data
  Structures, Database System Fundamentals, Expert Systems, Japanese I & II,
  Machine Learning, Natural Language Processing, Software Process and Design,
  SQL, Supercomputing, Syntax of Natural Languages, Virtual Reality.

Projects:
  o Conceived graphical version of "Scotland Yard" board game.  Amiga and IBM PC
    platforms.  Development completed in three weeks by five-man team.
  o Developed GUI for decision tree induction software in C and Tcl/Tk.  Unix
    platform.  NASA research grant.
  o Assisted in the design and implementation of C++ models for natural
    language induction.  Developed Tcl/Tk GUI for said models.  Unix platform.
```

Figure 8.4, continued

```
EXPERIENCE

Summer 1998       Director, Computer-Ed Lake Forest
                  Computer-Ed Inc., Woburn, MA
                      o Organized and directed a new technical training program for
                        children in Illinois.
                      o Responsibilities included staff hiring, procurement of
                        equipment, facilities management, orientation, and curric-
                        ulum development.
                      o Success of program rescued over $150,000 in revenue.


Winter 1998       Graphics Specialist, Brush Imprinting Plant
                  Colgate Pharmaceuticals, Canton, MA
                      o Responsible for design and layout of customized toothbrush
                        logos using Adobe Illustrator and Photoshop.
                      o Maintained SAP customer database.
                      o Prioritized orders to adhere to tight production schedule.
                      o Coordinated efforts of sales, graphics, and production dep-
                        artments to ensure high quality and timely delivery of
                        products.


1995 - 1997       Educator, Japan Exchange and Teaching Programme (JET)
                  Sadowara, Miyazaki, Japan
                      o Hired by Japan's Ministry of Education to work with the
                        Sadowara Board of Education.
                      o Developed course material.
                      o Conducted classes in elementary school, middle school, and
                        adult education curricula.
                      o Periodically served as translator/interpreter.
                      o Editor of prefecture-wide English-language newsletter.
                      o Conceived of and organized weekly, prefecture-wide round-
                        table discussions to improve the quality of English education
                        in Miyazaki.


Spring 1995       NASA / MDS Research Team Member, Department of Physics & Astronomy
                  Johns Hopkins University, Baltimore, MD
                      o Investigated methods for the classification of galactic morph-
                        ology in Hubble Space Telescope data.  Design and augmentation
                        of software written in C with supporting Perl scripts.
                      o Completed software used to aid in the automatic classification
                        of HST data thereby freeing researchers from this task.
                      o Results published in Monthly Notices of the Royal Astronomical
                        Society, 281, 153.


1992 - 1994       Teaching Assistant, Computer Science Department
                  Johns Hopkins University, Baltimore, MD
                      o Prepared and graded material for multiple courses, including
                        Intermediate Programming in C++.
                      o Organized and conducted additional lectures in all courses.


1993, 1994        Educator, Computer-Ed
                  Lasell College, Newton, MA
                      o Taught a variety of classes, including Advanced Programming
                        in C++ and Artificial Intelligence Programming in CLIPS.
                      o Organized extracurricular activities for groups of over 150.
                      o Director of Counselor Training, 1994.



INTERESTS

Cycling, downhill skiing/snowboarding, foreign film & subtitling, travel.
During the summer of 1997, organized and executed a solo cycling tour from Hong
Kong to Beijing.


References furnished upon request
```

Figure 8.5

HTML resume #2.

Actress's resume includes photo...   ...and personal information

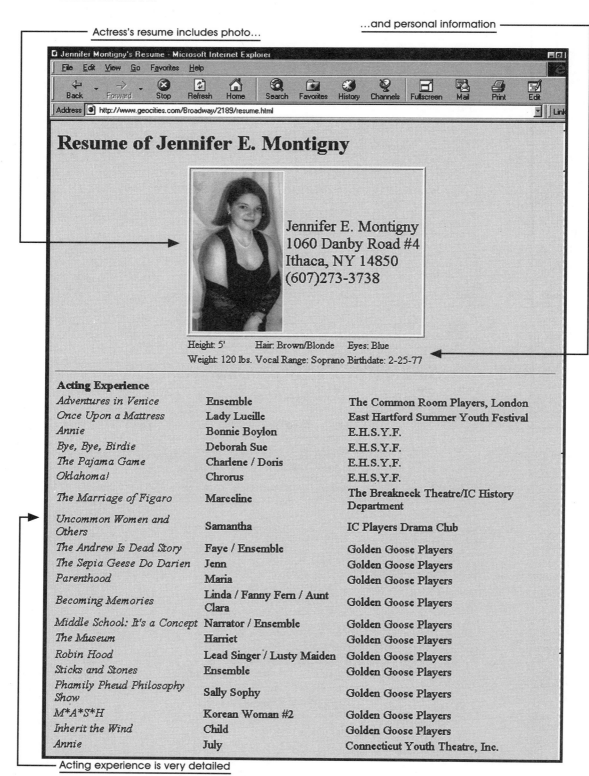

Figure 8.5, continued

Shows different types
of experience,
besides acting

Scenes

The Thickness of Skin	Laura	with Susannah Berryman, 1997
The Glass Menagerie	Laura	with Judy Levitt, 1996
Ambrosio	Antonia	with Barbara Anger, 1996
From *Win, Lose, Draw Little Miss Fresno*	Doris	with Barbara Anger, 1995

Technical Experience

Stage Manager	*Adventures in Venice*	The Common Room Players, London
Stage Manager, Tech Director, Lighting Designer, Set Designer	*Anne of Green Gables*	Lake Bryn Mawr Camp
Stage Manager, Tech Director, Lighting Designer, Set Designer	*Rogers and Hammerstein Revue*	Lake Bryn Mawr Camp
Stage Manager, Tech Director, Lighting Designer, Set Designer	*Joseph and the Amazing Technicolor Dreamcoat*	Lake Bryn Mawr Camp
Sound Crew	*The Bartered Bride*	Ithaca College Theatre
Electrics Crew, Spotlight Operator	*1776*	Ithaca College Theatre
Spotlight Supervisor and Operator	*The 6th Annual RHS Talent Show*	The RHS Service Club
Spotlight Supervisor and Operator	*The Mr. RHS Pagent*	The RHS Senior Class
Spotlight Operator	*Trixie the Teen Detective*	The Golden Goose Players

Directing Experience

The Marriage of Figaro by Beaumarchais; A staged reading produced in association with the IC History Department, April, 1997

Parenthood an original One-Act produced at the Golden Goose Players' Evening of One-Acts 1995

Sistertales an original One-Act produced at the Golden Goose Players' Evening of One-Acts 1994

Playwriting Experience

With a Little Help an original One-Act in progress, 1998

Water an original, absurd One-Act with Jonah VanSpreecken, 1998

The Lighter Side of the Trojan War an original One-Act, 1998

Music Is My Life an original Monologue featured in the Golden Goose Players' collection *It Could Happen To You*, 1995

Parenthood an original One-Act produced at the Golden Goose Players' Evening of One-Acts 1995

Sistertales an original One-Act produced at the Golden Goose Players' Evening of One-Acts 1994

Clytemnestra's Way an original Video Script awarded First Place in English Prose at the Connecticut State Latin Day 1994

(continues)

Figure 8.5, continued

Use of humor is okay for a theatrical resume

Training

Playwrighting with J. Fred Pritt (1998)
Aesthetics and Criticism with J. Fred Pritt (1998)
British Styles of Acting with Mel Churcher (1997)
Acting II with Susannah Berryman (1997)
Acting I with Judith Levitt (1996)
Intro to Acting II with Barbara Anger (1996)
Intro to Acting I with Barbara Anger (1995)
Advanced Acting with Margaret Kline (1994-5); including multiple public performances culminating with an appearance at the Connecticut Drama Association Festival 1995
Intro to Theatre II with Margaret Kline (1994); concentration on Acting
Intro to Theatre I with Margaret Kline (1993); concentration on Technical Theatre
Catholic Choir at Ithaca College's Muller Chapel 9PM services, including holidays (1995-)
Women's Choir with Eileen Sullivan (1991-5); performing a variety of pieces including Madrigals, Classical, Jazz, and Showtunes
Mixed Choir with Eileen Sullivan (1991-5), Thomas Faris (1988-91), and Anne Baldwin (1986-88); performing a variety of pieces including Classical, Madrigals, Jazz, and Showtunes
Private Voice Lessons with Salvadore Cicciarella (1994-5) and Marion Hanson (1995); studying Classical, Operatic, and Showtunes
Intro to Design with Craig Clipper (1996)
*Availiable upon request: Ithaca College Transcript including related courses and grades

Special Skills

Recent Spokesmodel for *Drippo Orphan Gruel*, Played Guest Kazoo with the Massachusetts Institute of Technology Marching Band, Can twirl a flag (Member of the RHS Marching "Ram" Band Color Guard 1993-5), Has experience in elementary Jazz and Ballet, Learns rapidly, Currently holding a 3.6 GPA, Multiple appearance on Dean's List and member of Oracle Society, Works well with others, and runs with scissors.

Return to Jenn's Homepage

Like me?
E-mail at Ifferjenn@aol.com

Includes a link to the home page...

...and e-mail

Figure 8.6

HTML resume #3.

Animated fishtail and bubbles.
Nice artwork because resume is
for design

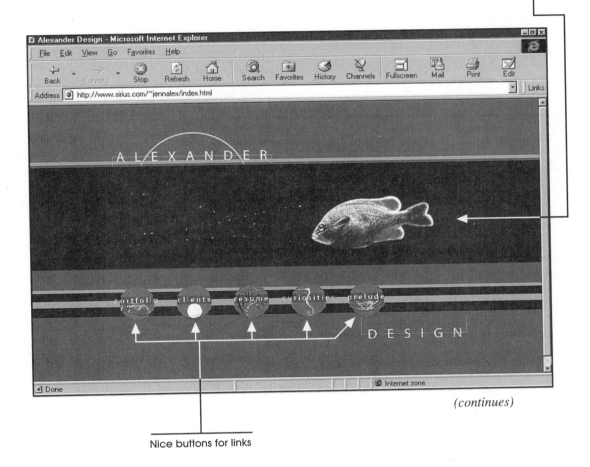

(continues)

Nice buttons for links

Figure 8.6, continued

Phone number is prominently displayed

Jennifer Alexander - Microsoft Internet Explorer

File   Edit   View   Go   Favorites   Help

Back   Forward   Stop   Refresh   Home   Search   Favorites   History   Channels   Fullscreen   Mail   Print   Edit

Address http://www.sirius.com/~jennalex/resume/resume.html

JENNIFER ALEXANDER
designer

4 1 5 . 3 3 3 . 1 5 7 9   jennalex@sirius.com

education

B.F.A. Scene Design - The North Carolina School of the Arts

experience

portfolio
clients
curiosities
prelude
entrance
exit

Alexander Design

Freelance Web Design: All aspects of site concept and production. (4/96-Current)

Projects include:

- Organic Online -**Designer**
  Developed concepts, created and implemented designs for proposals, banners, and active websites. (8/97-12/97)

  Clients include:
  Feld Entertainment (aka. Ringling Bros and Barnum and Bailey)* - Proposal
  Hyundai* - Proposal
  eBay* - Banners
  Palm Pilot* - Proposal
  Netgrocer - Production

  *Contact for visuals

- eMergingmedia -**Designer**
  Created template designs, as well as new elements for pre-existing designs (11/97-2/98).

  Clients include:
  Intershop - Designed templates
  the goodguys - Created elements for pre-existing designs
  Brightware - Proposal

- Symantec -**Designer**
  Designed logo and web presence for the Authorized Training Center division of the company. (6/97-8/97)
  URL: http://www-cu.symantec.com/javacentral/atc/intro.html
- Sage Interactive/Bay Networks -**Designer**
  Worked in conjunction with these two companies to create a web environment to be used as an online sales tool. (6/96-9/96)

Figure 8.6, continued

Links to examples
of work

- Numenet/Oracle -**Designer**
  Developed a look and feel for a business resource in
  collaboration with these two companies. Illustrated graphics
  for Numenet's Home site. (5/96-7/96)
  URL: http://www.sirius.com/~jennalex/numenet/brr-bl2.html
  URL: http://www.numenet.com

Cybernautics

Lead Designer/Project Director : Project direction, graphic
design, interface design, site architecture, animation, and HTML.
(9/96-4/97)

Projects include:

- Turner Interactive -**Project Director**- *Space Ghost*
  Directed project from concept through completion. Guided
  the overall artistic vision, managed a team of artists, designers,
  and writers, and created most of the design work.
  URL: http://www.sirius.com/~jennalex/sgfinals
- Netiva -**Project Director**
  Developed overall design concept, led a team of designers,
  supervised the web commerce area of the site as well as the
  BBS implementation.
  URL: http://www.netiva.com
- NetChannel -**Interface Designer**
- Microprose -**Production Graphics and HTML**
- Diamond Multimedia -**Production Graphics and HTML**

Mt. Lake Software

Designer: Created original content and design for a young web-
savvy crowd. (7/95-5/96)

Projects include:

- Cyberteens -**Designer**
  Created several award winning Shockwave animations and
  developed the design interface for the main body of this
  website geared for teenagers.
  URL: http://www.cyberteens.com/ctmain.html
  URL:
  http://www.cyberteens.com/multimedia/shockwave/index.html
- Cyberkids Launchpad -**Designer and Content Developer**
  Compiled links for this vast kid safe resource, wrote
  commentary and designed banners.
  URL: http://www.cyberkids.com/Launchpad/Launchpad.html

(continues)

Figure 8.6, continued

CMP Media/Woodwind Internet Services

Designer and Illustrator: Basic Web development for a wide
range of clients (7/95-3/96)

Projects include:

- NetGuide **-Designer**
  Designed prototypes for an online web service
- Bank of America **-Designer**
  Basic HTML and graphics manipulation
- Ketchum Kitchen **-Designer**
  Basic HTML and graphics manipulation
- Weblust **-Designer**
  Created a few graphics, but wrote commentary for much of
  the site.
  URL: http://www.weblust.com/links/women.html
- Woodwind Internet Services **-Designer**
- George Coates Performance Works **-Designer**

n o t i c e s)

Shocked Site of the Day
4 Star Magellan Site
C|Net's Best of the Web
Nominated for the Global Information Infrastructure Awards

*"...One very imaginative and fantasia-like Shockwave movie runs on a page
created by Cyberteens...."*-The New York Times

(s k i l l s

Computer Skills: Photoshop 4.0, Illustrator 6.0.1, Painter 4.0, Director 5.0,
HTML 3.2, Autocad 13, Strata Studio Pro

Related Skills: Drawing, Painting, Sculpting, Model Building, Drafting, Carpentry,
Basic Electronics, Lighting Design, Sound Design, Public Speaking, Directing,
Writing

R e f e r e n c e s   a v a i l a b l e   u p o n   r e q u e s t)

Good idea to
include a positive
review of work

Figure 8.7

HTML resume #4.

Street and Web page addresses

Contains illustration samples

Note copyright,
due to artwork

Prominent
phone number

(continues)

Figure 8.7, continued

Two versions of resume
highlighting different skills

Angie Mason - Computer Resume - Microsoft Internet Explorer

File   Edit   View   Go   Favorites   Help

Back   Forward   Stop   Refresh   Home   Search   Favorites   History   Channels   Fullscreen   Mail   Print   Edit

Address   http://www.angiemason.com/res_comp.htm

Angie Mason

36 Manner Avenue Garfield, New Jersey 07026-1410

www.angiemason.com
angie@angiemason.com

Education

Parsons School Of Design B.F.A. Illustration
New School for Social Research course work
Ridgewood Art Institute studio classes
Summer Arts Institute of NJ intensive five week painting program
Center for Book Arts book binding workshop

Experience

Software

Photoshop creating, compositing, editing and scanning pixel images
Illustrator + Freehand creating vector graphic images and page layouts
Quark + Pagemaker composing, editing and printing page layouts
Acrobat generating and printing pdf files
BBEdit + Hot Dog Pro HTML programming and web page + site design
Painter creating and manipulating pixel images
Fontographer creating and editing fonts

Hardware

Skilled with **both Macintosh and Windows** operating systems.
Presently own a Mac, a Windows PC and a color scanner.

Media

Watercolor, color pencil, acrylic, computer, gouache, collage,
pen and ink, marker, printmaking, oil, clay, wood and fabric

Employment

UN Productions Creative Producer print, net + media production + design, original character design
Snailworks Publishing Production Artist orig. character + font design, scanning, color corrections
The Puppet Company Assistant Internship restoration of puppets and general office duties
The Childrens' Museum of Manhattan volunteered to assist with childrens' activities
Pearl Paint displays, customer relations, general retail duties

Awards

Deans' List @ Parsons School Of Design
Parsons 98 Catalog Chosen to represent Illustration Dept.
Parsons Tuition **Scholarship**
Mutual Life Benefit Award for excellence in the arts

973*253*1244

All images + writings © 1995-98 Angie Mason

Figure 8.8

HTML resume #5.

Good idea to list all means of
contact in one place

Cartoon is better
than photo because
it adds interest

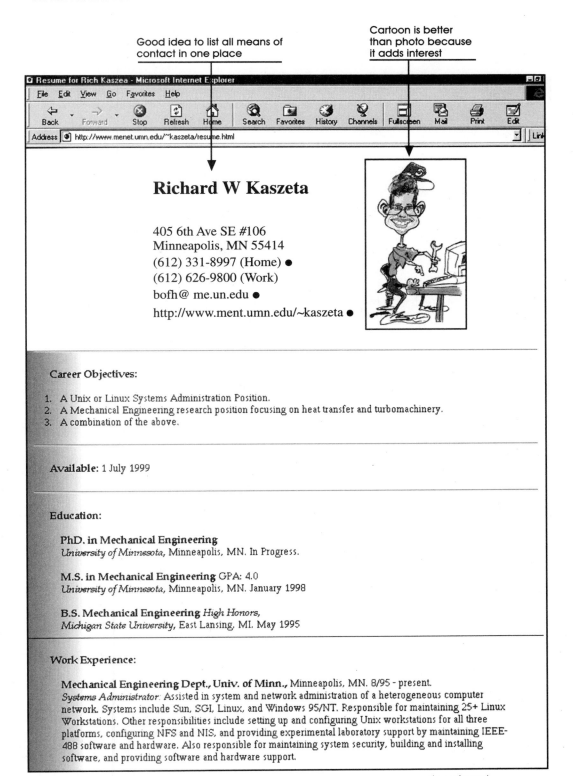

Resume for Rich Kaszea - Microsoft Internet Explorer

File   Edit   View   Go   Favorites   Help

Back   Forward   Stop   Refresh   Home   Search   Favorites   History   Channels   Fullscreen   Mail   Print   Edit

Address   http://www.menet.umn.edu/~kaszeta/resume.html

Richard W Kaszeta

405 6th Ave SE #106
Minneapolis, MN 55414
(612) 331-8997 (Home) ●
(612) 626-9800 (Work)
bofh@ me.un.edu ●
http://www.ment.umn.edu/~kaszeta ●

Career Objectives:

1. A Unix or Linux Systems Administration Position.
2. A Mechanical Engineering research position focusing on heat transfer and turbomachinery.
3. A combination of the above.

Available: 1 July 1999

Education:

PhD. in Mechanical Engineering
University of Minnesota, Minneapolis, MN. In Progress.

M.S. in Mechanical Engineering GPA: 4.0
University of Minnesota, Minneapolis, MN. January 1998

B.S. Mechanical Engineering *High Honors,*
Michigan State University, East Lansing, MI. May 1995

Work Experience:

Mechanical Engineering Dept., Univ. of Minn., Minneapolis, MN. 8/95 - present.
Systems Administrator: Assisted in system and network administration of a heterogeneous computer
network. Systems include Sun, SGI, Linux, and Windows 95/NT. Responsible for maintaining 25+ Linux
Workstations. Other responsibilities include setting up and configuring Unix workstations for all three
platforms, configuring NFS and NIS, and providing experimental laboratory support by maintaining IEEE-
488 software and hardware. Also responsible for maintaining system security, building and installing
software, and providing software and hardware support.

(continues)

Figure 8.8, continued

Mechanical Engineering Dept., Univ. of Minn., Minneapolis, MN. 7/96 - Present.
National Science Foundation (NSF) Fellowship: Conducting research on turbulent fluid flow and heat transfer in gas turbine flows (Wake-Induced Turbulent Boundary Layer Transition in Low-Pressure Turbine Blades).

Mechanical Engineering Dept., Univ. of Minn., Minneapolis, MN. 3/96 - 6/96.
Teaching Assistant: Assisted in the teaching of the graduate level course ME 8332: Radiation

Mechanical Engineering Dept., Univ. of Minn., Minneapolis, MN. 8/95 - 7/96.
Graduate Research Assistant: Conducting research on turbulent fluid flow and heat transfer in gas turbine flows (film cooling).

Oak Ridge National Laboratory, High Flux Isotope Reactor, Oak Ridge, TN. 5-8/95, and 5-8/94.
Assistant Systems Administrator and Engineering Intern: Responsibilities included Unix systems administration for Linux and AIX machines, engineering software development, and conducting mechanical analyses of spent fuel storage arrays.

Oak Ridge National Laboratory, High Flux Isotope Reactor, Oak Ridge, TN. 9-12/93.
Engineering Intern: Developed and implemented a x-ray based technique for verifying the thickness of cadmium sheeting in spent-fuel storage shrouds.

Michigan State University, Thermal Engineering Research Laboratory, East Lansing, MI. 9/91-5/95.
Research Assistant: Assisted primary researchers in a variety of thermal engineering projects, including thermal property measurements of live tree tissue, electro-rheological (ER) fluids, R134a refrigerant, and silver-tin solder. Also developed software for interpretation of Mach-Zender interferometry images.

Computer Related Experience:

Operating Systems: Various flavors of Unix including Solaris, SunOS, IRIX, and Linux; and MS-DOS/Windows;

Computer Hardware: Sun, SGI, IBM PC, IEEE-448 devices.

Networks: Ethernet, ATM, TCP/IP, Internet, and Appletalk.

Computer Languages: Perl, C, C++, FORTRAN, [c]sh, HTML, Java, and Pascal.

Personal: Own and administrate a private Unix system in my home. Also a software developer for the Debian Linux Project.

Miscellaneous: TeX/LaTeX, Internet News, Anonymous ftp, WWW, GPIB, Process Control, ssh, PGP/GPG, and other assorted topics.

Heat Transfer Related Experience:

Experimental Methods: Hot Wire Anemometry, Various Flow Visualization Techniques, Thermocouples, and Computer Controlled Data Acquistion.

Graduate Course Work: Courses have focused on heat transfer (conduction, convection, and radation), thermal design, experimental methods, turbulence, fluid dynamics, and computational modelling of fluid flow and heat transfer.

Figure 8.8, continued

Notable Web Publications and Tools:

X Window System Terminals: A New Use for Old and Outdated PCs, published in the April 1998 Linux Gazette.

The Crappy Divesite Home Page, a guide to inexpensive diving in lakes, quarries, and rivers. Listed as one of the top 50 scuba-related web sites by Rodale's Scuba Diving Magazine, and featured in the Aqua magazine's series "Diving Across America" (April/May 1998).

VR Chia Head, a Java applet which allows you to interactively "spin" our department's Chia Head. Selected for inclusion on Bonus.Com, the web site for kids.

CoffeeCam, a web page showing the real-time status of our office's coffee maker. Winner of the Editors' Choice Award from Goto.Com.

The ME/AEM Pressure Server, a page which shows both the real-time atmospheric pressure and the last week's pressure history, which is used to support departmental research activities, with interfaces via C, http, telnet, and the unix command line.

Recent Technical Publications:

Kaszeta, R.W., Oke, R.A., Burd, S.W., and Simon, T.W., "Flow Measurements in Film Cooling Flows with Lateral Injection(draft)," ASME Paper 98-GT-54, presented at the 1998 Turbo Expo, Stockholm, Sweden. (also available as postscript).

Burd, S.W., Kaszeta, R.W., and Simon, T.W. "Measurements in Film Cooling Flows: Hole L/D and Turbulence Intensity Effects." ASME Paper 96-WA/HT-7, presented at the 1996 IMECE.

References: Available upon request.

Richard Kaszeta kaszeta@me.umn.edu

E-mail link at bottom of
resume is a good idea

Figure 8.9

HTML resume #6.

E-mail address only; this should
include a phone number

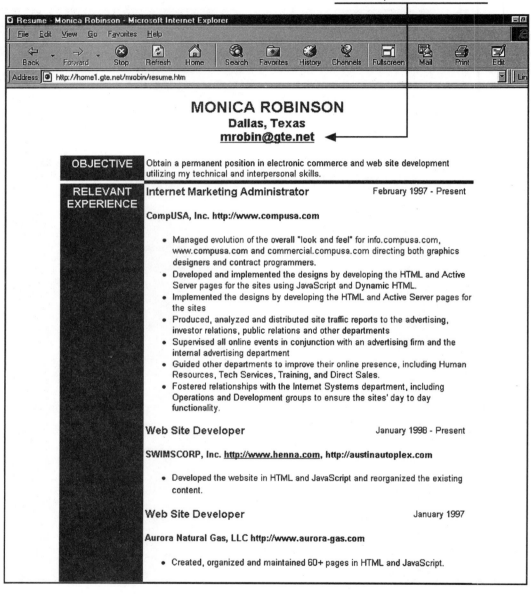

Figure 8.9, continued

Frames give a professional,
attractive appearance

TECHNICAL SKILLS

Languages
- HTML 3.2
- JavaScript
- Dynamic HTML

Software

- Macintosh OS 7.0+
- Windows 95, NT
- Netscape Browsers
- MS Internet Explorer
- Numerous Helper Applications
- Numerous Plug-Ins
- Adobe PhotoShop
- Paint Shop Pro
- MS Office applications
- WebTrends

- Microsoft Internet platform
- MS Internet Information Server 3.0
- MS Commerce Server
- MS SQL Server
- MS Index Server
- MS Active Server Pages
- MS FrontPage
- HomeSite
- Lotus Notes

Hardware

- Apple Macintosh PowerMacs
- PCs and Compatibles

STRENGTHS
- Computer/internet enthusiast and quick learner
- Responsive to customer demands and feedback as it relates to the functionality of the website
- Conscientious planner and organizer
- Project-oriented self-starter
- Exceptionally versatile, analytic and congenial

EDUCATION

Master of Arts Degree in Biochemistry   May 1997

The University of Texas at Austin, Austin, Texas
Cumulative GPA: 3.05/4.00

Bachelor of Science Degree in Chemistry   June 1994

Washington and Lee University, Lexington, Virginia
Cumulative GPA: 3.18/4.00 Dean's List 4 years

ACTIVITIES & INTERESTS   Fitness, charity fun runs, community service, horseback riding, and creative cooking

Chapter 9

Job-Hunting Netiquette

You wouldn't dream of dropping in unannounced on an employer in the middle of a business day and expect an audience. Yet, through the miracle of e-mail, such casual interfaces are now entirely possible. When employers access a new mail message and find your resume, you have effectively gotten in to see them. If you were fortunate enough to get a busy employer's undivided attention, you would not take liberties with this important person. You would be extremely mindful of your behavior during your interview. However, when people use the Internet to conduct an electronic job search, they often make mistakes in etiquette and conduct that they might not otherwise make in person.

Conversation on the Net—"chat," if you will—is highly informal. In cyberspace, people use nicknames and feel free to speak very candidly to others. This is due largely to anonymity in computer-mediated communication. The thinking is "They can't see me, they don't know me, and they can't find me." There is something remarkably freeing in knowing that. So, people tend to let down their guard and say and do things they wouldn't ordinarily say or do in face-to-face conversation. Be aware, though, that the same rules of etiquette governing face-to-face job hunting also apply in the electronic labor market. Remember that the employer is evaluating you from the first word on your subject line to the last statement on your resume. You are not there to give those all-important nonverbal cues to the employer. Your written words on a computer screen must represent you. Those words, in effect, become you, so you should give serious thought to how you want them to represent you.

Suppose a total stranger approached you on the street, slapped you on the back, and called you by your name as though she had known you intimately for years. Then, suppose this same person proceeded to ask you for a big favor involving money and finished by saying she would be calling you soon. Overly informal language directed to an employer is a serious breach of job-hunting etiquette. It is akin to slapping an employer on the back when you don't even know him. Employers don't like it one bit.

General Rules

In the real world of work, manners are expected. If an applicant is too familiar, the employer will be turned off. Such behavior is presumptuous. Even though you may think that the dynamics of your relationship with an employer are different by virtue of being conducted in cyberspace, you must remember that the basic power structure remains the same. Certain behavior is expected of you. Here are some rules of etiquette for electronic job seeking:

✔ **Never address the employer by his or her first name.** "Ms. Jones:" or "Dear Mr. Brown:" is appropriate. *Never* "Hi, Joan."

✔ **Always use your full name when signing correspondence.** Using only your first name presumes intimacy.

✔ **Watch return addresses.** A few of the Net resumes we checked out had "clever" names. We found a "Smart Guy" and a "Wise Guy," for example. Consider the effect these nicknames have on employers. They start forming a first impression based on these seemingly insignificant "clues." They wonder, "Is this guy maybe too 'smart' for our organization?" It is a risk better not taken. Use your own name.

✔ **Never e-mail a resume "for a friend."** We noted several subject notations that said this very thing. This is the same thing as taking a friend along to an interview or calling a company for someone else "just for information" (practices that employers loathe). If you must send a resume or correspondence by someone else's access, have that person forward it for you. Your name and identifying information will appear on the resume or letter itself. The employer will figure out that this is where you can be reached.

Along these same lines, if you accessed your employer through a resume service that the employer paid for, do not share this referral with other job seekers. Employers pay for the privilege of having the service screen for them. You have been approved and are expected. Your friend has not and is not.

✔ **Avoid slang expressions.** "I'll get back to you" is rude. "I will contact you again at the end of next week" is more appropriate.

✔ **Forget about using "smileys."** Smileys, or "emoticons," are those facial expressions made by using punctuation marks—like this: :-). Turn the page to the side to see the smiling face. Smileys are used to add expression, emotion, and feeling to written statements. It is inappropriately casual for you to introduce smileys to your communication with an employer.

✔ **Write in complete sentences.** People communicating electronically tend to use a type of verbal shorthand, such as, "Available after next week. Thanks for attention." Take the bit of extra time and keystrokes it takes to respond properly.

✔ **Never presume on the employer's time.** Always ask if what you propose is convenient. "I would like to arrange an interview at your earliest convenience," not "Give me a buzz so we can talk" or "I'll be expecting your call."

✔ **Don't make demands.** For example, don't tell employers to respond to you by a certain date. "I haven't even met this person yet, and they're ordering me around," says Kimberly, a human resource interviewer with a national retail chain. "It is better to make polite requests rather than aggressive demands. Manners really count in e-mail messages." Let employers set the agenda. It's their call.

✔ **Be humble.** Never assume employers are waiting breathlessly for you to come along and "save" their companies. A little humility goes much further than a lot of bravado.

✔ **Don't be a pest.** Don't inundate the employer with a string of messages. Once you have sent your resume, you may follow up at well-paced intervals—about every three to five days. Remember, this person is receiving hundreds of these things. Give the individual a little time to get back to you.

✔ **Don't assume that the employer will remember you.** In subsequent messages, it will be necessary to reference your prior correspondence, the kind of work you do, and any communication or instructions the employer may have sent to you. Julie, a supervisor in a large HMO, says, "I get these message fragments and have a hard time trying to figure out what the person is referencing, what we had previously discussed. It really helps if I have a copy of at least part of our prior message. That way, I can put our conversation and the applicant in context." Always identify yourself clearly, with both names, in every message.

✔ **Check your e-mail several times a day, every day.** If you let your messages sit for several days, you may risk losing a job opportunity or alienating a potential employer. Things move pretty fast in the Internet world. You need to keep pace.

✔ **Never keep employers waiting.** Answer your e-mail messages promptly. You know how it feels to watch for that "new mail" message. Most people wouldn't dream of ignoring a phone call from an employer; they would answer it right away. Yet they tend to let their e-mail in-basket pile up, or they read their messages and don't answer them until later. Keep on top of your mail. It's only polite.

✔ **Be polite and observe proper manners.** "Thank you" is a completely legitimate phrase. The time it takes an employer to read an e-mail message and respond is just as valuable as any face-to-face encounter.

✔ **Be friendly, but not too familiar.** Adopt a professional, yet cordial writing style. These people are human beings just like you. They are interested in you. Be careful, though, about crossing the line. Don't ask personal questions, and never volunteer personal information about yourself.

✔ **Strike the right balance.** Be assertive but not aggressive. Enthusiastic but not pushy. Professional but not stiff. Agreeable but not a doormat. Knowledgeable but not a know-it-all. Persistent but not annoying. Above all, be respectful. Don't forget: This person may be your future boss.

Newsgroup Fundamentals

Sometimes you will use newsgroups in your job search. Newsgroups are online conferences devoted to particular subjects, including employment-related topics (see chapter 4 for more information about newsgroups). Some are support groups, where weary job seekers can air their gripes and frustrations about the crummy labor market. Many others are places for actual job and resume postings. Following are some tips for proper behavior in and use of newsgroups.

Follow the Employer's Instructions

Read! Sounds simple, doesn't it? When you spot a "perfect job," however, you may be in such a rush to respond that you miss the all-important message that says, "Please fax or mail resumes," or "No e-mail except messages!!!!!!" (We counted the exclamation points on that one. Think the employer means business?) If you ignored or missed that message, your resume would not be considered, regardless of your qualifications. The employer reasonably deduces that, if you can't follow simple instructions in the application process, you certainly won't be able to do so on the job. Furthermore, it just plain ticks employers off!

Several announcements said, "Local applicants only," meaning that people outside a specific geographical area would not be considered. The employer probably wanted to avoid relocation expenses. Sometimes they simply want people familiar with the local sales or labor market. One posting said that only in-house applicants would be considered. In this case, the company is a large, international firm with a staff of thousands. Their employees all over the world can read this message and respond to it, but no outsiders should. When you respond inappropriately, it inconveniences the employer and disappoints you. Read the instructions carefully and follow them!

Follow Newsgroup Usage Instructions

Established newsgroups, including those that post jobs, frequently have rules governing their use. Often, they will post *frequently asked questions (FAQs)* that help new users learn the ropes. Don't be the kid in class who raises his hand to ask a question the teacher answered yesterday. Take the initiative and read the "about the [newsgroup name]" section carefully, and play by the rules of the group. If you don't find an FAQ list, post a short note asking for one. People who have been using a newsgroup for a while get tired of seeing the same questions posted again and again.

Networking

Oops! There's that word. All too often overused in the world of work and job hunting, the networking concept was made for the Internet. While perusing a new newsgroup, that computer whiz you were chatting with last night on the conference sees a posting for a software designer, which fits exactly with your qualifications. A quick e-mail from her gives you access to a position you might have otherwise missed. Alternatively, you might respond to a job posting, and have the employer tell you thanks, but you're not the right one for the company. By all means, ask for a referral. So often, employers know each other and hear of other openings within the industry. If they know of a job that might be right for you, they'll usually pass it on.

Choose Your Group

Maybe you've been spending all your time in a generic "jobs" group, although another newsgroup exists that serves your particular career or field of interest. Special conferences exist in which participants discuss issues pertinent to their specialized discipline or sphere of work. In these exclusive newsgroups, users forward information they have found at other sites on the Internet. Of course, this information includes job postings. Here, you will find only those jobs that are relevant and appropriate to your field.

Surf the Net and Find Your Own Niche

It's just like moving into a new neighborhood. You have to get out there and make friends—contacts who can help you move forward in your new community. By the same token, if you come across something that isn't suitable for you, pass it on. In the unique culture of the Internet, individual users are, in a sense, part of a "neighborhood," a community linked together by avid interest in this remarkable form of communication. Much like people in a real-world community, Net users watch out for one another. They have to do their "community service." If you help your electronic neighbor "raise a barn" today, the same community will rally 'round to help you raise yours tomorrow.

Postings Are Public

Remember that what you write is likely to be viewed by many, many people. These can be people who know you or the employer you are trying to target. Keep your postings professional and never publish private e-mail messages.

Writing Tips

In the world of face-to-face interviews, the applicant's appearance— grooming and facial expression—is all-important in a chance at the job. Some employers rate appearance as high as seventy-five percent in determining whether the applicant is selected. Appearance is easily controlled through intelligent, pertinent grooming choices. In an electronic job search, however, your entire appearance is limited to what is written on the screen. Let's take a careful look at how to write on the Internet.

The problem with the written word is that it is static. Once it's on the page and you hit the Send key, it's there forever. Someone wise once said, "Never put anything in writing!" What lies behind this extreme caveat is the fear that the written word cannot be altered. There is also the fear that, with the written word, no opportunity exists for the writer to mediate the message. In other words, however the receiver interprets it is how it will be received. We are reminded of the quotation: "I am sure you believe that you understand what you think I said. But I'm not sure you realize that what you heard is not what I meant."

Messages on the Net are especially open to misinterpretation. The receiver can't hear the inflection of voice or discern a chuckle from a sneer. He can't see the raised eyebrow or a roll of the eyes. There is not even handwriting to be analyzed! All that is there is words. You must be thoughtful and cautious when constructing your messages. Here are some ideas:

✔ **Don't e-mail mistakes!** Be sure that you write your messages in complete sentences, using proper grammar, punctuation, and spelling.

If writing is not your forte, you might consider composing all messages in your word processor first, where you can spell check them and, in some cases, even check style and grammar before pasting them into e-mail. Some mail systems on the Net already have word processing functions like these built in.

✔ **If you don't know, don't guess.** Just as your messages have the potential to be misunderstood by employers, you also can misunderstand theirs. If something comes to you that you just don't "get," query and ask for clarification. Don't try to bluff your way through a response. Chances are you'll get it wrong and end up looking bad.

✔ **Avoid being "funny."** A clever remark on your end can arrive as impudence on the other. Better to play it straight, unless and until you have established some kind of relationship with the employer through several messages and have a sense of her brand of humor.

✔ **Watch line length.** It is a good idea to limit the length of the lines in your message to approximately sixty spaces rather than typing until the cursor automatically wraps to the next line. Your message might be somewhat indented when it arrives at the other end. Different systems "read" line length differently, so your neatly composed message can reach its destination looking sloppy. Press Enter at the end of each line, allowing for a neat right margin and no line extension to the end of your screen. If you're composing your message in a word processor in order to paste it into an e-mail message, set your right margin at about three inches.

✔ **Don't use Caps Lock.** In the language of electronic communication, capitalized words are read as shouting. The only place all uppercase letters are permissible is in your subject line. Don't forget that in many e-mail programs there is no way to add emphasis, such as underlining or italicizing. Your written sentence must convey meaning on its own.

✔ **Watch your tone.** Don't whine or gripe. Employers get plenty of messages that read, in part, "Haven't you come to a decision yet? I have been out of work for more than six months, the bills are due, the car's broken down, the dog's sick…," or, "This is my third message. When are you going to get back to me?" This is not the way to win a job.

✔ **Write for several readers.** Often the receiver is not the only person who reads your message. The human resources manager may forward it to the department supervisor who then gives it to the line supervisor. These people can be of different gender, age, and ethnicity. At the very least, they are all individual personalities. Each has a different frame of reference on the job. Your message should be generic enough to be read, understood, and appreciated by all of them.

✔ **Stick to the point.** You're here to do business. Get to it. Don't meander all over with irrelevant chat. If you want to insert a personal note, fine. Just stay focused on your stated purpose—finding a job.

The issue of netiquette has been written about extensively on the Net. Articles are frequently excerpted and posted to various newsgroups and forums. The reason is simple: When many people are sharing the same arena, occasional misunderstandings, conflicts, and mistakes are bound to occur. Chuq Von Rospach has been involved with Usenet and the Internet since 1978. In 1987, he wrote an article giving advice and suggestions on Internet etiquette, particularly in the Usenet newsgroups. Even though Von Rospach's essay was written a long time ago, even given the speed with which things change on the Internet, we still find much of it to be applicable to netiquette today. We have selected excerpts from his article, "A Primer on How to Work with the Usenet Community," to sum up the importance of netiquette (reprinted with permission from their site).

Never Forget That the Person on the Other Side Is Human

Because your interaction with the network is through a computer, it is easy to forget that there are people "out there." Situations arise where emotions erupt into a verbal free-for-all that can lead to hurt feelings.

Please remember that people all over the world are reading your words. Do not attack people if you cannot persuade them with your presentation of the facts. Screaming, cursing, and abusing others only serves to make people think less of you and less willing to help you when you need it.

If you are upset at something or someone, wait until you have had a chance to calm down and think about it. A cup of coffee or a good night's sleep works wonders on your perspective. Hasty words create more problems than they solve. Try not to say anything to others you would not say to them in person in a room full of people.

Be Brief

Never say in ten words what you can say in fewer. Say it succinctly and it will have a greater impact. Remember that the longer you make your article, the fewer people will bother to read it.

Your Postings Reflect Upon You—Be Proud of Them

Most people on Usenet will know you only by what you say and how well you say it. They may someday be your co-workers or friends. Take some time to make sure each posting is some-thing that will not embarrass you later. Minimize your spelling errors and make sure that the article is easy to read and understand. Writing is an art, and to do it well requires practice. Since much of how people judge you on the Net is based on your writing, such time is well spent.

Use Descriptive Titles

The subject line of an article is there to enable a person with a limited amount of time to decide whether or not to read your article. Tell people what the article is about before they read it. A title like "Car for Sale" to rec.autos does not help as much as "66 MG Midget for sale: Beaverton OR." Don't expect people to read your article to find out what it is about because many of them won't bother. Some sites truncate the length of the subject line to 40 characters, so keep your subjects short and to the point.

Think About Your Audience

When you post an article, think about the people you are trying to reach. Try to get the most appropriate audience for your message, not the widest. If your message is of interest to a limited geographic area (apartments, car sales, meetings, concerts, etc.), restrict the distribution of the message to your local area. Some areas have special newsgroups with geo-graphical limitations, and (some) software allows you to limit the distribution of material sent to worldwide newsgroups. Check with your system administrator to see what newsgroups are available and how to use them.

Be Careful with Humor and Sarcasm

Without the voice inflections and body language of personal communications, it is easy for a remark meant to be funny to be misinterpreted. Subtle humor tends to get lost, so take steps to make sure that people realize you are trying to be funny. The Net has developed a symbol called the smiley face. It looks like ":-)" and points out sections of articles with humorous intent. No matter how broad the humor or satire, it is safer to remind people that you are being funny.

But also be aware that quite frequently satire is posted without any explicit indications. If an article outrages you strongly, you should ask yourself if it just may have been unmarked satire. Several self-proclaimed connoisseurs refuse to use smiley faces, so take heed or you may make a temporary fool of yourself.

Only Post a Message Once

Avoid posting messages to more than one newsgroup unless you are sure it is appropriate. If you do post to multiple newsgroups, do not post to each group separately. Instead, specify all the groups on a single copy of the message. This reduces network overhead and lets people who subscribe to more than one of those groups see the message once instead of having to wade through each copy.

Summarize What You Are Following Up

When you are following up someone's article, please summarize the parts of the article to which you are responding. This allows readers to appreciate your comments rather than trying to remember what the original article said. It is also possible for your response to get to some sites before the original article.

Summarization is best done by including appropriate quotes from the original article. Do not include the entire article since it will irritate the people who have already seen it. Even if you are responding to the entire article, summarize only the major points you are discussing.

When Summarizing, Summarize!

When you request information from the network, it is common courtesy to report your findings so that others can benefit as well. The best way of doing this is to take all the responses that you received and edit them into a single article that is posted to the places where you originally posted your question. Take the time to strip headers, combine duplicate information, and write a short summary. Try to credit the information to the people that sent it to you, where possible.

Use Mail, Don't Post a Follow-Up

One of the biggest problems we have on the network is that when someone asks a question, many people send out identical answers. When this happens, dozens of identical answers pour through the Net. Mail your answer to the person and suggest that they summarize to the network. This way the Net will only see a single copy of the answers, no matter how many people answer the question.

If you post a question, please remind people to send you the answers by mail and offer to summarize them to the network.

Read All Follow-Ups and Don't Repeat What Has Already Been Said

Before you submit a follow-up to a message, read the rest of the messages in the newsgroup to see whether someone has already said what you want to say. If someone has, don't repeat it.

Be Careful About Copyrights and Licenses

Once something is posted onto the network, it is effectively in the public domain. You should also be aware that posting movie reviews, song lyrics, or anything else published under a copyright could cause you, your company, or the Net itself to be held liable for damages, so we highly recommend caution in using this material.

Cite Appropriate References

If you are using facts to support a cause, state where they came from. Don't take someone else's ideas and use them as your own. You don't want someone pretending that your ideas are theirs; show them the same respect.

Mark or Rotate Answers and Spoilers

When you post something (like a movie review that discusses a detail of the plot) which might spoil a surprise for other people, please mark your message with a warning so that they can skip the message. When you post a message with a spoiler in it, make sure the word "spoiler" is part of the Subject line.

Spelling Flames Are Considered Harmful

Every few months a plague descends on Usenet called the *spelling flame*. It starts out when someone posts an article correcting the spelling or grammar in some article. The immediate result seems to be for everyone on the Net to turn into a sixth-grade English teacher and pick apart each other's postings for a few weeks. This is not productive and tends to cause people who used to be friends to get angry with each other.

It is important to remember that we all make mistakes, and that there are many users on the Net who use English as a second language. If you feel that you must make a comment on the quality of a posting, please do so by mail, not on the network.

World Wide Web Netiquette

As with every other area of the Internet, whether e-mail or newsgroups, there are certain forms and rules of behavior that users of the World Wide Web observe. These are still emerging because the Web is still in development. When you access the Web, you will begin to see almost immediately how some types of behavior can range from vaguely annoying to downright rude. These few tips are offered to help make you a good neighbor in the community of the World Wide Web.

Keep Your Page Simple

Most visitors to Web sites have had the exasperating experience of getting "locked" on a page that takes forever to load. If you use large pictures and complicated graphics, you are going to waste other people's time and just beg for them to hit the Stop icon and get out. Using smaller graphics speeds the load time and gives your visitors the option of clicking on them to enlarge them.

Limit Your Links

Too many links to boring or redundant sites discourage perusal of your own site. Sometimes, you'll visit a page where seemingly every other word is highlighted. This is clearly not necessary. Furthermore, a smorgasbord of unrelated links just confuses people. They figure, "There's far too much to see here," and they get tired and leave. Only include those links that truly have some meaning to you or to your visitors.

Respect the "Low-Tech"

Remember that not everyone has a graphical browser. Some folks still can access only text on the World Wide Web. If you use an image map—that is, a graphic containing links imbedded in the pictures themselves—for your links, not everyone will be able to use it. Be sure to include text links in your pages.

Include Your E-Mail Address

Let your readers know how to contact you if they have questions about your documents. Your e-mail address should appear at the bottom of every page.

Send Them Home

After you've had visitors, you should show them the way home. It's only polite. Put a link at the bottom of each page back to the top of your home page.

Update Your Page, and Keep It Simple

Do a little maintenance every so often. Make sure that all your links are still "live" and the information you have included is current. Put the date of the latest revision on the page.

The Net: User Guidelines and Netiquette is a publication by Arlene Rinaldi that contains excellent advice on appropriate behavior both on the Internet and the World Wide Web. Among other things, Rinaldi advises that you not only limit the size of graphics, but also that you put the file size (such as 2 MB or 10 KB) in the description when you are putting sound or video files in your document. This way, users will know how long it will take to download your file. URLs themselves can be problematic. Rinaldi suggests keeping them simple, with few changes in case (upper- and lowercase letters) because some sites are case-sensitive. She further advises users to include their URLs within the document itself so that if a visitor wants to print the page, the URL will be handy for future reference.

You can access Arlene Rinaldi's publication on the World Wide Web at

    www.fau.edu/netiquette/net/

or, type in "Arlene Rinaldi netiquette" at a search engine, and you will find many postings of her publication.

Be Respectful of Others

Remember that all sorts of people with all sorts of opinions and points of view can access your documents. Obscenity, profanity, bigotry, and other breaches of civility have no place in any community. You risk not only insulting untold numbers of people, but possible prosecution under various laws. Present yourself in a dignified and appropriate manner. You're putting up a "window to the world." Let others look in without shame or embarrassment.

Chapter 10

Internet Interviewing: By E-Mail, Phone, Videoconference, and in Person

Whether you're preparing for a face-to-face or electronic interview, a certain amount of self-analysis is essential. In addition to having a firm idea of the kind of work you want to do, you should have a profile in mind of the ideal company you want to work for. You should also be well acquainted with the product you will be marketing at the interview—namely, you. Here are some questions you should try to answer about yourself prior to the interview:

✔ What are my short-term goals?

✔ What are my long-term goals?

✔ Am I willing to relocate? Commute? Travel?

✔ How do my hobbies and outside interests make me a better candidate for this job?

✔ What factors from my previous job(s) can I use as evidence of my fitness for this job?

✔ What are my own personal traits that apply to the position in question? Do I prefer working alone or as part of a team? Do I enjoy working with the public? Do I enjoy detailed work, a supervisory position, physical work rather than cerebral work? Am I happier when I can exercise some creativity? Do I prefer structure and firm guidelines, or am I happier setting my own schedule and working with little or no supervision?

✔ What are my intentions toward this job? Do I plan to stay here and forge a career or use this as a stepping stone in my career path?

✔ Is the philosophy of this company in line with my own philosophy? This question relates not only to how you perceive the nature of the working relationship of employer to employee, but may also involve ethical considerations. For example, Claudia turned down a lucrative career position with an oil company because it had caused an environmental accident.

✔ What are my chances for advancement?

✔ Is there a good match between my skills, knowledge, interests, and abilities, and the challenges of this position?

In interviewing, as with other practices in job hunting, Internet communication once again differs markedly from face-to-face communication. In the usual sequence of events, your paper resume is received by mail, and if the employer is interested in you, she schedules a face-to-face interview. She may ask one or two clarifying questions when she calls to schedule the interview, but for the most part, any in-depth questions are held off until the face-to-face interview itself. Let's compare this standard practice with the Internet process.

With electronic interviewing, the sequence is largely the same: you respond to a job posting, submit a resume, and are interviewed. What differs is the manner in which the process takes place. You find the job opening through a newsgroup or online placement service on the World Wide Web rather than in a newspaper ad or at an employment agency. Your resume is in an electronic format, sent by e-mail to the employer or pasted into a template at their Web site. You can expect to be interviewed, at least initially, through e-mail. In fact, several preliminary e-mail interviews will probably take place before you meet with the employer in person.

This chapter examines the electronic interview and helps you prepare for dealing with it effectively. You also are given pointers on telephone interviewing. Bear in mind, though, that electronic interviews never entirely take the place of the face-to-face kind. You still need to be proficient at answering questions and thinking on your feet when you meet the employer in person. Therefore, the last section in this chapter helps you prepare for that all-important face-to-face meeting with the employer, based on the context of each situation. Now, let's take a look at the e-mail interview.

The E-Mail Interview

When an employer receives your e-mail resume, it is screened for basic qualifications. If it is found satisfactory, you will be contacted by e-mail before you are called in to interview. Employers do not proceed directly to the interview from the resume because e-mail provides the perfect means for pre-interview inquiry. Pre-interview screening is almost never done in the world of face-to-face job seeking. The result is that, for many employers, the interview process is long and can involve some disappointing "surprises"— things the employer didn't discover about the applicant until the actual interview.

Clarifying Your Resume

The Internet pre-interview is conducted through a series of e-mail messages between the employer and the applicant. Much of this correspondence is to clarify certain points on your resume, but the employer gathers a lot of information about you during these exchanges. For example, suppose you respond to a posting for an administrative assistant position. You e-mail your resume, which outlines your experience related to the job, to the employer. Let's say, however, that the employer is looking for a specific type of desktop publishing experience and you haven't listed it on your resume. It is a fairly simple matter for him to send you an e-mail asking whether you have experience in that type of desktop publishing. The employer may also decide to ask you for a bit more detail about that last position you held in the university public affairs office. You respond with the requested desktop publishing information and also flesh out your job duties at the university. You might then detail the way in which you used the desktop publishing program to compile the monthly newsletter and student profiles for the student-of-the-quarter awards.

This give-and-take is exactly what happens in the face-to-face interview. The employer starts with the framework of the resume, and then you fill in the details when you arrive for the interview. E-mail interviews provide opportunities for you to give more detail than was previously possible before the interview, possibly increasing your chances of getting the position. Electronic interviewing can assist both the employer and the job seeker in the recruitment process. For employers, it saves valuable time that would be spent clarifying pertinent details of your experience before the "meat" of the interview. The employer can also find out whether you are indeed suited for the position in question before going to the expense of bringing you in for a face-to-face interview. You, on the other hand, can find out before an actual interview if the position in question is a good match for your skills and whether you are interested in the company or the job.

Exchanges Can Be Conversational and Friendly

Although e-mail interviews are written, with delays between questions and answers, they are still very much conversational and often informal (see the "Voice E-Mail" section, later in this chapter). Thus, employers and job seekers frequently discover enlightening things about one another in addition to job-related information. For instance, if an applicant inquires about childcare centers in the employer's area, the employer assumes the applicant has a family.

Sometimes an inquiry about area museums, galleries, or other local attractions can spark a discussion of mutual interests between the employer and the applicant. If, for instance, an employer in Minnesota suggests that bass fishing in his area is great around the time your interview is scheduled, you'd have to be pretty dense not to figure out that fishing is an enjoyable hobby for him or that he thinks you might enjoy it.

A common exchange between job seekers and employers pertains to the medium in which they are meeting. E-mail conversations frequently involve discussions about the types of computers and software being used, preferences for one program over another, hobbies involving the computer, experiences using the Internet, and even computer games. Remember that the employer talking to you is computer savvy. She relies on this medium for recruitment and, no doubt, uses it extensively in other applications. Chances are the employer has a personal computer at home. This is an excellent opportunity to demonstrate your knowledge and expertise as well as your genuine interest in the world of computers and the Internet.

Be Careful, Positive, and Polite

One of the most obvious things employers can discern about you through e-mail interviews is your writing skill level. This can be tricky, especially if you are not the best writer. It's a good idea to compose responses in your word processor first and then copy them to an e-mail message. Make sure they are spell checked and proofed for proper grammar before you send them. Save your message as a text document so that it can be transmitted. Remember: The moment you click Send, e-mail messages are irretrievable. Read everything over at least twice before you send it; it's impossible to take back written words.

Keep your general attitude positive. As in a face-to-face interview, you should never interject negative statements into your messages. Keep references to former employers positive. Be assertive in discussing your abilities. Focus on what you have to offer, rather than on any shortcomings you have.

Be unfailingly polite. Keep in mind that this *is* an interview. The employer may have initiated more informal conversation, but you don't want to cross the line between friendly informality and impudence. You're building a first impression here. Present yourself in a courteous, dignified manner.

Tips on E-Mail Interviewing

Through e-mail interviews, employers get a look at your general manner, writing skills, even your philosophy and attitude toward work and their organization. True, it's all taking place on a computer screen, but make no mistake: You are being interviewed. Many of the same rules that apply to face-to-face interviews apply here. Following are some tips for electronic interviews.

✔ **Be distinct.** Do not give vague answers to direct questions. Help the employer understand fully what it is you do and how hiring you will benefit the organization.

✔ **Provide details.** It is intensely frustrating to employers to get one-word responses to questions and have to "pull" information out of the applicant. The employer has contacted you in order to get more detail on some aspect to which you've alluded on your resume. Elaborate. By the same token, you should be aware of when the employer is asking you closed-ended questions, such as "Have you worked with Windows applications?" This question calls for a yes/no response. Answer it as though it had been asked as an open-ended question—that is, "What types of word processing packages have you worked with?" Expand on your yes or no answer.

✔ **One thing at a time.** Sometimes, interviewers write one question that is dovetailed with another question—for example, "Did you leave your last position to go back to school?" Here, there are really two questions: "Why did you leave your last job?" and "Have you returned to school?" It is up to you to respond to each of these questions individually.

✔ **Give just enough (but not too much) information.** There is really no need to tell the whole story in an e-mail message. The idea is to get invited to a face-to-face interview. State the highlights and always offer to give more information when you meet the employer.

> *Tip:* When it comes to questions of a technical nature, in which the employer is asking you to demonstrate knowledge of a particular skill needed to perform the duties of the position, be explicit. If you don't provide this information in the e-mail interview, you won't be invited to a face-to-face interview.

✔ **Give examples.** "The proof of the pudding is in the eating." The best way to convince an employer that you have the skills, knowledge, and ability needed for the position she's trying to fill is to cite examples from past job performance that demonstrate your experience and qualifications.

The employers we spoke with were enthusiastic about e-mail interviews. They view them as a real boon to the application process. Many of them spoke of a sense of "getting a better handle" on an applicant through a series of Internet "conversations." Jeannette, a human resources manager with a health care corporation, put it this way:

> We use Internet messages to delve a little deeper than the resume, to get a better "feel" for the applicant. We ask things like: "Do you have this specific experience?" "When did you work with this or that?" "Please clarify." By the time we're at the [face-to-face] interview stage, we feel we already know the applicant and have a better understanding of his or her background.

Jeannette noted that most of the correspondence she receives is polite and professional, a point of view echoed by several employers. Andy, owner and manager of a medium-sized computer services company, added that the tone of the exchange is also important. He, like most employers, is put off by "overconfidence and people who appear to have real ego problems." Sometimes applicants exaggerate in the hopes of making a good impression and beating out the competition. Unfortunately, this is a mistake that can backfire badly. Says Andy, "Don't overblow it and try to make more out of your experience than you really have. The same goes for bragging. Don't do it. Just discuss your background honestly."

E-mail messages are an expedient way to stay directly in contact with an employer. Most job seekers have had the unpleasant experience of writing a follow-up letter to an employer, only to never hear a word from that company again. An employer might also simply say, "We'll get back to you in a couple of weeks." Human Resources professional Craig Bussey says:

> When a hiring manager says "we'll get back to you in two weeks," don't believe it. It always takes longer because of the day-to-day things that go on in a company. Unscheduled phone calls from applicants can also be a problem because of the amount of time they consume. If [an applicant] takes the time to write me a letter, I should take the time to answer it. The problem, again, is the lapse of time.
>
> ...e-mail is unobtrusive. I can read and answer e-mail at my own leisure. I don't have to go to a secretary to compose a letter for me. I can do it in my own words. I can be a lot more responsive in e-mail. It's just much easier on hiring managers.

Other Screening Methods

Some companies use interactive multimedia programs to conduct their pre-interview screening. With these programs, you can be tested electronically for your fitness for a particular job. The test is performed on an interactive CD-ROM at the employer's place of business, or sometimes can be completed at the employer's Web site.

PII Interactive Interview and Evaluation Software Tools provides such technology to employers. Their applicant assessment aids can be used to test applicants or to train human resource interviewers in how to interview. Candidates answer specific, industry-related questions, and then those answers are scored to see whether the employer has any further interest in interviewing the applicant in person. Some questions test how the applicant would act in certain hypothetical situations, such as customer service. This is a new twist on the interview question: "What would you do if...?"

Best Buy, Inc. uses a computerized telephone pre-interview program. Applicants answer questions via telephone and their responses are recorded. After the initial screening, candidates are contacted for an in-person interview and testing. These interactive pre-interview tools help busy hiring managers because they need to spend time interviewing only those candidates who are most appropriate for the job. Eventually, though, if you make that first cut, the human element is still there in the face-to-face interview.

Declining a Position

Suppose you decide that, after having gotten a more detailed look at the company, this job is not for you. After all, this often happens with employers who decide against calling an applicant in for an interview after several e-mail contacts. You should certainly notify the employer that you have decided to decline the position. Just walking away from your "conversation" is rude and unprofessional; besides, word does get around in business, and you don't want to risk a smear on your reputation. E-mail the employer a polite thank you for considering you, and decline any further interviews.

The telephone interview is a standard part of the electronic interview process for getting any type of job. In the following section, you receive advice on how to succeed in this significant part of the pre-interview phase.

The Telephone Interview

Following the e-mail interview stage, a telephone call is invariably placed to the applicant for further clarification. This is not standard procedure in traditional hiring practice. It is much more common with the Internet because the applicant is often remote to the employer. This is a function of the "global marketplace" feature of the Internet, where job seekers can browse for jobs anywhere in the world. It is frequently not practical (for the employer or the applicant) to hold face-to-face interviews, so employers make a phone call first.

Telephone interviews present some new problems for job seekers. In this instance, the employer doesn't have nonverbal cues, such as your facial expression, body language, or general appearance. What they do have are your voice, words, and, maybe most importantly, your presentation. The following suggestions may help you succeed in the telephone interview.

Be Prepared

A major problem with telephone interviews is that they are rarely scheduled. You can be taken by surprise and expected to perform well at any time. The solution is to prepare in advance for the conversation.

Keep a notebook containing job-related information near the telephone. This should include a current copy of your resume, a list of references, data on the company, and copies of all prior e-mail correspondence with this employer.

> **Tip:** Mary recommends to all her clients that they keep a record—in a loose-leaf binder or file box—of all pertinent job-search information, including contacts, dates, notes, and a follow-up file arranged by date of next contact. Keep this file up to date!

Practice answering questions. Rehearse a couple of different responses to pat questions. Make some notes of questions you might want to ask employers.

Brush up on your telephone manners. Answer by saying "Hello," not "Yeah." Don't just bark your name into the receiver, either.

Involve your family and roommates. It is annoying to have children answer the telephone and then demand to know, "Who is this?" Teach them to say simply, "Just a moment, please," and call you to the phone immediately. Explain to everyone how important it is that you receive all messages if you are not there. Teach everyone how to take a proper message, including the name of the person, company name, and a complete phone number. Leave a message pad and pencil next to the phone.

During the interview itself, take notes as you talk with the employer. Your notes will help with the current phone call and be useful for future reference.

Skip the tinny background music and celebrity impersonators on your answering machine. Avoid cute or entertaining messages. Say your name or phone number clearly so that employers will know they have reached you and not a wrong number.

If you have multiperson voice mail on your telephone, put your name first on the list of options. The employer won't have to wait through a long list of instructions before leaving you a message. You might consider stating, "Please leave your name, phone or fax number, or e-mail address," in your message. It is also a good idea to warn employers to expect either voice mail or an answering machine on your phone (for example, by putting "voice mail" in parentheses after the phone number on your resume).

Phone Interview Tips

When you call the employer back, follow these tips:

✔ **Modulate your voice.** Try to sound enthusiastic. Speak distinctly. Visualize yourself sitting in front of the person to whom you are speaking. Put a mirror by your phone. You will find yourself sitting up straight, being more focused, and even smiling into the phone. The interviewer just may be able to "hear the smile" in your voice.

✔ **Ask for a face-to-face appointment.** Everyone makes a better impression in person than on the phone. If the employer appears ready to end the conversation and hasn't yet scheduled an interview, ask if it might be convenient for you to meet with him in person in the near future.

There is no doubt that the Internet will revolutionize the job-finding process. Opportunities are easier than ever to find. All you need to know is where to look. Once you find the opening, you have only to contact the employer electronically to get your foot in the door. After the initial contact, e-mail smoothes the way and provides important pre-interview glimpses of both the employer and the applicant.

Voice E-Mail

Just when you thought you were safe and anonymous at your computer terminal, along comes the latest element in electronic interviewing: voice communication. Several software programs are now available to provide voice e-mail. Voice E-Mail 4.0 from Bonzi Software can be installed on current versions of **America Online, CompuServe, Netscape, Microsoft Internet Explorer, Microsoft Exchange, Outlook 97, Outlook Express, Eudora Pro, Eudora Light, Lotus Notes, cc:Mail,** and any other **POP3-compatible e-mail**

program. For $29.95 you can download it and add voice e-mail capability to your e-mail account, allowing you to send audio messages using your own voice.

Audio e-mail programs compress your message to transmit it over the Internet. Voice E-Mail 4.0 uses "lossless" compression so that none of the original sound is lost. Programs that are not "lossless" get rid of some parts of the sound data in order to compress it, and the result is a poor-quality sound that contains hisses or other noises.

To download and use Voice E-Mail 4.0, you need a sound card and microphone, 8 MB of RAM, 10 MB of free disk space, and Windows 95, 98, or NT.

To receive and play back a voice e-mail message, you must have a sound card and speakers. Bonzi, the company that makes Voice E-Mail 4.0, offers a free download version of the Voice E-Mail player that will allow you to open, uncompress, and play back messages sent to you, even if you don't have the full version of Voice E-Mail 4.0. For more information and to hear a sample of Voice E-Mail 4.0, check out the Bonzi Web page at `www.bonzi.com`.

With voice e-mail, you can also send pictures and photographs.

Note: In general, you will use voice e-mail only if the employer sends you an audio message and you have the capability to return it. Not all companies have voice e-mail, and it is not advisable to send voice messages to an employer first. Keep to standard e-mail and wait until the face-to-face or telephone interview to let the employer hear your voice.

Desktop Videoconferencing

With the capability of Internet job search has come a global applicant pool. Thanks to the Internet and World Wide Web, employers can now expect to receive applications from around the country and around the world. However, it's just not cost effective to fly in every applicant for an interview. *Desktop videoconferencing* makes it possible for employers to interview candidates face-to-face right on their computer screens.

With videoconferencing, employers can interview one or several applicants in different parts of the country in real time. *Point-to-point* conferencing involves two participants. *Multi-point* conferencing involves three or more

participants. A videoconference is like a picture telephone. All participants can see and hear each other. The transmission of a videoconference is accomplished through the use of a *reflector*—a server on the Internet that allows multiple CU-SeeMe users to connect to it at the same time—which functions as a traffic controller for videoconferencing sessions. Everyone connects to the same reflector to take part in the conference.

Three or more participants can be involved in a conversation that takes place in a virtual conference room, with everyone taking part as if they were sitting next to each other. In order to take part, each partner needs a camera, a microphone, speakers, and videoconferencing software.

CU-SeeMe

CU-SeeMe is a videoconferencing program that was developed at Cornell University. It was originally written for the Macintosh by Tim Dorcey, under the sponsorship of Richard Cogger of the Advanced Technology group in the Network Resources division of the Information Technology department at Cornell. CU-SeeMe was conceived initially for distance learning. However, it has found application throughout the business community as a conferencing tool. Most recently it has come into popular use on the Internet in chat rooms.

When CU-SeeMe introduced the concept of *videochat*, each person in a chat room, in addition to typing and receiving messages from other people in the chat room, was able to see and hear them as well. As desktop videoconferencing programs have become more affordable, videochat has become more common in Internet chat rooms.

CU-SeeMe software allows for multipoint seeing, hearing, and sharing. It can be used over the Internet or any private network or intranet. CU-SeeMe enables you to see live videos of several people on your computer screen at the same time! You can also hear them, talk to them, or send typed messages. A typical CU-SeeMe package includes a color video camera (which attaches to the parallel printer port), CU-SeeMe V3.1.2 for Windows 95/98/NT 4.0 software, a CD-ROM, and printed User Guide.

System requirements for CU-SeeMe Pro include:

Windows 95/98 or Windows NT 4.0, Pentium processor, 133 megahertz (MHz) minimum (166 MHz recommended for H.323 connections), 32 megabytes (MB) of RAM, and 10 MB of hard disk space. For network connections, you need TCP/IP (Winsock-compliant IP address), 33.6 Kbps (minimum) modem, LAN, cable, or ISDN connection (56 Kbps recommended for H.323 connections), and PPP for a dial-up connection.

To send video, you need a digital camera (color) or desktop color video camera and video capture card. To send audio, you need a microphone, 16-bit (minimum) sound card, and drivers. To receive, you need speakers or headphones and a 16-bit (minimum) sound card and drivers.

Other Videoconferencing Programs

Many other videoconferencing programs are available. System requirements for these programs are similar to those for CU-SeeMe. Here is just a partial list of the available programs:

ARMADA Cruiser 100 & 150
Being There Pro
Bell Canada Desktop
   Videoconferencing
Bitfield Video Communications
CollabOrator System 1000 & 2000
Communique!
CorelVIDEO
C-Phone
Desktop Multimedia Conferencing
   (DMC)
DynoVision
ERIS Visual Communications
   System
FarSite
Focus PC
Global Phone Turbo
InPerson
Internet VideoPhone
Lucent Technologies MMCX
Mediafone / Mediafone Trio

MediaStar
Meet-Me Mac / Meet-Me PC
MegaConference
MINX Video Network Systems
NetMeeting
Panasonic Vision Pro 7800
Panorama
Paragon
PictureTel Live200
ProInnovision 200
ProShare 200
ShareVision Mac3000 / ShareVision
   PC3000
ShowMe
SmartStation 384
Symposium Multimedia Conferencing
TELES.VISION B5
VidCall
Vidphone
VideoPhone (Cail)
VideoPhone (Connectix)

It Could Happen to You: Videoconferencing Tips

Don't think that a videoconference won't happen to you. If you don't have the equipment at home, you might be asked to go to a local branch of the company, a college, or a television station, or even a local duplicating shop that provides videoconferencing services.

Desktop videoconferencing poses some special considerations for job seekers. The visual element is there, but the image and sound are not always the best. It is difficult for even a seasoned television pro to come across well on video, so take some time to prepare for your videoconference. Pay special attention to your grooming. You might even go so far as to use

powder to keep your complexion from shining. Answer questions directly. Smile, even though the absence of a person may make you feel somewhat awkward. Be aware of pronunciation. Try to "put yourself in the room" with the interviewers, who may be across the country. This is an interview, so conduct yourself professionally. Affect a friendly manner, but be respectful and careful in constructing your answers. Prepare answers to questions in advance. And relax! Not having all those people in the room with you kind of takes the pressure off.

Some employers conduct videoconferences by use of a satellite, rather than a program like CU-SeeMe. The means are different, but the effect is the same: You are in a room in one part of the country, and your interviewer(s) are in another. You will probably be called in along with several other job seekers because employers tend to do all of their video interviews at one time to save costs. If you find yourself in a waiting room with various other candidates, don't let it throw you. Just think of it as the employer's "lobby." Be cordial and professional.

This technology has changed the way some interviews are conducted, but in the final analysis, it eventually all comes down to two people communicating face-to-face in a traditional interview. You still have to sell yourself to the employer.

With that in mind, we need to take a careful look at the traditional, face-to-face interview.

The Face-to-Face Interview

This is it. The big moment is at hand. You have navigated the vast highway of cyberspace and located a job. Your resume opened the door to an opportunity, and you made your way past a sea of other applicants. Subsequent e-mail interviews with the employer opened the door wider. Now you wait confidently to walk through that door to a face-to-face interview. Well, perhaps "nervously" better describes your frame of mind as you contemplate the coming appointment. What will the interviewer ask? How will you respond? Have you made the right grooming choices? How will you handle that all-important salary discussion? You wonder what the interviewer will be like, how heavy traffic will be on the way there, and whether this is really the company for you. At least we *hope* that is what's going through your mind before an interview. You should be trying to think ahead, to prepare for every eventuality. Sadly, many job seekers fail to prepare adequately for interviews. The result is that they fail to get the job or end up in a job that is less than satisfactory. For a successful job interview, preparation is key.

On the other hand, some applicants "over-train"—read all the books, attend every seminar, and spend so much time in preparation that there remains no spontaneity at all in the interview. These job seekers run the risk of failure because they end up giving rote, canned responses that interviewers have heard many times before.

Consider the following scenario: "Tell me," the interviewer asks, "what would you say is your greatest strength?" As the job applicant launches confidently into a response, the interviewer listens with a sigh. This is her sixth interview today and this is the third time she has heard the same response. Not *just about* the same, *exactly* the same. She wonders how she will get past the rote, automaton-like answers to the real person across the desk from her. In fact, she has almost begun to reject applicants on the basis of such a canned response to her questions. Have all job seekers read the same book or gone to the same class, she wonders?

The experience of this interviewer is hardly unique. So many self-help guides to the interview process are available that applicants have begun to take on an assembly line appearance. The Internet is filled with advice about interviewing. For the most part, the advice is good, but it is sterile and generic. The problem is that no interview fits a pattern. You must also remember that some of this online advice does not come from experts in the field, but from average people who feel like voicing their opinions on the subject. All interviews are individual. Each has its own character and tone. Thus, a single, prepared answer can't possibly work for every interview. What is missing is any consideration of the context of each individual interview.

In the following pages, we will take a *situational approach* to the employment process. You will be encouraged to analyze the context of the particular situation and to weigh the factors evident in each interview before making a decision on how best to respond to questions. Considering the context will also help you realize how to best handle the other components of the employment process, such as grooming.

Evaluating the Interview Situation

Any number of factors, or clues, can help you assess the interview context. Some are quite obvious and readily observable in the setting itself. Others require some advance preparation and forethought on your part. The three most helpful components to evaluating the interview situation are

1. Researching the company

2. "Reading" the surroundings

3. Sizing up the interviewer

We now examine each of these variables to get a clear understanding of the interview context.

Researching the Company

An excellent way to research a potential employer is to talk directly to the people who work there. You can accomplish this through an informational interview or simply by chatting with members of the organization. The purpose here is to find out about the workings of the company—its corporate philosophy, the general working environment, and even the salary and benefits structure.

The following is a list of general areas to consider when formulating questions appropriate for an informational interview:

✔ Description of the kind of work performed—outline of positions within the organization.

✔ Types of background necessary to apply. Include degrees, certificates, and so forth in addition to work experience.

✔ Personality traits desirable in employees.

✔ Available career paths and training options.

✔ Most rewarding aspects of the job.

✔ Most frustrating or difficult aspects of the job.

✔ Best way to do well and advance in the organization.

✔ The organization's main competition.

✔ The organization's salary/benefits structure.

✔ The organization's mission statement.

The last item is valuable in forming a picture of the company's philosophical base and is essential to gauging the context of the interview.

Face-to-face informational interviews are set up with either the personnel director or the head of the particular department that interests you. An informational interview is usually a scheduled, structured period of about fifteen to twenty minutes. That's a big chunk out of a busy human resource person's day.

Job seekers often have difficulty getting an appointment for an informational interview. You can, however, send a brief e-mail message outlining your purpose and questions. These e-mail discussions are much more favorably regarded because of the time factor. Neither does the human resource person fear that the applicant will take the opportunity to press for a job, contrary to the stated purpose of gathering information. Consequently, interviewers feel more comfortable discussing the company through the medium of e-mail.

In your message, make the employer aware that the purpose of the "interview" is *only* to derive information about the company. You must also remember that the aim here is not to ask for a job, but to find out everything possible about the organization in order to make yourself the best competitor for the job. Employers regard these queries as an expedient means of getting a look at the sort of applicants who are available, and as an inexpensive way of establishing good public relations, always a priority with businesses.

The other way to go about informational interviews is with the staff themselves. If the staff actually serve the public directly, it is a simple matter to approach one of them as a customer and informally ask what it's like to work for that company. You should make no secret of the fact that you're looking for work and may be considering their organization or a similar one. In fact, you should talk to everyone. Many an opening has been found through networking and passing the word. For example, if someone has a friend with a brother who works for the company of interest to you, that's one way of getting an informational interview with a staff member. Sometimes a phone call to any department in the organization, but preferably to the one that interests you, is sufficient. Just remember to be honest. If you don't state the real reason for the interview up front, such behavior will be remembered later.

Reading the Surroundings

Want to know the lay of the land before the actual interview? By all means, pay a visit to the site. Most companies have an open door to the public. You can drop in as a consumer or curious passerby. An excellent time to pay a call is on the day of the informational interview, but a brief visit to the site before the scheduled interview time, just to look around, is essential.

Of course, during the interview itself, you have an excellent chance to really get a feel for the corporation. If you are astute, you can pick up clues that reveal a great deal about the company. Consider the physical layout of the interviewer's office. Is it very orderly, neat as a pin? Somber? Professionally decorated? Poorly lit? A total mess? These factors all dictate behavior based on context. Let's consider some other environmental clues:

✔ Are the offices discrete rooms with doors, or are they separated by low, uniform dividers?

✔ What is the pace of the visible staff? Brisk? Relaxed? Calm? Frenetic?

✔ Is there music? If so, what mood does it reflect?

✔ What is the decor, such as furniture, paintings on the walls, and carpeting? Is there any decor to speak of?

✔ Are there constant interruptions, or is the interview room cloistered?

✔ How are the employees dressed?

✔ Look at the parking lot. Are there separate, marked spaces for management and supervisors?

✔ What is the break room like? Are there comfortable chairs or tables? Is it neat or cluttered? Is it clean? Are there magazines or music or some other form of entertainment? What about a bulletin board? If there is one, what sort of information is posted there?

✔ Is there a time clock?

✔ Do phones ring constantly or rarely?

✔ Is there conversation among employees?

✔ Is there noise, or can you hear the clock ticking?

Some of these clues give rather obvious information. If, for example, the phones ring constantly and the employees tend to run rather than walk, you could fairly surmise that the atmosphere is harried and probably stressful. It may require some thought to put these factors together and deduce a cohesive, accurate picture of the organization. For example, the use of uniform height dividers for offices rather than walls generally denotes a company with a "team" philosophy, where all employee input is valued and hierarchy is downplayed. Workspaces are similar to encourage interaction between management and staff. On the other hand, a parking lot with clearly delineated spaces for management and supervision might be indicative of a tight hierarchy within the corporate structure, where supervision is favored and workers know their place. Sometimes an office with a hopelessly anal-retentive demand for order and structure can stifle an individual with a strong need for flexibility and creativity. If, however, such order appeals to you, you would be well advised to mention your penchant for the orderly.

So far, we have laid some crucial groundwork in trying to discover the context of an interview situation. It remains for us now to get a handle on that all-important person across the desk as the final piece of the context equation.

Sizing Up the Interviewer

It is intrinsic to human nature to take the measure of the people we meet. We do it all the time, automatically. We develop an instinctive way of reading others that is sometimes the saving of us and at other times can prove to be our undoing. It is this instinct that makes us form instant, lifelong relationships with some people, or causes us to give a wide berth to others because we get a "funny" feeling about them. With some careful consideration and planning, these instinctual feelings can be honed into a useful tool for gauging the personality and character of interviewers and, by extension, their expectations of potential employees. Let's examine some clues.

✔ **E-mail demeanor.** You can tell a lot about your interviewer by his e-mail messages. Some interviewers are very warm, writing in a conversational style, addressing you by your first name. Others are witty, mixing little jokes and humorous remarks in with job-related questions. Still others get right down to business—no chit-chat or informality. Before you ever meet the interviewer, you begin to form an opinion about the person, based on his or her approach and style. It still remains for you to check him or her out face-to-face, though.

✔ **Office appearance.** Let's begin with the physical setting of the interviewer's office. Some put a desk the size of a 747 between themselves and you. This is a clear message to you to keep your distance. A straight-backed, rigid chair for the applicant says, "Let's get down to business, and then you leave so I can get back to mine." Here, you would be advised to adopt a crisp, businesslike style, with brief, professional answers. And, for heaven's sake, don't touch that desk!

A homey, comfortable environment—kids' pictures on the desk, executive toys, soft chairs, and a sofa—sends another message entirely. There may not even be a desk between the applicant and the interviewer, but rather two chairs grouped around a coffee table. This environment invites more intimacy. It says, "Be yourself. Tell me about who you are so I can get to know you." Here, your manner, though still professional, should be relaxed and open, more personable. It would be a mistake with this employer to sit ramrod straight and give cool, truncated responses to the questions.

✔ **The Interviewer.** You must, of course, evaluate the interviewer himself. As a job applicant, you should be like a sensory sponge, drinking in every detail of the interviewer, processing these details in order to figure him out. How is the interviewer dressed? What is his or her hairstyle like? What is his or her body language telling you? Consider the following suggestions about what to look for in an interviewer:

- What does the interviewer do between questions while you are speaking? Look directly at you? Fiddle with items on the desk? Take notes, or stare out the window?

- Are his shoes shiny, buttons all in place? Or is his hair messy, clothing rumpled?

- Does the interviewer smile and make eye contact, or does he tend to look away and maintain a sober, noncommittal expression?

- Does the interviewer make "chit-chat" or stick strictly to business with rapid-fire, closed-ended questions?

- Are you invited to call the interviewer by his or her first name?

- Are you invited to sit down and offered a handshake, or does she begin immediately asking questions?

Sometimes, a room is designated as the "interview room" and is not the personal workspace of the interviewer, so it might not always be possible to draw conclusions about the person based on his working environment. You can, however, be alert to personal clues that are visible on the interviewer. Look for personal style, manner of speech, eye contact, and facial expression. These are all clues that can help you determine what your behavior should be during the interview.

Hypothetical Interview Situations

Now, using what we have learned so far, let's set up some hypothetical contexts based on our observations and think about what sort of interview these situations might dictate.

Situation I

Through research, you learn that a single individual founded this company on a shoestring. The company has grown dramatically and is now a national, public enterprise. The founder and CEO, who is still very much a viable presence in the organization, maintains a hands-on style of leadership. Company perks are many, with employee bonuses given for exceptional performance.

The office building is fairly new, and the offices are decorated in contemporary style and colors. Low, uniform dividers separate the working spaces. There is an air of subdued energy, with the employees engaged in busy but not frantic activity. You observe some conversation but no music. Personal accoutrements in the workspaces are limited to one or two pictures and some plants, but otherwise, desks and work areas are more or less uniform. There are two designated spaces in the parking lot—one for the office manager and one for the employee of the month.

In the informational interview, you learned that this company offers flextime, an on-site gymnasium, childcare assistance, and an incentive program for employees who want to take college courses. An open-door policy exists for every supervisor and manager, all the way to the top of the organization.

The interview is held in a comfortable office, which, the interviewer explains, is her own office. There are lamps rather than overhead lighting, plants, a desk in the center of the room, and two club chairs and a coffee table near the window. A full-length mirror hangs on the back of the door, which has been closed for privacy. The interviewer is a woman; she is extremely well groomed and wearing a fashionable red business suit. She greets you with a warm smile and handshake, asks you to address her by her first name, and ushers you to the chairs by the window.

Contextual Conclusions

These factors point to a context in which you must make particular choices. You already know that a self-made entrepreneur started the company, so you should emphasize your strengths as a motivated self-starter. The tone of the office suggests that energy, enthusiasm, and ambition must be stressed as personal qualities you possess. You might want to mention some examples of outstanding job performance, such as an instance where your efforts resulted in a monetary savings to your former employer, because it has already been determined that this company rewards excellence. Of course, interest in physical fitness would be nice, but what is called for here is a more general sense that you are the sort of person who strives for a "personal best."

On the job, your grooming should be first-rate (and hopefully you've done a good job of grooming yourself for the interview, as well). This interviewer takes personal appearance so seriously that she has a mirror in her office for periodic checks. Note, however, that the color of suit she has chosen is far from somber or serious. This is a clue that this company affords some latitude for personal style and individualism. (You should, however, beware of mirrors placed directly behind the interviewer. This is a "trick" to see if you are easily distracted or self-absorbed. Avoid glancing at your reflection, primping, or looking at your image as you answer questions. Yes, some applicants actually do that! Keep your attention focused on the interviewer.)

Now let's examine a different interview context for comparison.

Situation II

In this case, your research revealed that the company is a well-established local accounting firm with two branch offices in the same county. A company-supplied brochure emphasizes the firm's stability and reputation. Nothing is said of profit or growth except in very general terms, because the pamphlet is merely an introductory statement to prospective clients. The company president has been appointed by a family board of directors and handles the interviewing himself.

The offices are located in the same building the company has occupied for more than twenty-five years. Colors are dark, and carpeting is neutral and worn. Several formal paintings decorate the walls, but no personal effects are visible on any of the employee desks or in their workspaces. There is very little noise, except for the sound of computers, typewriters, and telephones. Office chatter is minimal and conducted in hushed tones. The pace of the workers is subdued.

The interviewer is a man in a dark blue suit and plain navy tie. His clothes are conservative and appear a bit dated. His office contains a large desk, a painting on one wall, and several certificates from community agencies and a business license on the other. His desk holds no personal items. You are seated across the desk in a straight-backed mahogany chair, which has been placed about two feet from the interviewer's desk. The employer previously declined your request for an informational interview, so you have spoken to one secretary and the security guard. They tell you that there is very good job security with the company, but it takes a long time to move up. On the way to the interviewer's office, you note that the break room is really nothing more than a partitioned area furnished with commercial tables and gray chairs. State labor law regulations and notices of upcoming meetings are posted on the bulletin board. There is a time clock just inside the door.

Contextual Conclusions

Clearly, this data represents a completely different context from the previous situation. Free-form answers emphasizing creative thinking ability and ambition are not called for here. What you should stress is your desire for long-term employment and company stability. Respect for authority and the chain of command, plus the personal qualities of dependability and loyalty, would be prized in this organization. Because this company has a time clock, you should also mention punctuality as a strength. Your answers should be pointed and brief. Grooming called for here is conservative and simple. And don't touch that desk!

Questions in Context

Of course, the interview questions themselves must always be evaluated in terms of the context of an interview. Some of the more commonly asked questions should ideally yield somewhat different responses, depending on the circumstances of each interview. We will look at a few commonly asked interview questions and decide on appropriate answers based on your knowledge of yourself and the interview context.

What Is Your Greatest Strength?

Answers to this question require a bit of tailoring from one situation to the next. No pat answer will work every time. With this particular question, the interviewer is looking for two things in your answer. The strength in question could be either professional or personal. In formulating a response to this question, you must weigh not only the interview situation itself, but also the type of job being discussed and your own real strengths. Let's consider a couple of possible answers.

Professional: In the case of an interview for a highly technical position, a job-related strength—demonstrating expertise in a particular skill—would be the best choice of response. An auto mechanic might say, "Besides being able to do a complete engine rebuild, I can machine valves and do milling to specifications. I am also very strong in electrical systems diagnosis." Here, the applicant has focused on strengths as they relate to performing the job. Similarly, a bank teller would focus on his or her ability to balance consistently and correctly. A machinist should emphasize the ability to work to tolerance. All of these job-related strengths tell an employer that the applicant isn't just talking. Referring to specific skills not only demonstrates competence but also knowledge of what the position entails. There is still, however, the second component of this answer to consider—your personal strengths.

Personal: If an employer were hiring a machine to do the job, a simple recitation of professional strengths would suffice in this answer. Employers, however, hire people, and people come equipped with different strengths as well as weaknesses. It is essential, therefore, that the interviewer reveal the person, not just what that person can do. If you misunderstand this fundamental concept of interviewing and hiring, the game is lost.

Put another way, you may have heard or even said yourself, "Employers hire friends. It's not what you know, it's who you know." Quite right. Employers do not hire people they don't like or trust, that is, people they don't "know." Your primary job during the interview, then, is to communicate to the employer who you are. You do this by emphasizing personal qualities that make you a desirable candidate for the job.

One way to understand the importance of your personal qualities as an applicant is to put yourself in the position of the employer. Let's say you wanted to hire someone to clean your house. What if you had to go out on a public street, stop the first person you saw, and ask that person to clean your house. You would give him or her some money and the keys to your home, and send your new employee off. You're thinking, "No way!" Yet, that's exactly what employers do every time they hire someone. They "give the keys" to a stranger and offer that person money to do a job. Just as your first concern would be with the *kind* of person you were sending into your home (letting his cleaning ability take a back seat), so are employers acutely interested in you as a person, not just in what you can do.

The "strengths" question requires some self-knowledge on your part, as well as the ability to communicate this to the employer. The auto mechanic in our first example, for instance, should point out to the interviewer that he or she is not only a competent mechanic, but also a dependable employee who can be counted on to be at work as scheduled. The bank teller would be wise to emphasize cash-handling ability as well as strong interpersonal skills, because tellers are in the public eye. A secretary could stress discretion and the ability to handle multiple tasks. These qualities are all crucial to an employer, but are not evident on the surface of things.

Self-awareness and consistency are both important in considering answers to tough questions and interview context. A secretary who stresses neatness as a strength but has a button missing has clearly made a blunder. You should always be sure that your answers reflect reality. In other words, it is best to be honest when listing your personal qualities to an employer.

Be acutely aware of the dynamics at work in the whole process. Let's again consider the applicant at the interview where the phones ring constantly, harried people bustle around, and the interviewer is continuously interrupted by work. Offering punctuality, say, or interpersonal skills as strengths wouldn't score nearly as many points at that particular interview as offering the ability to work well under pressure.

So, you must be able to select a strength from a whole host of possibilities and then make sure it is really a strength you possess and one that fits the context of the interview. Here are some suggestions for personal strengths that employers find appealing:

Dependable	Detail-oriented
Motivated	Flexible
Good listener	Punctual
Self-starter	Loyal
Organized	Personable
Discreet	

The following are abilities you might want to emphasize:

> Work independently
> Think creatively
> Work well under pressure
> Make decisions
> Shoulder or delegate responsibility
> Work effectively with people at different levels

Never say, "I like to work with people!" Not only is this a cliche, the unspoken response of many employers is "What else would you be working with, aardvarks?"

Remember to evaluate yourself fairly and honestly, and choose your representative qualities wisely. No employer likes to be conned.

Now let's look at another common interview question.

What Did You Like Most about Your Last Job?

This question practically directs you to think about the context of the interview. Yet, the answers many applicants give eliminate them from consideration by the employer. Some common answers given here are "Oh, I just loved the people I worked with" or "I really liked my boss." or "They had good benefits." The first two answers tell the interviewer that the applicant's last company was a neat place to work, so why is he or she here? The last answer indicates that this applicant is out for what she or he can get from the company. Neither answer shows any thoughtfulness in relation to the current context.

Again, it is incumbent upon you to think about the company to which you are applying and what the conditions might be like on the job in question. You must then evaluate the components of your last job to see whether there is a correlation with this one. Consider the following examples:

On her last job, Debra, as division secretary, was responsible for putting together a departmental newsletter that told about current events and outlined unit goals and accomplishments. She now finds herself in an interview for administrative assistant to a department manager. Knowing that she will be responsible for generating and editing a great deal of correspondence, wouldn't she be wise to volunteer that she liked the newsletter aspect of her last job?

Claudia worked for a small operation with only a few people on staff. The employees did virtually everything in the operation. Consequently, Claudia had different assignments every day. She is currently interviewing with an

organization that has many departments and a diversified product line. Explaining that she liked the varied job responsibilities and prided herself on being flexible in her last job can only help her secure this new one.

Evaluating Yourself

A truly fair and honest assessment of yourself, coupled with an understanding of the context of each interview, will result in an encounter with the employer that will be beneficial and satisfying to both of you. By all means, read all the information you can get on interviewing. Take seminars and find out the common questions and responses. Just remember that, like you, each interview is unique and deserving of individual attention as well as respect.

Negotiating a Salary

Let's assume you get that long-awaited job offer; now you need to make sure you get the salary you want. People seek out particular companies and careers for many different reasons. We hope you find a job that fulfills you both personally and professionally and that you actually look forward to going to work every day. However, the reality is that most people go to work to *make money*. Accordingly, you should know something about the process of negotiating a salary. Based on his book, *Win-Win Negotiating* (John Wiley & Sons, 1985), Fred Jandt offers the following advice:

We can't provide you a complete negotiator's manual in this book. What we can provide you are some guidelines to keep in mind when you're offered a job and want to negotiate salary or conditions of employment.

You need to determine whether or not negotiation is even appropriate. Some organizations make a non-negotiable offer. You're asked to "take it or leave it." Others make a non-negotiable salary offer, but do negotiate certain conditions of employment such as benefits, moving expenses, commuting expenses or telecommuting options, office space, and any other possibility—except salary. And, of course, there are others who are open to negotiating any aspect. How do you find out? Don't assume; do your research. Ask current and former employees.

With this knowledge, but before you respond to a job offer, you must first do an honest assessment of your position. First, you need to evaluate your options. Negotiators often speak of one's BATANA or Best Alternative To A Negotiated Agreement. By this, they mean that anyone involved in a negotiation MUST understand the consequences of *NOT* settling. Another way to say this is "What options do you have?" This must be an honest assessment. This evaluation should help you determine how you negotiate with the employer.

The weakest position, of course, is to have no money, no other offers, no other applications being considered elsewhere, and no leads. Be realistic. You want to get fair compensation, but you can't afford to have the employer withdraw the offer.

On the other hand, the strongest position is to have another job offer. If you do have another offer in hand or are very sure that one is forthcoming, you can afford to take a stronger stand. Actually, if that other offer is completely acceptable to you, you should tell the truth, that is, tell the employer that you have another offer.

> *Caution:* All professional negotiators will tell you, never lie! If you bluff, you may lose. If you lie, you will be found out eventually, and we don't think that you would want your new employer to discover that you can't be trusted.

Second, you need to set realistic objectives. Professional negotiators know that having carefully researched and determined their objectives results in better outcomes than trying to negotiate for the "best deal you can get." The negotiator who is prepared knows the range and average salary for the position and knows what others doing the same work in the organization receive. How do you find this out? By now, you know to expect us to say to search the World Wide Web for salary information. Before you negotiate, you must have first done your research and set realistic objectives.

You need to determine the authority and expectations of the person you are negotiating with. Does the person have the authority to negotiate salary and conditions of employment, or are they limited in their authority? We recommend a simple but effective approach: Ask, but, of course, ask politely. You don't want to come off as a potential employee who is going to be difficult to deal with. Second, you need to determine the other party's expectations about negotiation. Do they typically make a low first offer, expecting the applicant to ask for more? Or do they typically make a mid-range offer and expect to discuss it with you but not negotiate it with you? Or, do they typically make what they believe to be a fair offer and resent someone who expects to negotiate? You must find out. So far, you've seen that most of the work of negotiation occurs before one word is spoken.

Negotiations can be divided into single-issue and multiple-issue types. Single-issue negotiations are about one issue only, such as salary. Multiple-issue negotiations offer more opportunities for mutually satisfying outcomes because they offer more ways to construct the outcome.

Single-issue negotiations are most often settled by compromise. If the employer offers to pay $10 an hour and you've asked for $13, if both the employer's offer and your demand are reasonable, and if

both of you expect to negotiate and settle, it's probable that you'll walk away with $11.50—the average of $10 and $13.

Most negotiators prefer to deal with multiple issues. Having multiple issues on the table makes it possible for the parties to link movement on one issue in exchange for movement on another issue. In multiple-issue negotiation, for example, if you are concerned about commuting in heavy traffic, you can offer to drop your demand for flexible hours if the employer agrees to include you in company-sponsored van pools.

Notice in the above example that not only are you trading movement on one issue in exchange for movement on another issue, you've reached an outcome that is in both your interests. You don't have to drive in heavy traffic, and the employer may receive incentives or recognition for encouraging mass transit. This should tell you something about multiple-issue negotiation. Not only do you make trade-offs, you attempt to reach an agreement that benefits both parties. This type of negotiation is called *win-win negotiation*. Not only do you both "win," you begin to establish a working relationship that can continue to benefit both parties in the future. This style of negotiation puts equal emphasis on the relationship as it does on the outcome itself. Remember, negotiating for a salary should be the beginning of a long-term relationship.

What are the other issues that can be relevant to salary negotiation? Almost anything, but here's a list of the obvious ones:

- Bonuses
- Company car and other commuting options
- Computer and other home office equipment
- Flextime
- Holidays
- Insurance
- Job-search assistance for family members
- Medical, dental, and eye care health programs
- Moving expenses
- Profit sharing
- Retirement programs
- Scholarships and tuition programs for family members
- Uniforms and other special clothing
- Vacation time
- Working conditions, such as office size and location

To make multiple-issue negotiation work, then, you need to set more than salary as your objective, and you need to be able to drop issues and to trade off movements on one issue in exchange for movement on another issue. How does this work? Most professional negotiators use what are called "what if" questions. Think about asking a question like this: "What if I were able to put aside my concern about the cost of commuting; are there ways for me to control my own hours some-what so that, if traffic is heavy, I'm not penalized for being late?" The "what if" question has many advantages: It clearly communicates you are not inflexible in your demands; it communicates that you want to work with the employer to solve what can become a shared problem; and it communicates your desire to be a reliable employee.

Other skills you need to develop to make multiple-issue negotiation work are listening, asking questions, and paraphrasing what you've heard the employer say. Many people assume a skilled negotiator is a skilled "talker." If anything, it's the opposite. A skilled negotiator is a skilled listener. Listen carefully to what the employer says. Ask questions to clarify what you don't understand. To be sure you understand what the employer said, paraphrase in your own words and ask if your understanding is correct. Remember that the agree-ment is what the *employer* thinks it is—not what you think it is.

That should alert you to remember that any agreement you reach is, as negotiators say, "not real until it's in writing." Don't sell your house and move on a verbal understanding that a job is waiting for you. The employer may have understood your agreement to be that you'll be hired for the next available opening—whenever that is. You may have understood the agreement to be that you're hired now.

We all want our employers to be fair and honest. Employers expect the same of their employees. That relationship is often established in salary negotiations. The Golden Rule really does apply here: Treat the employer as you want to be treated as an employee. Remember, too, that salary negotiations reveal how the employer will be treating you. If you feel you're not being treated fairly in salary negotiations, what reason do you have to believe you'll be treated fairly on the job in the months ahead?

Chapter 11

Advice for College Students

The World Wide Web is a rich source of information for college students and recent graduates. Where you should look depends on your career plans. Perhaps you have decided to stay in education and are searching for positions for research assistants and teaching assistants at colleges and universities. The Web has listings for these. Some graduates look for work in specific geographical locations. Still others want to confine their job search to a certain discipline—for example, mathematics or science. You can conduct your search geographically, by discipline, or in several other ways. Perhaps you are still an undergraduate and need help focusing on a particular career or want to use the Web to find an internship where you can gain experience before you graduate. You can find information about all these areas on the Web.

Places to Look

This section gives you some specific sites and directions for online job search, especially for college students. This list is only a representative sample. Bear in mind that there are many more sites you can mine for jobs.

Entry-Level Jobs

The Student Search System posts entry-level jobs and internships for college students. It posts openings in the computer-related, manufacturing, mechanical engineering, business, and electrical fields, and it offers a listing of temporary positions. You can find it at

www.studentsearch.com/

You may also want to check the USENET newsgroup `misc.jobs.offered.entry` for jobs requiring zero to three years of experience.

Jobs by Discipline

Perhaps you've devoted your education to becoming a specialist in one particular field, and you want to confine your job search to that one discipline. Searching for jobs on the Web by discipline is a relatively simple matter. The easiest way to search is to use a search engine, such as AltaVista and key in your chosen discipline and the word "jobs" or "employment" (for example, "Mathematics jobs"). Try different combinations, using "employment" or "job opportunities". There are dozens of sites out there for just about every discipline. Here are a few examples of sites that concentrate on specific disciplines.

Math

Visit the Web site of the American Mathematical Society at

`www.ams.org`

Click on Employment and Careers.

Science

The National Science Foundation Web site is located at

`www.nsf.gov/`

Click on Directory and Staff, then on NSF Vacancies.

You can find opportunities at this site for the Student Temporary Employment Program (STEP), which provides opportunities to gain meaningful work experience while continuing your studies. The Grants and Awards feature at this site also provides information about the forms and applications process.

Physics

PhysLINK, which bills itself as "the ultimate physics resource on the planet," is located at

`www.physlink.com`

Click on Physics Jobs. Here you'll find postings of graduate positions in research, plus internships, fellowships, and teaching assistantships.

Journalism

The National Diversity Newspaper Job Bank is at

    www.newsjobs.com

NDNJB makes a special effort to reach minority circles through colleges and universities. You must submit a resume to obtain a password.

Internships and Summer Jobs

If you're a student, you should try to spend some time in an internship. Employers view internships in your field as job experience—just the thing that can give you an advantage over other applicants.

Fortunately, the Web can help you find an internship opening. Some of the job data banks also list internships. To find internships online, simply enter "internships" at a search engine. You get an enormous list of sites offering information on internships. To narrow your search, enter the specific type of internship you desire. For example, we entered "internships communication" at AltaVista and found thousands of pertinent sites for communication internships.

For a large listing of internships, summer jobs, fellowships (including White House Fellowships), and volunteer positions, check out The Riley Guide to Alternative Work and Career Opportunities at

    www.dbm.com/jobguide/misc.html#intern

A database called 4Work also posts internships for students. You can reach it at

    www.4work.com

CampusCareerCenter Worldwide is a global job clearinghouse where employers post information about job openings, contract positions, and internship programs all over the world. The site also offers job interview and career counseling tips. Reach them at

    www.campuscareercenter.com

In addition to internships, you can find those all-important summer jobs online. Cool Works posts over 35,000 summer jobs—from waiting tables at Yellowstone to mopping decks on a Louisiana river barge. Reach them at

    www.coolworks.com

College Placement Offices

The place to start your job search is at your own college career center. In the past, college career centers had shelves filled with binders that were crammed full of job vacancy announcements. Today, those shelves are likely to hold computer manuals!

Your campus career center is a wonderful resource for doing a job search in general. Such a center provides not only on-campus recruitment information and student job opportunities, but career guidance and testing as well. Many career centers today offer free Internet job-search services for students and alumni. Some schools offer unlimited perusal of their databases, while others limit this service to currently enrolled students. Still others offer campus placement services to alumni for a fee. Let's look at an example of a well-respected college placement office.

University of South Florida

USF has a student population of 37,000. The University has a large and active online career center. In 1998, the Career Center received listings from employers for approximately 38,000 positions. USF job seekers had access to many more positions via links on the USF site. The university is relatively young, compared to other U.S. schools. USF was an early believer in online recruiting. Drema Howard, Career Center Director, says that the school's comparative youth may have something to do with that:

> Other schools may be older and have more ivy on their walls, but by almost any definition, the University of South Florida is one of the most dynamic institutions of higher education [in] the United States today. It is one of the few American universities created in the Twentieth Century. The average age of the student body is twenty-five, and approximately seventy-five percent are employed while pursuing a degree.

The Career Center provides a broad range of services to students and alumni as well as the general public. Says Howard:

> The University of South Florida Career Center offers a Twenty-First Century career service to its students, alumni, faculty, and employers. [The center offers] face-to-face personal career planning and job search assistance. The Career Center also uses online technology to manage recruitment activities and disseminate information to all of its constituents. Through *Making Connections* via the Career Center's home page, students and alumni may access the *JobLine* and additional *JobLinks* to learn about part-time, work-study, Careerships, and full-time professional employment opportunities.

The USF Career Center provides other career-related help to students, in addition to access to job postings. "Students may also apply for and schedule on-campus interviews [and] learn about services and upcoming special events," says Howard. "They may also view lists of employers participating on Networking Fairs and obtain details about employers' on-campus information sessions."

Howard goes on to say that employers also benefit from the services available at USF:

> Employers receive candidate resumes electronically, and both employers and faculty use the site to learn about services, on-campus recruitment deadlines, and interview dates. During the peak campus recruiting season, we average daily traffic of about 400 to 450 students.

Some of the USF Career Center job database is limited to students and alumni. Students and alumni who are formally registered with the Career Center and have uploaded their *Electronic Disk Resume* may search that area. There is an area for nonregistered job seekers, too.

Besides links to major job databases, such as Monster.com, USF provides links to government jobs, state and federal jobs, Florida cities' newspaper classified advertisements, internship sites, summer jobs sites, and international job-search sites.

Let's explore the University of South Florida Career Center's site. We conducted a search for a Therapist/Case Manager position.

Figure 11.1

USF's Career Center Home Page, located at www.career.usf.edu.

On the home page, we clicked WebWalk! We saw the screen shown in figure 11.2.

Figure 11.2
WebWalk page.

Then we clicked on Full-Time Employment, and got the login screen in figure 11.3.

Figure 11.3
Login screen.

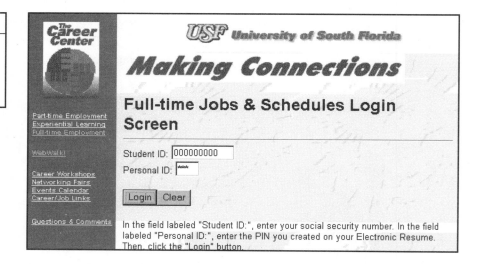

We followed the instructions for logging in at the bottom of the page, and then saw the Jobs Menu shown in figure 11.4.

Figure 11.4

Jobs Menu, showing career clusters.

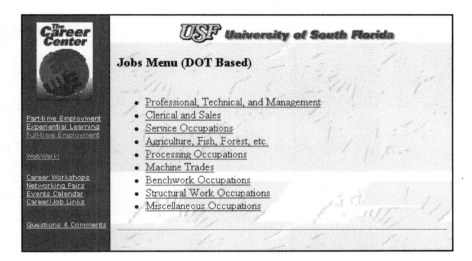

We clicked the first cluster—Professional, Technical, and Management— and got the screen in figure 11.5.

Figure 11.5

Job groups within the Professional, Technical, and Management cluster.

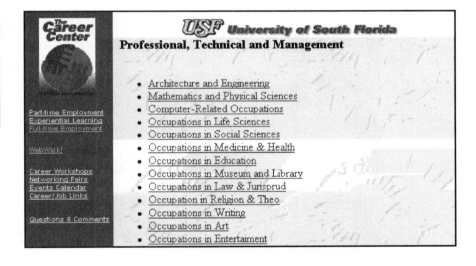

We clicked Occupations in Social Sciences and got the screen shown in figure 11.6, which lists the job openings in that category.

Figure 11.6

Job listing screen for the Social Sciences cluster.

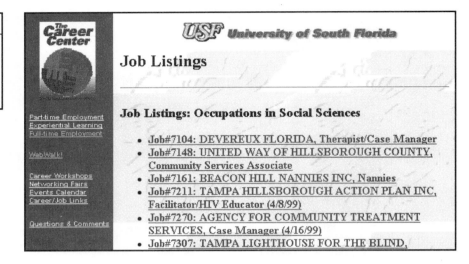

We clicked on the first job posting in the list and went to the screen shown in figure 11.7. More information about the job and the company are shown in figures 11.8 and 11.9.

Figure 11.7

Job listing for Therapist/Case Manager.

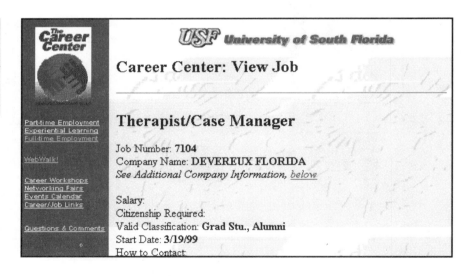

Figure 11.8

Therapist/Case Manager job description.

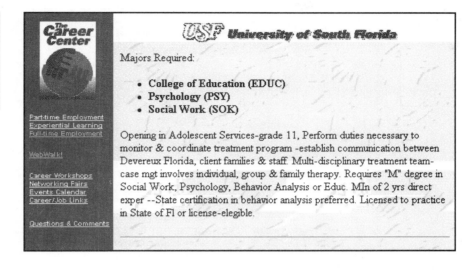

Figure 11.9

Company contact information for Therapist / Case Manager job.

Online Placement Information: JOBTRAK

JOBTRAK is a daily posting of jobs available in many college career centers. To access JOBTRAK's job listings, you must be a student or alumnus of one of the participating colleges and universities. JOBTRAK has over 2,000 new job postings daily and provides job-search and resume tips, graduate school information, and direct links to company career centers. Access the site at

`www.jobtrak.com`

Figure 11.10

JOBTRAK's home page.

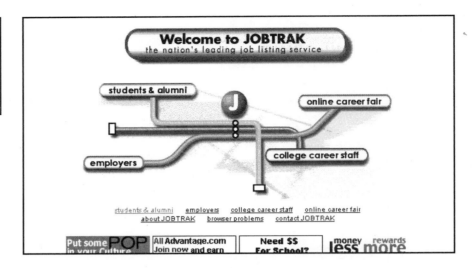

Contact your college career center or student employment office for a password. (Most career centers allow "pathway" access from on-campus computers.) If you have already filled out your User Profile or posted a resume, you need only to enter your user name and password at the JOBTRAK site to enter immediately.

Major Online Career Services

Many online recruiting services are available to you on the World Wide Web. Some are free to job seekers; others charge a minimal fee for wide distribution of your resume or for special assistance in preparing it. In chapter 3, "Getting Job Information from Corporate Sites and Job Boards," you'll find extensive job data bank listings, and in chapter 4, "Usenet Newsgroups," you will find newsgroup listings. Some are especially appropriate for college students. Let's look at a couple of large online services that cater exclusively to college students.

College Grad Job Hunter

College Grad Job Hunter is a database that caters to college students and recent grads. College Grad Job Hunter posts entry-level jobs and includes information on resumes, interviewing, offer negotiation, and more. It's located at **www.collegegrad.com/**. Figure 11.11 provides a look at this Web site.

Figure 11.11

College Grad Job Hunter's home page.

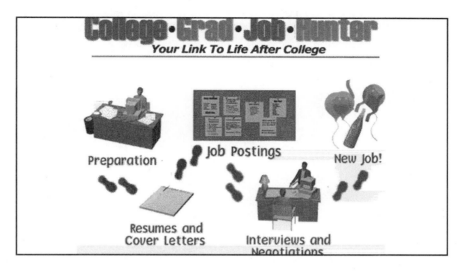

Click on Job Postings. You'll see the screen in figure 11.12. Then select Entry Level Job Search.

Figure 11.12

Job Postings page at College Grad Job Hunter.

At the Entry Level Job Search screen, you can search using keywords.

Figure 11.13

The Entry Level Job Search screen with keywords "public relations" entered.

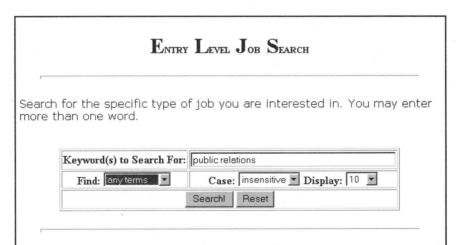

When we entered the keywords "public relations," we were presented with the first ten matches, the first of which contained public relations job postings (see figure 11.14).

Figure 11.14

Search screen results for keyword "public relations."

Keywords (any terms, case insensitive): **public relations**

(395 files searched; 23 matches found)

Matches 1 - 10

- **World Cancer Research Fund – WCRF International Management Development Trainee Program**
Keyword Matches: 8; Size: 3 kb; Last Updated: 14 Apr 1999
World Cancer Research Fund WCRF International Management Development Trainee Program Company Description: World Cancer Research Fund (WCRF) is the only non-profit organization dedicated solely to the prevention of cancer by means of healthy diets and

BridgePath

BridgePath is a recruitment service for college students that's headquartered in the San Francisco area.

Figure 11.15

BridgePath's home page.

BridgePath's mission is to increase employment opportunities for current students, recent graduates, and new alumni. The company looks for applicants with less than ten years' experience. BridgePath calls these people "the most recently educated, dynamic, and cutting edge segment of the workforce."

BridgePath markets its services directly to recent graduates and alumni by visiting colleges and making its presence known at places where alumni and students are likely to be. The company works with career centers, student organizations, young alumni groups, and alumni organizations.

Mel Ochoa, Director of Public Relations and Communications at BridgePath, explained the company's focus on recent grads:

> Many of our clients are looking for young alumni because, in the age of automation, young alumni and recent graduates are becoming more important. They are being taught more specific skill sets in school than previous generations were, and have a better technological base at a younger age. Roughly 90 percent of college graduates can use Microsoft Word, Excel, Access, the Internet, and e-mail. These qualified job seekers save the employer high training costs.

BridgePath also focuses on "passive" job seekers, those who are either not inclined or don't have the time to go through the process of actively sending out applications and searching through many databases to find jobs. Often, passive job seekers are employed, and don't want their current employers to know they are looking elsewhere. BridgePath attracts passive job seekers because it doesn't require tedious searching on the part of the job candidate. These job seekers can have job postings sent directly to them as the openings occur.

BridgePath is not just a bulletin board of job openings. Rather, it enables employers to e-mail job and internship announcements directly to students based on their skills and interests.

A noteworthy difference between this and other online services is that BridgePath does not collect resumes. Instead, the service collects detailed information from you when you register. This information is entered into a database, which employers can then search. When you are notified of employer interest in you, you send your own resume via e-mail directly to the employer.

When you register with BridgePath, you provide your e-mail address so that employers are able to contact you when suitable openings occur. You fill out an online questionnaire, which takes five to ten minutes to complete and includes questions about where you would like to work, your major field of study, what industries you are interested in, and your skills. When an employer has an opening, he uses pull-down menus to select the desired criteria. It's important that you check your e-mail often for BridgePath referrals and respond to those job announcements that interest you.

A very important feature of BridgePath is that your privacy is preserved until a suitable employer is interested in your qualifications. Employers search "blind" resumes, meaning that your name and other contact information is shielded. Ochoa explains:

Recruiters are not given students' personal information at this point. Then, recruiters type a personal e-mail alerting targeted students of a job or internship opening. After e-mails have been sent, it's up to the students to decide whether to submit their resumes via e-mail. Most importantly, students only receive e-mails from employers who are interested in them.

Because employers are charged per e-mail, it is in their interest to target their searches carefully. Thus, you are likely to get only serious inquiries.

You can access BridgePath at

www.bridgepath.com

Insider Tips from a Professional Recruiter

Jim Shunk is the manager of Hewlett-Packard's Corporate College Recruiting Department. He has been with the company for seventeen years, most of them in human resources. He joined Hewlett-Packard right out of graduate school himself and has interviewed hundreds of college students and recent graduates, so he is a prime source of advice to student job seekers. Mary talked with Jim about college recruiting, and he offered several valuable insights into how students can prepare to succeed in the job interview.

Mary: How should a college student or recent graduate compensate for lack of career-related skills?

Jim: Internships and/or co-op assignments are the best way to acquire career-related skills. While in school, honing one's skills in research, writing, public speaking, team projects, and project planning will come the closest to "mirroring" the work environment I see at HP.

Mary: How do you regard internships?

Jim: I think that a student's time spent in an internship or co-op assignment will be the most valuable time they have in school. I can't exaggerate their value or importance in competing for jobs. Here at HP, we hire a lot of summer interns, and it really gives the students a "leg up" on other students when it comes to getting a job with HP.

Mary: What should a college student emphasize? GPA, honors, service, organizations—what?

Jim: Schoolwork is number one. We, and most other top companies I speak with, still value the GPA highly as a predictor of success. We understand that a student with a 3.2 GPA and many other outstanding factors may be a better hire than a 4.0, but the GPA is used as a strong screening factor in determining who will get interviewed on campus and who will be "pulled up" on a computer search of candidates. After schoolwork, I would have to say that relevant work experience is next; either in internships or in a full-time position before or during school. Next would be leadership positions and contributions in school and/or student organizations. Finally, community service.

Mary: *What questions should an applicant ask you?*

Jim: A student interviewee should always be prepared with specific questions about the interviewer's organization, either at a corporate or divisional level. It is a real turnoff for a student to not have any questions. It is interpreted by recruiters as lack of interest or knowledge. All recruiters and interviewers may not always leave time in the interview for the student to ask questions, but the student should always have five or six questions ready.

The questions can vary greatly, but my favorites are these:

- Where is this organization headed? What is its vision for success?

- What are the main challenges this organization is facing?

- What do you see as the main opportunities to contribute in this or similar positions?

- What are the opportunities for continued learning? What are the most common career paths? How does the organization support upward and horizontal career development?

Mary: *Is there anything a student can do while still in school to enhance employability after graduation?*

Jim: Work like a dog at their schoolwork. Don't just learn areas of knowledge, but improve skills: for instance, listening, speaking, writing, and working in groups.

Mary: *What are some common mistakes students make in preparing resumes, grooming, and interviewing?*

Jim: Resumes can easily be too long and not include enough nouns—computer job searches are typically performed on nouns: ceramics, acoustics, computer architecture, and SAP, for example. "Under-dressing" for an interview is probably the most common mistake we see in grooming. Not coming with questions for the interviewer, and not showing that they have learned something about the company and thus are able to answer questions or ask questions with the company perspective in mind are the worst mistakes that can be made in interviewing.

Mary: What do you see as a real "interview breaker?" (What will guarantee a student won't succeed?)

Jim: For HP, behaving in an arrogant manner, not being able to demonstrate critical thinking or basic technical understanding, not listening well and thus not answering the question that was asked, and not demonstrating knowledge of and interest in what our company does are real "killers."

Mary: How much interviewing do you do via e-mail? By phone?

Jim: [E-mail interviews are] more a logistical information exchange (convenient times to have a plant trip, for instance). For HP, I don't think video interviewing or e-mail interviewing will ever replace our desire to have a face-to-face interview (both on-campus and at the plant site). Our hiring managers routinely conduct a twenty- to sixty-minute phone screen between the campus interview and an offer for a plant trip. We will be doing more video interviewing in the future. For us, it will most commonly be used for interviewing students for internships (we don't routinely fly internship candidates out for plant trips), for screening international candidates before offering a plant trip (a European hiring manager conducting a video interview with a European student attending a U.S. school), or when several managers spread out all across the country want to interview a student simultaneously.

Mary: What overall advice can you give students concerning career search?

Jim: Be honest. Don't "oversell" yourself, or you may get in way above your head. Think about the kind of company you want to be associated with, and be willing to make short-term sacrifices in terms of salary or geographic location in order to get a position with a company you want. The mid- and long-term opportunities will be there if it's a good company and you work hard. Find out who your manager will be; she or he will be the company to you, so it's important you know something about that person before you accept a job.

Tips for a Successful Student Job Search

When talking to recent college graduates, we are often reminded of the scene in the movie *The Graduate,* in which Benjamin's (Dustin Hoffman's character) uncle has one word of advice for his newly graduated nephew: "Plastics." The meaning of that one-word admonition in the '60s was that Benjamin was assured a bright future if he landed a job in the plastics industry.

Unfortunately for today's graduate, no such assurance exists. With a tight job market and more companies downsizing, graduates today must be more competitive than ever to gain an edge in the labor market. This section provides insights on how to use your college degree and relative inexperience to your advantage.

Resume Tips

A resume for a recent graduate needn't be sparse on experience or skills. Some thought and preparation will make your resume competitive with experienced veterans.

Realigning Your Resume

Obviously, most recent graduates don't have as much job experience as seasoned employees who have spent the past few years in the labor market instead of in school. You might think that this is problematic for writing a competitive resume, but to write a proper and honest resume that attracts employers, you really only need to rethink the standard resume format and be more creative in describing the jobs you have had.

Education First

For starters, remember that, as a recent graduate, you want to lead off with your education. Here, you will not use the standard two-line space that gives only the name and address of the university, degree, and graduation year. Education, after all, is your strongest offering to the employer. Elaborate. Indicate classes you think most closely match the company's needs. Include those special Saturday seminars and extra classes you took to really delve into advertising. Feature the paper you presented at a regional university conference. Discuss the special departmental honors you received. This is your big offering. Give it some attention. The employer will too.

Part-Time Jobs Are Still Jobs

You may not think that those part-time jobs you held during school have any relevance to your future career, but your employer is interested in them. You merely need to learn how to present them. For example, your experience as second assistant manager at the athletic shoe store, where you were in charge of two high school underachievers, can be mined for important generic job duties and attributes. You handled cash, budgeted, scheduled, controlled inventory, supervised, performed evaluations, opened and closed, served customers, and made sales. You had to be responsible, dependable, accurate, fair, organized, motivated, and adept at customer service, to name just a few of the attributes you brought to that job. The same is true for your jobs in restaurants or the college bookstore. Look carefully at each of your part-time student jobs and think about the responsibilities you held. How do they relate to your future job prospects? Can you find something relevant to put on your resume? Employers appreciate this.

Internships and Special Projects

What about the special projects you worked on as a student? Mary recently worked with an engineering student who had participated in two projects for private companies that had gone to his university for help with specific engineering problems. That was work experience, directly related to his job objective. Maybe you held an unpaid internship related to your major? It should go without saying that you include all internships and externships as job experience on your resume. They exist to give undergraduates experience in the world of work for which they are preparing.

Your work experience is no less valid than any other job seeker's. It is up to you to present it in a way that shows its relevance to your prospective employer.

Interview Tips

Job interviews are daunting to everyone, but they provide opportunities for college students to shine. Here are some tips to help you succeed in your post-graduate job interviews.

Be Professional

You have mastered some complex theories and principles during college. The world of work is waiting for you to make a contribution with your knowledge and training. Unless you can convince the employer that you know how to be professional on the job, however, you won't get your shot. You look professional by making a strong showing in the interview with the proper grooming, preparation, and communication with the employer. To do a good job of interacting with the employer, use the presentation skills you acquired in school.

Positive Qualities

Too many college students focus on all the reasons they might not be selected—which mostly revolve around experience. Employers base their hiring decisions on a variety of attributes, however, not just experience alone. In fact, decisions are made every day to hire someone with less experience and better personal qualities, rather than a more experienced candidate with other problem traits. Remember, employers want you to tell them why you would make a good candidate for the job. Applicants with experience need only point to work history examples that illustrate their fitness for a job. You can do the same thing using your experience as a student.

Part of being a successful job seeker is knowing how to make the most of your assets. Examine your career as a student. Look for those things that made you a success at school, and then translate them into employment terms. Let's examine some positive qualities of student applicants.

Ability to Work with Deadlines

College students live in a world of schedules—papers due, projects pending, exams coming up. You are responsible for deadlines every day of your student life. Deadlines are also a reality in the work arena. You're good at meeting them. Offer this strength to employers.

Ability to Handle Multiple Tasks

During school, you worked on several projects for different classes simultaneously. "Why do they all want major papers and projects at the same time?" is a common student lament. This can be turned into an advantage in the job interview. Illustrate your ability to keep assignments straight and get everything in on time.

Ability to Achieve Goals

Your entire education revolved around the goal of graduating. You worked toward achieving that goal. You studied your head off to be top of the class. Employers like applicants with goals.

Ability to Work as Part of a Team

Remember those group projects in school that made you groan? It was difficult working with all those different personalities. You sometimes felt that not all members gave equally. In the world of work, you will frequently be part of a team effort. Many employers have adopted the Total Quality Management (TQM) philosophy of management. In TQM, as well as in most other work situations these days, teams work toward solutions of problems. You will already have similar experience from school.

Ability to Adapt

When that class you had to have was closed, you somehow made the adjustment and still graduated on time. Your many professors exhibited huge personality differences, yet you managed to work successfully with all of them. You were able to fit your work schedule around your school schedule and survive on less sleep and money. Let's face it: The whole college experience involves adapting to many different conditions and changes.

No Bad Habits to Unlearn

All this time you've viewed your relative inexperience as a handicap, while employers often view it as a plus. Sometimes, seasoned employees want to do things their own way. This can cause real problems on the job. Inexperienced applicants are more easily molded into the company's way of doing things.

Enthusiasm

Recent college graduates burst onto the work scene, eager to try out in the real world the theories they studied at school. Employers welcome enthusiasm and energy. It gets the blood of the organization going. Too often, long-term employees are set in their ways, out of ideas, and lack energy. Companies need the infusion of fresh ideas and the dynamism of college hires to keep them energized.

Knowledge of New Theories

College students get the whole picture when studying a discipline. They are often exposed to the latest theories and schools of thought in their fields. Employers like to be kept in touch with cutting-edge information through their employees.

This is where your expertise with the Internet comes in especially handy. Colleges and universities had a real advantage with this new technology because they were among the first organizations to use it.

Two employers we spoke with said they had recently gotten online and were still feeling their way along. One department manager who had a job opening posted in a newsgroup told Mary he really wasn't the one we wanted to talk to.

"This is the first time I've ever recruited for my department over the Internet," he said. "There are a couple other people here who have, but I'm not really knowledgeable or comfortable with it, yet." This is precisely the situation in which you would have an edge as a recent college grad with lots of Internet experience.

Writing Ability

Here's where all those hours spent slaving over a word processor or typewriter pay off. You can write that new policy statement. You can submit that press release. You can edit the in-house newspaper. Writing skills are important in the workplace. Many employees lack well-honed writing skills, and your skills give you an edge.

Remember that you have already had a few chances to demonstrate your writing ability through e-mail correspondence with the employer. Do not throw those opportunities away. Construct your messages intelligently and carefully.

Fact-Finding and Information-Gathering Abilities

College students emerge from school adept at research. You had to be able to see all sides of an issue in order to present your own. Employers like employees who can research the information needed on a particular question and come back with an answer. Your education has prepared you for this.

The primary use of the Internet in colleges and universities is for research. Through the Net, you can access libraries throughout the world. You can contact media producers and tap into information databases of all kinds. You can become the research source at work because of your experience on the Net. This is a tremendous plus in your favor. Offer it at your interview.

Avoiding Mistakes

There are several mistakes to avoid as a job seeker. Consider those that follow.

What Can You Do for Me?

Mark, a human resource manager for a computer company, told us about an interview with a recent college graduate. The applicant looked good on paper: He had a degree from a prestigious school with good grades. During the interview, though, he wanted to know all the "wrong" things.

> He asked me what time he had to be at work in the morning and how long he'd have for breaks and lunch. He also had questions about vacation and sick leave policy. I got the feeling he wanted to know just how much time he'd have to spend actually working. Time off seemed to be more important to him than time spent making contributions to our firm.

This is not your job as summer camp counselor or night clerk at the motel where you could do your homework. This could be your future, your second home, for years. The same questions you asked as a student no longer apply. You have to demonstrate real interest in the company and voice your plans for making a contribution to it.

Says Elaine, head of marketing for a manufacturing company:

> So often, inexperienced applicants ask me what we can offer them. The real deal is that we want to know what we're getting. I need to be sure that the person across from me will give me full value for the training time and expense I will be investing in him or her. Yes, I plan to offer profit sharing, a company car, and an expense account. But, neither my company nor I plan to do that for "free." Time in the interview would be best spent telling me what I'll be receiving in return for a good job with a bright future.

I'm Here to Fix This Place

That same wild-eyed enthusiasm that attracts employers to recent graduates can also work against them. Sometimes in their zeal to make a contribution, new hires charge into the job with the attitude that they will make some changes and "rescue" the organization. Employers fear that they will upset the apple cart, alienating existing staff and perhaps valued customers. Don't be too quick to point out flaws in the organization, even if your intentions are good. If you have suggestions, pick your moment carefully. Go through the chain of command. Ask someone who knows the ropes to tell you the proper procedure for making a suggestion.

I Know Everything Already

Debby is an office manager who is responsible for training all new hires. She had the following to say about the know-it-all syndrome.

> Perhaps it's pride, but all too often, recent college grads are resentful of being corrected. At first, they are willing to take instruction and [are] appreciative when their mistakes are corrected. After a while, even though they still have a lot to learn, they're not as likely to take constructive criticism willingly.

Good employees generally have the attitude that something can always be learned.

Interview Grooming for Men

Okay, when you were king of the "frat" at college, your earring with the omega symbol was a real fashion plus. Most human resource managers, however, take a dim view of earrings on male applicants. True, you see some managers in the entertainment or information systems industries sporting gold or diamond studs. However, the fundamental rules for appropriate grooming in the employment interview are virtually the same for every industry across the board. Following are some tips for proper grooming choices.

Clothing

Degreed professionals are expected to wear a suit and tie to the interview. When you were an undergraduate, you could get away with a neat shirt and slacks for the retail job at the mall. This is no longer the case. Your grooming choices are carefully inspected. The amount of care you take in dressing appropriately for your job interview equates in an employer's mind with how much respect you have for the proffered job.

Even with a suit, mistakes can be made. For example, the monochromatic look—the same color suit and shirt—will not work in most job interviews, especially if the clothing is all black. Choose a color that flatters you. Avoid large patterns. A conservative pattern, such as a muted pinstripe, is acceptable, but if you choose a patterned suit, even a subtle one, do not wear a shirt with a pattern or design. Shy away from ties that have words printed on them or that resemble a vivid test pattern. Men have a lot more latitude nowadays in choosing ties with colors and patterns, but somewhat conservative ties still work best at interviews. Don't wear "bolos," string ties, or bow ties.

Choose a shirt in a pale color that complements both the suit and your complexion and hair color. Be certain that the suit is neatly pressed, collar and cuffs are not frayed, and all buttons are in place. Your shoes should be in good repair and polished. Athletic shoes are never appropriate, not even black or brown ones. Socks should be a solid dark color, without patterns, and not sheer. Never wear white socks to an interview.

With student loans to repay and little saved from minimum-wage jobs, most recent college graduates aren't exactly "flush." It is not advisable to spend a fortune on clothes. Shop at discounted men's clothing stores, or do your initial shopping at thrift shops. You can purchase nice suits for little money. Mary often brings examples of interview clothes she has bought at second-hand stores to the classes she teaches, just to show that it can be done. One suit she bought was a navy Brooks Brothers, which she picked up for $7.00! A quick trip to the dry cleaners, and you'll look great.

Hair

Face it. It's time to lose the ponytail and let the "fade" grow in. Most employers are conservative about hair. Beyond extremes of style, however, your hair should be clean, neat, and out of your face. Facial hair doesn't pose as much of a problem. If you have a mustache or beard, it should be neatly groomed.

Hands and Nails

Years of talking to interviewers have revealed a common complaint from employers about male applicants: they do not like long nails on men. Include attention to your nails as part of your overall grooming habits. Be sure your nails are clean. If you are an auto mechanic and an employer sees dirt under you nails, he thinks, "Yep, that's a mechanic." But if you are in, say, the health or food-service industries, one speck of dirt under the nails can throw the interview.

Jewelry/Cologne

Limit the jewelry you wear—one ring, one chain, and so on. Instead of the earring, wear your Phi Beta Kappa pin. Use a tie tack or bar. Turn off your watch alarm! Cologne should be worn sparingly. This is an interview, not a date.

Hygiene

You should be freshly shaved. If your beard grows in quickly, shave just before leaving for your appointment. Use deodorant and mouthwash. Get a good night's sleep before the interview.

Interview Grooming for Women

Now is the time to pitch the overalls and jerseys that were perfect for late nights in the library. As you leave college for the world of work, you must begin to change your image. Let's examine some professional grooming choices for women.

Clothing

Choices of business suits for women abound today. You are no longer limited to the navy suit with the white blouse and little scarf, once considered the "power suit" for interviews. By all means, use color; choose shades that complement your coloring. You must wear a suit with a skirt; slacks are not considered professional attire for interviews. Skirt length can be your undoing if it means you are constantly tugging at your skirt during the interview. Your undergarments should fit properly, and not slip or show above or below your outfit.

The blouse you select can be any shade, as long as it goes with the suit. You can wear "shells" or button-front styles. Patterned blouses are not as professional as solids, and you should never mix patterns of blouses and suits. A scarf is fine, as long as it doesn't overwhelm.

Polish your shoes. This is a grooming practice that is often overlooked by women. Be careful that your shoe heels are in good repair, with heel tips in place and no scuffing. Clean off the "black stuff" that gets on the backs of high heels when you drive. Heel height should be moderate. Hose should be the color of your skin tone. Do not wear colored, patterned, or seamed hosiery. Carry an extra pair of hose in the car. A run in the stocking is sloppy and distracting.

Hair

Avoid extreme hairstyles. Hair should be clean and controlled. It is distracting when an applicant fiddles with her hair during the interview. If you are interviewing for a job in health care or food service and you have long hair, pull it back.

Hands and Nails

Manicure your nails carefully. Employers really look at hands. Keep nails at a moderate to short length. If you wear nail polish, choose a conservative color that complements your outfit. If you are in the food-service or health occupations, you should wear clear nail polish or none at all, and your nails should be shorter. (A French manicure, with clean, white nail tips, works very well for these careers.)

Makeup

If the employer can see your face from a block away, you have on too much makeup. Use a light touch when applying makeup for an interview. Less is more. Avoid bright eye shadow and blush. Your lipstick should complement your clothing and nail color. If you're not sure how to apply makeup properly, consult a fashion magazine for tips on daytime makeup application.

Accessories/Jewelry

Your bag should match your shoes. If you carry a briefcase, you shouldn't also carry a purse. Pare down the contents of your purse so that you don't need to fumble for a planner or a pen.

Keep jewelry simple. Wear just a couple of pieces. Earrings should be close to the head, never dangling or extreme. Jewelry that is noisy or gaudy or moves is distracting to the interviewer. The idea is to keep attention focused on you, not your jewelry.

Keeping the Job

Now that the dust has settled and you're safely ensconced in your new position, take a good look around you. Take the measure of the company once again, this time from the inside. What does it take to get ahead and succeed in this new job? The task of finding a job required hard work and dedication. You will now need to apply that same determination and diligence to keeping it. Job retention is the final step in the job-search process. Following are some tips to make you indispensable to your new employer.

Job-Related Tips

What is it that puts an employee's picture on the "employee of the month" bulletin board time after time? Why do some workers get promoted rapidly while others languish at entry level? Companies pay attention to excellence on the job.

Hone Your Skills

Whatever skills you brought to the interview were sufficient to get you the job. The problem is that many employees stop there. Doing just enough to get in the door and no more will keep you at a fairly plodding pace in the company. Employers look for employees who go out of their way to improve their skills and job performance. These are the ones who get the promotions and keep their jobs during crisis periods. Volunteer for new in-house training if it becomes available. Take extension courses. Practice your craft, whatever it is, and become an expert at it. Try to "best your best."

Stay Informed

You got this job by means of the latest technology. Don't let your cutting edge become dulled. Read up on the latest techniques and trends. Do periodic research on the Internet. Stay up-to-date on the most recent events and changes in technology.

Contribute

Get involved in the discussion at staff meetings. Make suggestions for improvements—at least for your own job performance. Give your input when asked for it. Take an active part in your company's future. Bumps on a log don't grow.

Be a Team Player

Of course you want to be the one who stands out from the crowd. What you want to avoid is standing apart from the crowd. Share your ideas and always

credit others for theirs. Be generous in praise for your co-workers. The prevailing management concept in business today is Total Quality Management, or TQM. In TQM, everyone has a stake in the success of the company. You need to know how to play nice and share with the other kids to make this work.

General Tips

Besides job-related strengths, employers appreciate and notice personal qualities in their employees. Those employees who embody ethical, professional, and appropriate behavior on the job are the ones who excel.

Keep Your Private Life Private

Don't bring your personal "stuff" to work with you. Employers don't like to hire problems. Keeping the details of your private life confidential will inspire respect from those you work for and with. Also, resist the temptation to date fellow employees. Things get very complicated and uncomfortable after the personal relationship has cooled and you are still forced to work together.

Don't Become Involved in Office Politics

Stay professional and courteous to your co-workers and superiors. Try to distance yourself from petty grievances and conflicts between other people. Be the one who builds consensus instead of one of a few who create divisiveness.

Keep a Positive Attitude

Don't be the one who always says it can't be done. Rise to new challenges. Be open to change. Stay flexible and willing to grow. Help lead the way into the future, instead of being dragged into it.

Stay in Touch with the Internet

The Internet was your best buddy when you were looking for work. You developed many contacts there and discovered a whole universe of data on a wide variety of subjects. This information is invaluable to you now. Make frequent contacts with the Internet. Through it you can stay current on world events, learn about advances within your company's field, watch the stock market (including your company's holdings!), and nurture future job contacts.

Your college experience will serve you well as you enter the labor market of the future. At school, you have been exposed to some of the very latest in technological advances, particularly the Internet. This exposure is a distinct advantage in a competitive labor market. You bring with you a fresh approach and a willing spirit, something that longtime employees sometimes lack. Stay engaged and interested. Don't leave your education at the university—make learning a lifelong pursuit.

Chapter 12

Advice for Employers

Perhaps you have been considering using the Internet for recruitment but are daunted by the sheer immensity of it. After all, you keep hearing these huge numbers: *forty million people on the Internet*. You wonder, "If I put a job announcement on the Internet, how in the world am I going to interview and screen forty million job applicants?" You certainly don't have time to waste looking at all kinds of unsuitable applicants.

Electronic Recruiting

To many people, the question is "What do you do now to prevent a crush of unqualified applicants?" In the face-to-face world of recruitment and selection, employers are careful where and how they list position announcements. For example:

✔ They select agencies or "headhunters" who specialize in the kind of applicant pool they need.

✔ They pass the word through the "grapevine" to other employers that they are looking for good people.

✔ They write ads carefully, spelling out the minimum qualifications or setting the experience requirements very high.

✔ They place "blind" ads, where their name is not given.

✔ They begin with a "resume only" period, during which they do some preliminary screening to see how the applicant looks on paper.

✔ They contact college career centers where they think there might be a pool of graduates in their particular field.

These are the same steps you can take on the Internet. When you post your job opening in certain employment databases, you are prompted to enter certain keywords. For instance, if your applicant must have a master's in marketing, ten years of experience, and live in the St. Louis area, your order would appear with the keywords: "MA Marketing," "10 years exp.," "St. Louis." You can narrow the field of applicants considerably just by adding specific keywords. This is akin to writing your ad with precisely defined requirements. Within the body of the order, you can be even more detailed, thus further limiting your field of applicants.

Newsgroups and Online Employment Services

Recruitment is costly, in both money and time. For many companies, the World Wide Web has lightened this major burden by providing access to a larger qualified applicant pool and by giving hiring authorities better control of the process. Resume-management programs and online services have simplified the task of sorting through mountains of resumes. Employers can now search through hundreds of applicants and select the most qualified by typing a few appropriate keywords. What once took a company months to accomplish now can be completed in a matter of days.

You can find applicants online in a variety of ways, with services providing differing options and levels of assistance. In the following section, we review a few of those services.

A number of sources are available for posting your job openings on the Internet. Basically, these are newsgroups and commercial online recruiting services. Which one you choose depends on a number of factors, including cost, accessibility, and number of job openings available in your field. Following is an overview of the newsgroups available on the Web.

Newsgroups

Typically, newsgroups are places where people with common interests go to share information and resources. For recruiting purposes, newsgroups are arranged according to profession, degree of experience, or geographic location.

For example, there is a newsgroup for job seekers in the San Francisco Bay area called `ba.jobs`. Job seekers looking in the `ba.jobs` newsgroup know that the jobs are limited to a certain geographical area. Similarly, there is an `atl.jobs` group just for jobs in the Atlanta area, a `balt.jobs` listing for Baltimore positions, a `dc.jobs` group for jobs in Washington, D.C., and so on.

Job seekers with one to three years' experience can seek work through the `misc.jobs.offered.entry` newsgroup. People in the field of biology can look for openings on the `bionet.jobs` newsgroup.

Before joining any newsgroup, you should first read the frequently asked questions (FAQ) posting for information governing use of the group. Armed with this information, you won't violate any rules of netiquette while you are dealing with the group. For instance, the `misc.jobs.offered` group is only for posting job openings. If, as sometimes happens, a person or group makes an inappropriate posting—for instance, a message or a resume—the group moderator or a reader will fire off a warning message, known as a *flame*. The user will then be told which group to use for their purpose.

A major advantage to using newsgroups is that they are free to both employers and job seekers. The main disadvantage is that they are not organized. `misc.jobs.offered`, for example, contains a wide assortment of jobs that are not arranged in any discernible categories. Job seekers must search through the entire list to find those openings that are most appropriate for them. Sales jobs coexist right alongside computer positions and clerical opportunities. In newsgroups, the most recent posting appears first, with previous postings following in order of the date and time of posting. Lastly, newsgroups are not maintained, which means that your posting may remain on a newsgroup long after the position has been filled.

One of the largest of the newsgroups, `misc.jobs.offered`, contains a wide assortment of jobs. Listings are not arranged in any particular order, but the latest entries appear first. You are encouraged to include as much detail as you can about the job offered in the subject heading, including the location code for the job. Job seekers then scan the headings to find the jobs that interest them. Bear in mind that applicants self-screen from newsgroups, so you really can't control the people who contact you through this medium.

Here are some sample jobs from the newsgroup `misc.jobs.offered`:

● ●

misc.jobs.offered:
FROM misc.jobs.offered

5/21 Reading . . . Sat, 05 Nov 1994 08:53:28 ab.jobs
Thread 1 of 8
Waterloo, Ontario, Canada

Position of International Marketing Director available:

Plastic household products manufacturing company, with facilities in Canada and U.S., is looking for an individual able to fill the position of International Marketing Director, who will be directing marketing of the company products in the worldwide market.

Salary between 60K-100K depending on experience, plus other remunerations. Language aptitude and European experience welcomed.

Please do not respond to this post, but fax your resume directly to 000-000-0000. You can also e-mail your resume to us < >, while we cannot answer any questions, we can forward your resume to the company. Please put the words: "RESUME of <your name>" in the subject line. Thank you.

• •

From misc.jobs.offered
Lines 24 Advertising Designer-Alkon Corporation-OH
No responses
occ@nero.aa.msen.com Online Career Ctr at Msen, Inc. –
Ann Arbor, MI (account)

Advertising Designer

Excellent opportunity for an individual to start up an internal advertising department for a Columbus, Ohio-based manufacturer of PC-based control systems. Ongoing projects include company newsletter, print ads, brochures, direct mail pieces, and related materials. Creative skills are a must, and copy strength is a real plus. Candidates must have solid experience with desktop publishing systems, purchasing skills with outside suppliers, and the ability for self-direction.

Send resume and current work samples to:

(NAME OF COMPANY) Corporation
Attn: LB
ADDRESS
Advertising Designer
Columbus, OH 43204

No Phone Calls, Please.

OH 43204

• •

From misc.jobs.offered

misc.jobs.offered Thread 173 of 2924
Lines 37 Information Technology Consultants-CGA-MN
No responses
occ@nero.aa.msen.com Online Career Ctr at Msen, Inc. –
Ann Arbor, MI (account)

(COMPANY NAME), headquartered in New York City, is part of a major transnational information technology consulting firm. With annual revenues of approximately $2 billion annually and operations in 16 countries, (co. name) maintains a worldwide, world-class professional staff of over 20,000 consultants.

The company's information technology service offerings include custom software development, applications management, systems integration, outsourcing, reengineering, training and professional services across a broad spectrum of industries, including integrating manufacturing, financial services, retail, pharmaceutical, and the telecommunications industries.

We have needs for consultant to work in the MINNEAPOLIS, MN, area. We select only the most ambitious technical professionals who are willing to do whatever it takes to help solve our clients' business problems. You could qualify for one of our Consultant positions if you've trained AND have experience in one or more of the following: LOTUS NOTES, C++, Oracle, Ingress, CICS, DB2, COBOL, Visual Basic or Powerbuilder, IBM Mainframe, FoxPro, or Sybase. Successful candidates will have demonstrated business maturity, co-op or internship experience, leadership abilities, as well as excellent interpersonal and communications skills.

If you want to join a company committed to excellence and client satisfaction, if you enjoy a challenge and teamwork, and if you want to work with other exceptional people, we want to hear from you. Please send your resume to:

(COMPANY SNAIL MAIL ADDRESS) Minneapolis, MN 55401; or 000-000-0000 (FAX).

We are an equal opportunity employer. M/F/H/V

● ●

misc.jobs.offered Thread 174 of 2924
Lines 25 Programmer/Analysts
occ@mail.msen.com Online Career Ctr at Msen, Inc. —
Ann Arbor, MI (account in)

(COMPANY NAME) currently needs:

- Sys38 RPG Analyst
(Will function as a Programmer/Analyst/Operator)

- Programmer Analyst
(Must have worked as a Programmer with ORACLE.)

Contact: Staffing Specialist
(COMPANY NAME)
Akron, OH 44308-1719
000-000-0000 - voice
000-000-0000 - fax

● ●

misc.jobs.offered Thread 277 of 2924
Lines 37 Laboratory Safety Spclst-Univ of Medicine
occ@nero.aa.msen.com Online Career Ctr at Msen, Inc. —
Ann Arbor, MI (account)

LABORATORY SAFETY SPECIALIST

Two (2) Positions:
One at Newark campus and one at Piscataway/New
Brunswick campus

UMDNJ, the University of Medicine & Dentistry of New
Jersey, the nation's largest comprehensive health sciences
university, is seeking a laboratory safety specialist. Reporting to the local Campus Safety Officer, this individual will
identify, evaluate, eliminate and/or minimize occupational
and environmental hazards in laboratories and related
premises.

In addition to a Master's degree in industrial hygiene,
environmental or occupational health sciences, chemistry or
a related technical discipline, a minimum of three (3) years
of professional work experience in the field of industrial
hygiene, laboratory safety, or occupational/environmental
health prevention programs is required. A Bachelor's degree
and five years of experience in laboratory safety, industrial
hygiene, or occupational/environmental safety and health
are also acceptable. Thorough knowledge of laboratory
safety principles is imperative. Considerable knowledge of
industrial hygiene equipment uses and methodology as well
as the ability to calibrate and maintain monitoring equipment is necessary. Knowledge of PEOSH/OSHA, NIOSH,
ACGIH, and NJ DEPE/EPA regulations is also necessary.

Ability to prepare clear, accurate, and informative reports
including investigative findings, conclusions, and recom-
mendations along with superior interpersonal and oral
presentation skills needed.

UMDNJ offers a competitive salary and a comprehensive
benefits package. Please send your resume to:

• •

FROM misc.jobs.offered

Insect Management Discovery Research - Biology

Associate Biologist. We are searching for a scientist capable
of working as a team member and collaborating on a variety
of projects in a multidisciplinary environment. The successful candidate will be required to perform "in vitro" bio-
chemical assays for insecticide discovery and mode of
action studies. This person would maintain the equipment
and supplies needed to run the assays, including maintaining

insect and cell cultures and preparing media and buffers. Laboratory experience is required, and experience in performing receptor binding assays is preferred. In addition to these operational duties, computer literacy is essential.

Requirements: Candidates should have B.S. or M.S. in biology, i.e., pharmacology, biochemistry, neuroscience, or related disciplines.

Applicants should send their resume, including names of at least three references.

Remember that newsgroups are among the few places where you can list your jobs online for free. Some college placement offices allow you to post your openings in their private databases at no charge; others refer you to a fee-based service that they use, such as JOBTRAK; still others charge a fee to employers to allow a search of their resume databases, just as they do when companies do on-campus recruiting.

Commercial Online Recruiting Services

In the past, you might have used an employment agency to help you with recruitment. These companies find qualified applicants for employers and charge a fee for the service. Some agencies deal only with management-level people and are known as *headhunters*. Others specialize in temporary personnel. Such services also exist on the World Wide Web. They are easier to use, put more control in the hands of the employer, and bring in a much larger and better-qualified pool of applicants than traditional agencies. In general, they are also less expensive. Here's how they work.

When your company posts a job opening with a service such as Monster.com—one of the largest and most extensive of the online services—the form you complete contains a section where you can enter certain keywords, words that best summarize the qualifications needed for the position. You can also enter a full-text job description, making it as detailed and concise as possible. You also give your instructions for applying, usually by fax, online resume template, mail, or e-mail. You can specify "no phone calls," "e-mail only," or "please fax a resume." You can even place your order as a blind ad, one that doesn't give your company name or address. This job order is then posted to the online service's list of openings.

When job seekers use the employment service, they, too, enter keywords that summarize their skills, knowledge, and abilities. The employment service's software searches the database of job openings and matches the applicant with the job. Thus, only qualified candidates, based on their own strengths in the form of keywords, are referred to your job.

In addition to job postings, these online services have resume databases. These work in much the same way as a job database when searched. When you are looking for a candidate, you can do a search of resumes using keywords that best describe the job you have available. Your query turns up only those candidates whose resumes contain those same keywords. Some online services charge nothing to employers for a resume search. Applicants are almost never charged for job searches.

Some online services, notably BridgePath and JobOptions, now use a technology known as *push*. Push technology is used to send information to a client without the client requesting it. You can have resumes sent automatically to your computer rather than having to go out and search them out. In the same way, passive job seekers can have jobs sent to them automatically. Push technology has made the process of finding the right candidate on the Internet easier than ever.

Compared to conventional recruitment avenues, such as print ads, head-hunters, and outplacement firms, the cost of these online services is relatively small. Remember that cost and assistance provided varies among the different services.

Now that you know the basics of online recruiting, let's take a closer look at some actual services.

JobOptions

In chapter 3, "Getting Job Information from Corporate Sites and Job Boards," we introduced you to JobOptions (`www.joboptions.com`). JobOptions is a major player in online recruiting. Its site is one of the fastest growing on the Web. It is also one of the oldest, having been around since 1991, first as AdNet, and later as E-Span.

Michael Forrest is the energetic president of JobOptions. He took over leadership of the company and renamed it JobOptions in 1998. Forrest has been actively involved with online technologies since the late 1970s. He was the founding CEO of CareerPath.com (www.careerpath.com), and built what was then one of the most trafficked job and career sites on the Internet. He has served as a director with a "Big Eight" (now "Big Five") accounting and consulting firm; as a senior executive for an 1,100-office, national franchise organization; and as a division vice-president of an American Stock Exchange–listed company, where he was responsible for both domestic and international operations.

With over twenty years of professional business experience and a wealth of firsthand knowledge of some of this nation's most successful companies, Michael Forrest has a firm understanding of what businesses need in a recruitment service. Mary talked with Michael Forrest about JobOptions and how it helps employers.

Mary: *How are you positioned in the online job services market?*

Michael: JobOptions, in its genesis as AdNet, then E-Span, was the first online job and employment site, founded in 1991. Today, as one of the most trafficked employment sites on the Internet, it is the clear technology leader in terms of user interface...job searching, employer database, resume technology, and job and resume push technology.

JobOptions is a major employment hub with something for everyone. It is the clear market leader with respect to experienced professionals in technology, finance and accounting, and sales and marketing. From a sample of 100,609 voluntary disclosures from site users over the past six months, JobOptions knows that 77.7 percent of its users are thirty years of age or older, and that the top ten areas of industry experience for its user base are, in order: Computer/Technology, Engineering, Consulting, Internet/New Media, Accounting, Manufacturing, Advertising, Financial Services, Health/Medical, [and] Banking.

Mary: *Approximately how many employers are registered with you?*

Michael: More than 6,015 employing companies use our services in one form or another, but of course, the actual number of recruiter-users is many times that number.

Mary: *About how many resumes are in your system at any given time?*

Michael: We currently have more than 151,000 resumes that were posted directly to the JobOptions Resume Database. This number should not be confused with some of the well-known sites that claim much higher numbers, which actually result from scraping resumes from other sites and from newsgroups to give the appearance of deeper content. More than 200,000 users are currently registered on the site, many of whom elect to take advantage of our Job Alert push technology, but not our resume functions. Registrations are growing at the rate of 24 percent per month.

Mary: What would you say is the significant way in which you differ from most or all other services?

Michael: JobOptions offers a user interface that is simply "best of class"...navigation, searching, resume building, and so on. With the exception of search results pages, all pages are viewable on one screen. Both resume and job searches provide rich, easy-to-screen results pages, and include "Narrow Your Search" functionality, which allows for better, faster matching. We are different than other sites that offer yesteryears' laundry list of employer links. JobOptions is the only site that offers a truly functional employer database, searchable by location, industry, and by keywords actually indexed from pages on the employers' sites. Important, too, rather than sending candidates to lackluster employer profiles, JobOptions' employer database actually sends candidates directly to the employers' sites, where candidates can obtain a better feel for the company, its business, and its culture.

Mary: Is that the Hot Link feature? How does it work at JobOptions?

Michael: I assume that you're referring to what most sites refer to as "Employer Hot Links"...in other words, an alphabetical laundry list of company names that link (on most sites) to a plain vanilla employer profile that robs the employer of truly discriminating itself from all the others; that takes away the opportunity to give the candidates a true sense of the employers' (product), services, and so on.

Hot links are usually just names of companies you click on. They're twenty-six pages of two columns, nine screens long. JobOptions' 5,800 company links are meaningfully displayed at the search results screen. Job seekers can click the link there, when they are truly interested in the company, to find out more about it.

JobOptions offers an employer database that allows candidates to search by location, industry sector, and keywords.

> *Note:* The keywords that are searched on are actually indexed from the employers' own sites, thus relieving the employer of the painstaking process of deciding what keywords to use, and providing for better matching.

The JobOptions Employer Database builds a custom list of employers that is responsive to candidates' interests. From the search results, candidates can click directly to the employers' sites. "We've even built in an automatic resume-forwarding mechanism, so the candidate won't have to hunt around looking for the right place to send e-mail," says Forrest.

Another service JobOptions provides to employers is billboards, company advertisements that appear on the employment site. JobOptions' approach to billboards, or banner ads, differs from many other online sites in a few significant ways. They limit the number that can be displayed to alleviate clutter, they rotate them for best exposure, and allow employers to decide on which page of the site they want their ads displayed.

JobOptions also makes it easy to post job openings by e-mail—a real time-saving feature.

Mary: How does the e-mail posting option work?

Michael: Actually, employers can send formatted e-mail or FTP files to JobOptions to automate the job-posting process. This is an essential function for larger employers who post to a number of sites and find the keying-in process inefficient.

Mary: How about Multiple-Location and Multiple Categories Posting?

Michael: Employers are able to post jobs on up to five categories and five locations. Since our most popular package provides for unlimited posting, there are essentially no limits on the number of categories or locations under which an employer might post jobs.

Mary: How many resumes are sent to the employer via the Resume Alert function? Can the employer set that number?

Michael: The employer can elect to receive between ten and fifty resumes each week from each Resume Alert. Employers can set up a virtually unlimited number of resume alerts.

Different from most sites that merely send a notification of new resumes, our Real Resume Push Technology actually e-mails the complete resumes together with a comprehensive profile. This is particularly responsive to the "passive" recruiter or [human resources] generalist who simply doesn't have the time to get online and check regularly.

Mary: *Is there a way to prevent the employer from seeing the same resume over and over?*

Michael: Yes. All resumes on the JobOptions network are date stamped for the last time edited. Resume Alerts send only those resumes that are dated subsequent to the last alert.

Mary: *What do you most want employers to know about your service?*

Michael: JobOptions, even when combined with Monster.com, reaches less than 5 percent of the monthly Internet user base. It's not a question of which one site to use, but which sites to use. JobOptions, because of its ease of use and its "all-you-can-eat" pricing, is a must buy...the foundation of an employer's online recruitment efforts. JobOptions' already leading value proposition is further and dramatically enhanced with JobOptions' Private Label option, wherein we provide technology to employers that either don't have a site or that have no job-posting functionality on their site. This Private Label no fee/small fee option saves employers time, allowing them to post both to their own site and JobOptions at the same time.

JobOptions' (**www.joboptions.com/xoom**) co-branding network technology works to direct more eyeballs to their online ads, and delivers more and more unique resumes. JobOptions currently has some of the Net's largest sites in its network, and expects to add fifty to 100 additional sites by the end of 1999.

JobOptions is the clear market leader with respect to experienced professionals in technology, finance and accounting, and sales and marketing.

There is a lot of discussion about which site is best and which isn't. Employers want one best site and one best isn't going to make it. Companies need to be able to pick and choose their sites. JobOptions is a good value because it works.

Let's take a look at the employer side of JobOptions.com:

At the JobOptions home page, click on the tab labeled "For HR/Recruiters."

Figure 12.1

JobOptions' home page.

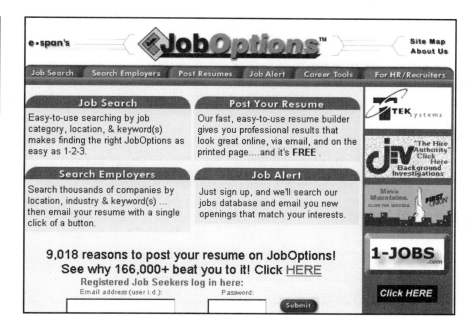

At the login page, you must enter your user ID and password. You get those by contacting a JobOptions regional account manager at the site and signing up.

Once in the employer area, you can search resumes by keywords. In our case, we used Indiana as the state and "new media" as the keywords.

You are then presented with a list of suitable potential applicants.

Figure 12.2

JobOptions resume search results, showing five possible candidates.

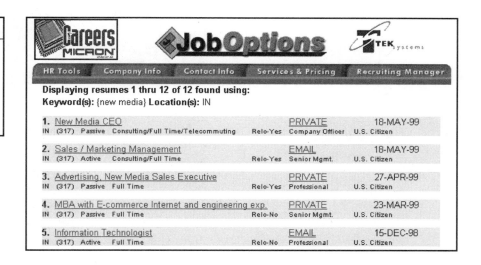

Figure 12.3 shows what a candidate profile, extracted from a resume, looks like.

Figure 12.3

A candidate profile.

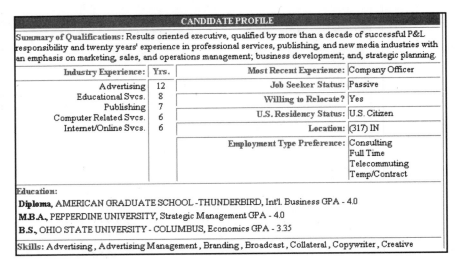

CANDIDATE PROFILE

Summary of Qualifications: Results oriented executive, qualified by more than a decade of successful P&L responsibility and twenty years' experience in professional services, publishing, and new media industries with an emphasis on marketing, sales, and operations management; business development; and, strategic planning.

Industry Experience:	Yrs.		Most Recent Experience:	Company Officer
Advertising	12		Job Seeker Status:	Passive
Educational Svcs.	8		Willing to Relocate?	Yes
Publishing	7		U.S. Residency Status:	U.S. Citizen
Computer Related Svcs.	6		Location:	(317) IN
Internet/Online Svcs.	6		Employment Type Preference:	Consulting Full Time Telecommuting Temp/Contract

Education:
Diploma, AMERICAN GRADUATE SCHOOL -THUNDERBIRD, Int'l. Business GPA - 4.0
M.B.A., PEPPERDINE UNIVERSITY, Strategic Management GPA - 4.0
B.S., OHIO STATE UNIVERSITY - COLUMBUS, Economics GPA - 3.35

Skills: Advertising, Advertising Management, Branding, Broadcast, Collateral, Copywriter, Creative

The job listing side of the JobOptions site is also easy to use. To enter your job listing, select the JobOptions Listing Manager.

Figure 12.4

JobOptions' Listing Manager.

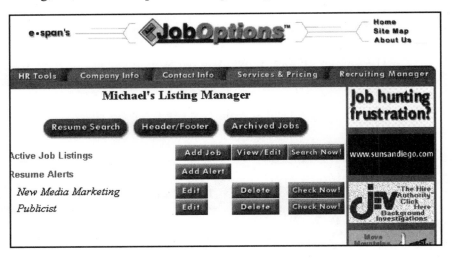

Here you can add or edit a job listing, work on archived jobs, or perform a resume search.

The price for the JobOptions service varies with the level of experience you choose. Single ads can run as long as sixty days for $150 per ad. Unlimited access, the most comprehensive package, costs $5,370 per year. For up-to-date price quotes, visit the JobOptions site at **www.joboptions.com**.

Other Commercial Online Recruiting Services

There are many other online recruiting sites on the Internet, offering a variety of services and features. These range from small, specialized sites,

such as the Science Professional Network (www.sciencemag.org), to large, comprehensive sites, such as Monster.com (www.monster.com). Prices vary widely, depending on service provided, size of the database, and search features.

Let's look at two big sites: Monster.com and CareerMart.

Monster.com
www.monster.com

First established in October 1994 as the Monster Board, Monster.com has become a major player in online recruiting. Monster.com uses software that allows you to load job descriptions from your desktop computer directly into the Monster.com database. The same desktop program enables you to search the resume database. Monster.com boasts a database of over 200,000 jobs and 30,000 employers.

Monster.com keeps your jobs online for up to sixty days. You can conduct keyword searches of the resume database, which Monster.com claims is over one million strong. You can also search by function, industry location, and date of resume posting. Monster.com is international, consisting of sites in Canada, the United Kingdom, the Netherlands, Belgium, Australia, and France, as well as the United States.

The cost to employers for Monster.com varies with the amount and kind of service you receive. For example, you can post a single ad for up to sixty days for $225. In addition, Monster.com offers a number of corporate value packages to increase your company's online presence. To set up an account and put a job listing on Monster.com, click on Post a Job at the home page, specify whether you are an employer or a recruiter, and then complete the fill-in-the-blanks screen. You pay for your ad by credit card or invoice.

CareerMart
www.careermart.com

CareerMart is an easily searchable database that contains an incredible half-million resumes. You can search on a number of categories, including states and keywords. With its automated resume reply feature, CareerMart uses push technology to automatically notify employers of appropriate resumes. The site also contains chat rooms, banners, and virtual job fairs.

Figure 12.5

CareerMart's home page.

The Advantages of Online Recruiting

The employers we have spoken to are enthusiastic about using the Internet to find candidates. Many of them report that they have found a richer and more diverse field of applicants online than they have with conventional recruiting methods. They also like the ease and speed that online recruiting affords them. The following are some of the benefits of online recruiting.

E-Mail: More Details, Less Time

The ability to use e-mail to conduct pre-screening interviews is a tremendous benefit to electronic recruiting. As you respond to the resume postings, you do so through e-mail, a much more expedient process than callbacks and "snail mail." Through the ensuing messages between you and the candidate, you get many more details than you normally would in a single phone call or by reading an application or resume.

The other advantage to e-mail is that the results are immediate. Generally, you can expect replies within eight hours, and usually even sooner because the job seeker is eagerly awaiting your "new mail" message. (Overseas responses usually take longer—because of the time difference, your recipient may be asleep when your message arrives.) With e-mail there are no busy signals or answering machines or waiting on hold. You simply post your reply or request and go on with your business.

Note: Remember that a human being is waiting on the other end for your answer. It is disheartening and frustrating to be left dangling while waiting for an employer's decision. It doesn't take a minute to send an e-mail if you have decided not to consider the applicant. A good way to handle this unpleasant task is to compose a courteous rejection note in your word processor that can be easily pasted into your e-mail program and sent to all the applicants you did not select. Be friendly and wish each one success. Such a message gives the job seeker closure.

Getting to the Right People

With conventional recruiting, you spend a lot of time interviewing the "wrong" people. Usually, when you're filling a position, you first receive a resume and perhaps make a brief phone call to schedule an interview with the applicant. Often when you finally meet the applicant, you find he or she doesn't have the qualifications or qualities you really need, but you are committed to that fifteen or twenty minutes of interview time because the applicant is there in your office. It is a waste of your time and the applicant's. Applicants are no more willing to waste their time than you are. Indeed, with the expense of job hunting and no income to offset it, sitting through a futile interview is even more troublesome to the job seeker than it is to you.

Thanks to e-mail prescreening interviews, you already have a "handle" on applicants before you ever meet them. You are able to delve into certain areas a bit more deeply, asking for examples that give you some evidence that the applicant possesses the skills and talents you're looking for. These prescreening e-mails are a service to the applicant as well. He may be able to expand on some point in the resume that may have been overlooked at first glance. He gets that "second chance" to impress you by giving you a little more specific information than can be provided in a resume.

Every employer we spoke with extolled the virtues of the e-mail prescreen. They found it a major convenience in terms of getting to the right people.

Your Computer Becomes "The Lobby"

Electronic recruiting has it all over the face-to-face variety when it comes to the lobby of your company. During conventional recruitment, applicants—qualified and otherwise—crowd your office, making it difficult to conduct normal business. Entire weeks get blocked out on calendars, meetings get postponed, and alternative space arrangements have to be made when a company is in "hire mode."

This is not the case with electronic recruiting. Your computer screen becomes your lobby, and applicants wait there. You access it at your convenience. The business of your organization does not grind to a halt while your receptionist deals with a lobby full of applicants.

We should mention here that we received some complaints from applicants who wondered why employers recruiting in an e-mail medium would specify "no e-mails" in their postings, as sometimes happens. If you have a rational reason for not accepting e-mail submissions, by all means state it in your order. It will make more sense to applicants and spare some hard feelings.

Less Time on the Phone

Thanks to e-mail, you won't be inundated with phone calls, as you are during conventional recruiting. Unless you have listed your phone number or have given it to certain candidates, job seekers will contact you only by e-mail. It's a good idea to specify "no phone calls" in the job order and not include your phone number if you don't want to get calls.

Cutting-Edge People

All the employers and recruiters we spoke to agreed on this point. If you find your applicant on the Net, you are probably getting someone who is comfortable with technology, familiar with current developments, and not afraid to try new things. These are people who already know how to work with that new computer you just installed to help with invoicing; in fact, they might well be able to help you troubleshoot problems with your system.

You Control It

With electronic recruiting, you call the shots. You decide when to pull your ad. You revise your announcement as needed. You can start recruiting immediately when you need to fill a position. You are not at the mercy of a newspaper ad or a busy calendar. You computer can receive applicants twenty-four hours a day, seven days a week, and hold them until you can deal with them. This puts considerably more control of the recruitment process in your hands and simplifies the task of finding your candidate.

Legal and Ethical Aspects of Electronic Recruiting

The Internet has grown so quickly that Congress and the judiciary have had difficulties regulating what can happen. With the even faster growth of the career portion of the Internet, it's no surprise that legal and ethical guidelines for recruiting on the Internet are ill defined.

What we can do is share the questions, experiences, and opinions of the job-search professionals we have interviewed:

Question: How should I deal with applicants who attach photos to their resumes?

Answer: Actors, models, and a few others are typically expected to submit photos, but today on the Internet an increasing number of applicants are attaching their photos to their electronic resumes simply because it can so easily be done. Most employers, of course, strongly recommend against it. We've seen resumes with what amounts to a family photo album attached!

Photos can be prejudicial—one way or another. If you've viewed an applicant's photo and then not hired them, they may accuse you of basing your decision on their looks. But it would be difficult to prove that an employer actually viewed a photograph, because most Web sites do not track the IP [Internet Protocol] addresses of hits.

Additionally, your Web browser can easily be set to not load any images. You'll see only an image icon where the photo was located. Therefore, it would be difficult to prove that, even if an employer did download a resume, it was downloaded with photos. Our recommendation, however, is to set your browser to not load images. This way you won't even have the photos to deal with.

Question: Are electronic resumes any less or any more inflated than paper resumes?

Answer: No one can know, of course, but the consensus seems to be that resume fraud may well be more likely on the Internet. A fraudulent resume can be circulated much faster and with a wider distribution than a paper resume. It's much easier to make changes on an electronic resume. To be safe, remember this: There is no more reason to believe every claim on an electronic resume than on a print resume.

Question: Does the same need exist for keeping a paper trail of contacts with candidates?

Answer: It's so easy to move around the Internet and not keep record of what was done that documentation becomes even more important. The recruiter must be careful to keep a good document trail and thorough notes. This means saving e-mail correspondence and documenting within the e-mail message itself the date and time of contact.

Question: *Is my company under any obligation to notify candidates we've found on the Internet that they're being considered for employment with us?*

Answer: It's important to remember that an employer—or anyone else—can look at a resume on the Internet and are under no obligation to notify the candidate that they have looked at it. However, this concern opens a broader area of discussion. Assume that a job seeker submits a resume in confidence to one company, and that this company subscribes to a service that provides automatic sharing of resumes. If one of the companies that now receives the resume is the job seeker's current employer and the job seeker is fired as a result of seeking employment elsewhere, does sharing a resume create any liability?

Question: *The demographics of the Internet show clearly that some groups of people typically do not have access. If our company recruits only on the Internet, regardless of the status of Affirmative Action laws, are we open to charges of discrimination?*

Answer: First, give credit to the country's libraries that are moving as quickly as possible to provide Internet access to people who might not be able to afford it. Second, recognize that some community organizations are beginning to collect and post resumes in databases. Third, some job databases like Online Opportunities collect resumes at such places as Urban League job fairs.

But unless your business is closely tied to the online industry, you would be missing qualified candidates if you recruited only on the Internet. Until access is more widespread, we recommend that online recruiting be just one part, albeit an important part, of your overall recruiting process.

Question: *We're a privately held business. We don't want our competitors to know even what positions we're recruiting for. Can we remain anonymous on the Internet?*

Answer: There are several options here. Headhunters routinely post job listings without showing the employer's name. If your company doesn't want to work with a headhunter, it could use its advertising agency and the agency's e-mail address. If the company wants to remain totally anonymous, there's always the option of having applicants reply through one of the anonymous remailers. For information on anonymous remailers, type "anonymous remailers" at a search engine prompt.

Question: We're recruiting on the Internet and are getting applications from all over the world. Do we have any special problems to be aware of with the international applications?

Answer: It's the same with any type of recruiting. The same laws and policies apply. Remember, however, that The Federal Immigration Reform and Control Act (IRCA) requires that you establish the legal right for all new hires to work.

Limitless Recruiting Opportunities

Recruiting over the Internet and World Wide Web can be the most expedient and rewarding means you have ever used for finding and hiring applicants. It is a cost-effective way of uncovering the best pool of qualified applicants available. This wonderful new technology has changed the face of the recruiting and employment process. Used properly, it can prove to be your company's most important tool.

Summary

The Internet is no longer an elite instrument of a few computer specialists or university personnel. In the last few years, it has become an indispensable tool for businesses and private citizens alike. The Internet—and the World Wide Web—provides an electronic marketplace for countless services and resources. As a job-search and recruitment tool, it is unparalleled.

As a member of the Internet community, you now have access to the most expansive assortment of jobs and applicants available anywhere. If you apply what you have learned about the process of job hunting on the Internet and have a positive attitude, you cannot help but succeed in this or any other labor market.

In the parlance of the World Wide Web:

Log in every day.
Search for the perfect company.
Link with the job that's right for you.

See you on the Web!

Glossary

W̲e offer this glossary as a limited glimpse of the information available about the Internet and World Wide Web. We have included terms that will help you understand the information offered in this book. The rate of progression and change on the Internet is rapid, and we hope you will keep in mind that this glossary is by no means complete.

Online glossaries are updated more frequently than those in print. Here is a sampling of a few.

Two Web-specific glossaries that can be found online are located at `www.infolink.org/glossary.htm` and `www.wbri.com/glossary.htm`.

For an extensive Web glossary that contains a variety of Web-related information, including common e-mail acronyms (for instance, ROTFL is the acronym for "rolling on the floor laughing"), check out Webguest's glossary at `www.webguest.com/glossr.html`.

Other Web resources include `www.jaderiver.com/glossary.htm` (specific to marketing types), `strategy.gemconsult.com/resources/indextemplate.cfm?FiletoOpen=glossary/index.htm`, and `webopedia.internet.com`.

access   A means of being able to connect to (or "get on") the Internet.

address   In Internet terminology, refers to a computer address for receiving e-mail; for example, `jobnet@aol.com`, which is pronounced "jobnet at A-O-L dot com."

agents   Tools that search out information on the World Wide Web; also known as "search agents" or "knowbots."

alt   (1) newsgroups that tend to be on controversial or lighter subjects—for example, `alt.fishing`; sometimes called bulletin boards or discussion groups; (2) the Alt key on your keyboard, used with another key to execute a command.

America Online   One of the more popular commercial Internet service providers.

anchor   Another word for hyperlink; the highlighted word or phrase that allows connection to another area of a Web page.

annotations   A note or comment that may be attached to saved Web documents.

AOL   The abbreviation for the Internet service provider America Online; pronounced "A-O-L."

applicant-tracking software   Special software programs that companies use to automate their staffing function and manage the storage and retrieval of resumes.

application   Software used to perform tasks specific to the user's needs; for example, a word-processing program or a Web browser.

archive   A place where files are stored.

article   A message posted to a Usenet newsgroup.

ASCII   *American Standard Code for Information Interchange;* one of the two main types of files (binary is the other); also known as a text-only file containing no special formatting codes, such as boldfacing or underlining.

AUP   *Acceptable use policy;* governs what activities may be permitted on certain Web sites.

AU Sounds   A format for audio clips transmitted across the Web.

authoring software   Software that allows creation of World Wide Web pages; HTML Writer and HTML Editor for the Macintosh are examples of authoring software.

bandwidth   The size of the frequency that determines how much data can be transmitted: the greater the bandwidth, the greater the amount of data that can be sent.

baud rate   The speed at which data is transmitted over telephone lines, measured in bits per second; baud rates vary, the more common rates being 14,400; 28,800; and 56,600.

BBS   *See bulletin board system.*

binary   One of the two main types of files (ASCII is the other); a program file, rather than a text file, that is indecipherable without a computer program.

bit   Short for binary digit; the smallest unit of information stored on a computer.

Boolean search   A database search that limits or expands the potential matches by use of the Boolean expressions AND, OR, and NOT.

bounced message   Undelivered e-mail returned to its sender.

bps   Bits per second; the unit of measure used to designate the speed of a modem.

browser   Web browser; a program that enables users to view and use information on the World Wide Web.

bulletin board system (BBS)   A service available through modem dial-up that can include read-only information, conferences, e-mail, live chat, and Internet access.

bullet   (1) a symbol (usually a dot) for marking lines or otherwise calling attention to a part of a text; (2) a condensed statement of information on a resume.

byte   (1) a character of data representing a single letter, number, or symbol; (2) a unit for measuring computer and disk storage capacity, usually in kilobytes (KB), megabytes (MB), and gigabytes (GB).

cache   A computer subsystem for storing frequently used information, such as Web pages, for faster access.

caps   Uppercase letters.

case-sensitive   A warning that upper- and lowercase letters cannot be interchanged; for example, some operating systems, such as UNIX, can read only lowercase.

CD-ROM   A *compact disc with read only memory;* a high capacity, optical disc for information storage and retrieval only.

chat   Real-time interactive communication; that is, as a user types the words, another user is able to read them and respond.

client   A computer having access to services over a network; services are received from a "server" computer.

.com   The part of an Internet address that indicates a site is registered as commercial; for example, `jobnet@aol.com`, indicating that AOL is a commercial organization.

command   A direction or order entered into a computer.

compressed   Files that are "squeezed" to conserve disk space and reduce transfer time; some common compression programs are WinZip (PC) and StuffIt (Macintosh). *(See zipped.)*

CompuServe   A commercial (for a fee) Internet service provider.

configuration   The way in which a single computer's hardware and/or software are set up.

cookie   Information returned to a Web server about the user when a specific Web page is accessed.

CPU   *Central processing unit;* the "brain" of the computer that interprets and acts on instructions.

cursor   A blinking indication of the user's position on the screen.

CU-SeeMe   The first program for Internet videoconferencing; developed at Cornell University.

cyberspace   A term created by sci-fi writer William Gibson (*Neuromancer,* 1982) for the electronic zone where information is exchanged and contacts take place through computers.

database   Data stored in a well-organized format that makes sorting, searching, and other operations easy to perform.

Delphi   One of the commercial Internet service providers.

desktop   The on-screen work area of a computer on which icons and menus enable users to access programs and files.

desktop videoconferencing   Various technologies that enable users to capture, transmit, receive, and display video and sound so that people at remote sites can interact as though in a face-to-face conversation.

dial-up connection   A connection to the Internet established by dialing into a server via standard telephone lines, such as that of an individual user from a home computer.

digital camera   A type of camera that stores images digitally (rather than using conventional film) and downloads it to a computer using special software.

direct connection   A permanent connection to the Internet via leased telephone lines, such as that of a business or office.

directory   An index to a location of files.

disk drive   The part of the computer that stores information on disk.

DNS   *See Domain Name System.*

document   (1) a file containing text, hyperlinks, or media—such as pictures and sound—on the Web; (2) a single file in your word processing program; for example, your resume is considered a document.

document window   The "window" on the Web browser in which documents on the World Wide Web are viewed.

Domain Name System   A system of names and addresses based on categories, such as Education (edu), Commercial (com), and Government (gov); the system also translates names into official Internet Protocol numbers.

download   To transfer a file from a remote computer to a local computer through a modem or network.

e-commerce   Electronic commerce; commercial activity that takes place over a computer network.

electronic interview   An employment interview that takes place through e-mail rather than in person.

electronic job application   A computerized employment application form on which the applicant enters information on-screen.

electronic resume   A special type of resume for use in computer-assisted job searches; an electronic resume does not contain the special formatting and font enhancements that your paper resume does.

e-mail   Electronic mail; a written message sent to one person or a group of people via a computer network or through the Internet.

e-mail address   An e-mail user's computer address. *(See address.)*

emoticons   Facial expressions made up of punctuation marks; these are used to convey emotion such as sadness or happiness in e-mail messages: **:)** and **:(** .

encryption   The process of encoding computer data to prevent unauthorized use.

error correction   A way of filtering out telephone line noise in modems.

error message   A message from the computer that the user has done something incorrectly or that a program has had an internal problem.

Eudora   A program for handling e-mail.

execute   To accomplish a command.

exit   To log out or leave a session.

external viewer   A program used for viewing audio-visual and graphics files, such as GIFs and JPEGs; LView Pro, Microsoft Photo Editor, and Apple QuickTime are external viewers.

extraction engine   The nucleus of applicant-tracking software; technology that pulls significant information from scanned resumes.

face-to-face   (or *ftf*) Communication that is face-to-face rather than by computer.

FAQ   *Frequently Asked Questions;* answers to the most commonly asked questions, compiled into one document for the users' reference.

fax modem   A modem (either external or internal) equipped to send and receive data encoded in fax format.

FidoNet   A large BBS network.

file   A collection of data, such as a document or program.

file server   A computer that stores data and programs that are shared by many users in a network.

finger   A program for finding and displaying information about the users of a computer; finger technology has been increasingly incorporated into Web pages and e-mail programs.

firewall   Security system software that prevents unauthorized access to a computer or network.

flame   An angry or hostile message or reprimand directed at an individual in a newsgroup or chat room.

floppy disk   A magnetic disk used in a disk drive to record and store information; the floppy disk drive is often designated as the A: drive.

font   A particular style and size of letters or characters; also known as *typeface.*

freenet   Community-based bulletin board systems funded and operated by individuals and volunteers; many offer Internet access free or at low cost.

freeware   Software (such as games and utilities) that you can download from the Internet and use without paying for it.

ftp *File transfer protocol;* a program allowing you to connect to another computer and view and copy files back and forth between the two computers.

GIF *Graphic Interchange Format;* a format used to transfer graphics in a compressed form across phone lines; identified by the .gif file extension.

global village The way in which our "real world" has been made smaller by the Internet and other communication technology.

groupware Software that makes sharing work on documents easier; some examples of groupware are Microsoft Exchange, Groupwise, and Lotus Notes.

hard drive The memory storage device built into a computer; usually referred to as the C: drive, although some computers can have more than one hard drive.

hardware The computer itself and computer equipment; that is, modem, monitor, printer, and scanner. *(See software.)*

header/headings The identifying data at the top of an e-mail message; that is, date, recipient, subject, and sender.

headhunter A recruiter who charges a fee to an employer for finding executive-level applicants.

home page The first document or page displayed when a browser accesses a site on the World Wide Web; usually contains a welcome message and a table of contents.

host (1) a computer with a permanent connection to the Internet; (2) an Internet service provider.

hotlist A list of interesting or new Web sites and their addresses (URLs), compiled by and posted at job databases and various other Web sites.

HTML *Hypertext Markup Language;* the authoring language that enables the creation of WWW documents; tells the browser how to read and display the various graphics, text, and links.

HTTP *Hypertext Transfer Protocol;* the basis of the World Wide Web, HTTP allows the transfer of linked hypertext documents.

hyperlink (link) A highlighted word, phrase, or graphic on a Web page; by clicking it, you are taken to a related Web page, either on the same site or on a completely different Web site.

hypermedia A system allowing transmission of linked multiple media, such as sound, pictures, and graphics, across the World Wide Web.

hypertext   The system of writing and displaying text in such a way that it can be transmitted and accessed by links that allow readers to jump from one piece of data to another.

icon   A symbol for a computer program that displays on a computer's desktop; by clicking it, a user opens the program.

inline images   Graphic images contained within a World Wide Web document.

interactive   A means of "give and take" between the user and the computer program.

interface   The connection between one compatible system and another.

Internet   The worldwide *inter*connection among computer *net*works.

Internet Explorer   Microsoft's World Wide Web browser for viewing pages on the Web.

Internet interview   An employment interview that takes place online rather than in person.

InternetMCI   A commercial network from MCI Communications.

Internet service provider (ISP)   A national or local company that provides access to the Internet for a fee; examples of national ISPs include America Online, AT&T Worldnet, and Earthlink.

Internet telephony   Use of the Internet and special software programs rather than the conventional telephone to exchange spoken information.

IP   *Internet Protocol;* the set of rules or standards that govern communication on the Internet.

IP address   *Internet Protocol address;* usually four groups of numbers separated by periods, such as 140.147.254.3—the IP address for the Library of Information System.

IRC   *Internet Relay Chat;* a many-to-many live interactive discussion.

job bank   A centralized listing of job openings.

job-search process   Includes online job search, resume, application, interview, and hiring.

JPEG   *Joint Photographic Experts Group;* format used to compress and store images and photographs so that they can be transferred over the Web; identified by the .jpg file extension.

keyword   A word denoting an important job or applicant characteristic (such as "marketing") used to narrow search criteria in a job bank.

kill file   Tells a newsreader which articles to skip in Usenet newsgroups; the user specifies whose messages are unwanted; also referred to as a *bozo filter*.

leased line   A phone line that is leased for an exclusive direct Internet connection, usually for a company rather than for an individual; for example, a T-1 line.

line length   The maximum number of characters that can be typed on a line of text. (Note that differing line lengths from one e-mail program to another can cause strange line breaks when the recipient opens it.)

links   The hypertext connections used to jump between Web documents.

Linux   A freeware operating system developed by Linus Torvalds of Sweden, based on UNIX.

list   Electronic mailing list or discussion group.

list administrator   The person who runs a list.

LISTSERV   List server; an automatic discussion list service capable of responding to requests for subscription.

live   An active link to another area of information on the World Wide Web.

load   To put information and data into memory for processing.

log in   (1) the process of signing on to a computer network; (2) the prompt for your user ID.

lurker   One who observes or reads a newsgroup or chat room without joining in the conversation.

megabyte (MB)   A unit of information storage equal to just over a million bytes of information.

megahertz   An indicator of the speed at which a computer processes information; abbreviated as MHz.

memory   The capacity of a computer to retrieve information from the hard drive or Internet and enable you to manipulate it.

menu   A list of sites, documents, or commands available.

message   An e-mail letter.

Microsoft Network, The   The commercial network from Microsoft.

MIME   *Multipurpose Internet Mail Extensions;* allows transmission of e-mail messages containing graphics, voice, and video.

modem   (from *mo*dulate-*dem*odulate device) the device for sending and receiving data over telephone lines.

moderator   Person who monitors and controls postings to a Usenet newsgroup.

monitor   The screen on which information is displayed in a readable form; monitors can be monochrome or color.

Mosaic   The first hypertext browser with picture and sound capability. *(See NCSA).*

mouse   A device used to point, select, and draw on the computer screen.

MPEG   *Moving Pictures Experts Group;* a digital compression format for motion media; a special application is required to view MPEG files on your computer.

multimedia   A combination of picture, sound, and text.

NCSA   *National Center for Supercomputing Applications* at the University of Illinois in Urbana-Champaign; developed the Mosaic browser.

Net   A shortened form of the word *Internet.*

netiquette   Internet etiquette; proper behavior on the Internet.

Netscape Navigator   The popular browser from Netscape; available in the Netscape Communicator suite that features e-mail and a newsreader.

network news   Discussion groups devoted to a single topic.

networking groups   Traditionally, individuals who work together to provide mutual support and job-search assistance to other members.

newsgroups   Discussion groups devoted to a single topic.

newsreader   A program that allows you to read and respond to messages in newsgroups.

node   Access area for computer hook-up to a network; network access is limited by how many nodes the network contains.

online   Being connected to the Internet or other computer networks.

online employment services   Fee-based employment agencies available online.

operating system   The software that controls the CPU and hardware of a computer, such as Windows 95/98, Windows NT, Mac OS, and UNIX.

page   A hypermedia document on the World Wide Web.

password   A secret word used to verify an authorized user's identification.

path   The sequence of menu choices selected to arrive at a particular information site; the location of a Web page on a server includes the domain name, the directories, and the filename.

PC   *See personal computer.*

personal computer   A single microcomputer that can function as a standalone or connected to a network; companies have moved toward giving each person a PC, rather than just a terminal connected to one huge mainframe computer.

point-and-click   Using the mouse to choose an option or select an action.

POP   *Point of Presence;* the point, or location, where users can dial into their service provider's host computer for connection to the Internet.

port   (1) a socket on a computer into which you can plug external devices such as printers and modems; (2) a dedicated line for linking up to a mainframe computer.

post   A message or article on a newsgroup.

PPP   *Point-to-Point Protocol;* a method, or protocol, that allows users to connect to the Internet by high-speed modem and telephone lines.

Prodigy   One of the commercial networks that provides access to the Internet.

prompt   The point where a command is entered, usually at a blinking cursor.

QuickTime   A digital viewer, developed by Apple Computers for the Macintosh and the PC, that allows the user to see video, such as AVI or MPEG files.

RAM   *Random access memory;* volatile memory that can be read and modified.

RealAudio   Technology that streams sound across the Web in real time as the sound file is downloading.

real-time   At the moment, as it is happening; chat programs allow for real-time online "conversations."

Restrac   A leading maker of applicant-tracking software.

Resumix   A leader in Human Skills Management and applicant-tracking software for staffing automation.

ROM   *Read only memory;* memory that contains data that cannot be modified.

router   A device that finds the most expedient route for the transmission of data between two networks.

scanning   The process by which an image, such as a photo or page of text, is captured by passing a set of photo cells over it; the scanner takes a "photo" of the document and sends it to the computer, where the image is then stored for future retrieval.

search engine   A program that searches Internet documents and data, based on a keyword (or keywords) request; some examples are Yahoo!, AltaVista, and Lycos.

server   A computer, connected to a network, that manages resources such as files or printers.

service provider   An organization that provides access to the Internet; commonly referred to as an Internet service provider, or ISP.

SGML   *Standard Generalized Markup Language;* internationally recognized standard for electronic publishing.

shareware   Software available for downloading that typically carries a small fee paid directly to the developer.

site   Location on the Internet where information is available through a Web browser and an Internet connection.

skill extraction   The process of retrieving job-related information from scanned resumes.

SLIP   *Serial Line Internet Protocol;* allows connection to the Internet by phone lines and modem rather than through a host.

smileys   Facial expressions that convey emotion in e-mail; made by using punctuation marks. *(See emoticon.)*

snail mail   Mail delivered by the postal service, as opposed to the lightning-fast e-mail.

spam The same message sent to many different newsgroups or e-mail addresses; akin to junk mail.

streaming media Compression technology that reduces digitized audio and video files so that they can be downloaded and reach your computer for playback in real time.

subject line A headline highlighting the topic of a message.

subscribe To add a name to a distribution list.

sysop Short for *system op*erator; the person in charge of a BBS, online service, or special-interest discussion group.

T-1 A dedicated line connection allowing high-speed data transfer.

tags Codes that identify how parts of an HTML document will look on the Web; that is, whether parts will be bold, larger or smaller font, and so forth.

talk Real-time interactive conversation; as a user "types" the words, another user is able to read them.

TCP/IP *Transmission Control Protocol/Internet Protocol;* the basic set of procedures, or protocols, that allow linkage of different computers across varying networks; governs all Internet applications.

Telnet A protocol that enables a user to log on at a remote location and access the Internet.

terminal emulation Enables a computer to recognize a user's terminal as compatible.

thread Various postings on a single topic on newsgroups and bulletin boards.

TIFF *Tagged Image File Format;* a format for storing graphics images, identified by the .tif file extension.

TIN *Threaded Internet Newsreader;* newsreader for reading postings on newsgroups.

UNIX An operating system originally developed for networking individual workstations.

unzip To uncompress an archived file.

upload To transfer a file from a local computer to a remote computer through a modem or network.

URL *Uniform Resource Locator;* the World Wide Web addressing system; the address of a World Wide Web site.

Usenet A worldwide network that functions as a BBS for special-interest discussions; predates the Internet.

user ID *See user name.*

user name A name used for logging in and gaining access to a computer system.

viewer A program that displays files as they were created by the originating application.

virus A program that infects computer files, causing problems to a user's computer, ranging from mildly annoying to vastly destructive. (Note: Never downloading files from unknown sources and maintaining updated anti-virus software on a computer are a user's best defense against computer viruses.)

voice e-mail Allows you to send your own voice speaking your e-mail message over the Internet, or to hear the voice of the sender.

VRML *Virtual Reality Modeling Language;* a language that allows for the creation of virtual "worlds" for exploring the World Wide Web.

WAIS *Wide Area Information Service;* an application using keywords to search databases.

Web browser The software used to access and view or "browse" HTML documents on the World Wide Web; examples include Microsoft Internet Explorer and Netscape Navigator.

Web document An HTML document, accessible on the World Wide Web.

webmaster The person in an organization who designs, administers, and maintains a Web site.

Web page HTML document that can be accessed or "browsed" on the World Wide Web; part of a Web site.

World Wide Web An organizing system with the Internet that makes it easy to establish links between computers; based on the concept of hypertext, the links between servers that allow fast and easy retrieval of data; also known as WWW and W3.

zipped file A file in compressed form, which makes it faster and easier to send it over the Internet.

Index

A

accessing. *See also* opening; starting
  Internet, 13–17. *See also* AOL; ISPs
  newsgroups, 64–66
    job banks, 66–67
adding. *See also* inserting
  colors (HTML tags), 152–153
  GIF images, 156–157
  horizontal spacing (HTML resumes), 153
  hyperlinks (HTML resumes), 154–156
  URLs to search engines, 160–161
addresses
  e-mail, 155–156
  Internet. *See* URLs
advantages
  Internet, 3–5
  online recruiting, 266–268
Alternative Work and Career Opportunities, Web site, 225
American Mathematical Society, Web site, 224
America Online. *See* AOL
America's Job Bank, 43–45
Angelfire, Web site, 158
anonymous remailers, 106
AOL (America Online), 28–37. *See also* ISPs
  e-mail, 35–37
  newsgroups, 64–66
  publishing resumes, 157–158
  spam, blocking, 107
  starting, 28
Arlene Rinaldi (netiquette) Web site, 193
ASCII, formatting (resumes), 86–87
Ask Jeeves, Web site, 21
AT&T WorldNet (ISP), 16

B

banks. *See* job banks
BizWeb, Web site, 43
blocking spam (e-mail), 107
boards. *See* job boards
Bonzi, Web site, 204
BridgePath, Web site, 234–236
browsers, 11
  Microsoft Internet Explorer, 13, 18
  Netscape Navigator, 13, 18
  newsreaders, 65–66
bulletin boards. *See* newsgroups
bullets (resumes), 116
Bureau of Labor Statistics, 95

C

calculators, salaries, 90
California, state employment, Web site, 43
Canada
  Career Page, Web site, 91
  Curriculum Vitae (resumes), 135–141
  government Web sites, 96
  ISPs, 14–15
  Job Bank, 45
  Jobs Catalogue, Web site, 91
Careerfile, 51
CareerMagazine Online, Web site, 91
CareerMart, 33–35, 265
CareerMosiac, 51
CareerPath.com, 46
careers. *See also* employment
  resources, 89–97

services, 232–236
    BridgePath, 234–236
    College Grad Job Hunter, 232–234
    recruiting, 262–267
CERN (Centre European Research
    Nucleare), 11
chronological format (resumes), 119
citysearch.com, 97
clarity (resumes), 117–119, 197
clothing, interviews, 245–246
Collabra (Netscape Navigator newsreader), 65
College Grad Job Hunter, 232–234
    Web site, 92
college students, 223–226
    career services, 232–236
        BridgePath, 234–236
        College Grad Job Hunter, 232–234
    disciplines
        journalism, 225
        math, 223
        physics, 224
        science, 224
    internships, 225, 240
    interviews, 240–243
    placement offices, 226–231
        JOBTRAK, 231–232
        University of South Florida, 226–231
    recruiters, 236–239
    resumes, 239
    summer jobs, 225
colors (HTML tags), 152–153
combination format (resumes), 120
companies. See also employers
    recruiting, 251–252
        advantages, 266–268
        online services, 253–265
        prescreening interviews, 266–267
    researching, 209–210
    Web sites, 39–43
Companies Online, Web site, 93
CompuServe, 17
computers
    education, 9
    online. See Internet; Web
conferencing. See videoconferencing
ConnectAmerica (ISP), 15
connections, Internet, 13–17. See also AOL; ISPs
Cool Works, Web site, 225
corporate Web sites, 39–43
creating HTML resumes, 151–157
Curriculum Vitae. See CV
CU-SeeMe (videoconferencing), 205–206
CV (Curriculum Vitae), 135–141
Cyber Patrol, 108
CYBERsitter, 108
cyberspace. See Internet; Web
Cybertown, Web site, 158

D

databases
    job banks, 55–59
    viewing, 90–91
    4Work, 225
declining positions, 201
Dejanews, 66
desktop videoconferencing, 204–207
Dictionary of Occupational Titles. See DOT
Digital Landlords, Web site, 157
Disney, Web site, 41–42
documents. See HTML; resumes; text
DOT (Dictionary of Occupational Titles), 95
Dun & Bradstreet Companies Online,
    Web site, 40

E

Earthlink (ISP), 15
EDGAR, 92–93
    SEC reports, 93
editing. See also proofreading
    HTML resumes, 159–160
    resumes, 115–119
    writing tips, 186–191
education
    computers, 9
    resume formats, 135–141
Electronic Disk Resume, 227
electronic resumes. See resumes
e-mail
    addresses, 155–156
    AOL, 35–37
    interviews, 197–201
        negotiating salaries, 219–222
        prescreening, 266–267
    resumes, 86–88
        hyperlinks, 155–156
        interviews, 197
        submitting, 86–88
    security, 106–108
        anonymous remailers, 106
    spam, 107–108
    success stories, 5–7
    voice, 203
    writing tips, 186–191
employers
    recruiting online, 251–252
        advantages, 266–268
        online services, 253–265
        prescreening interviews, 266–267
    researching, 92–94, 209–210
    screening methods, 201

SEC reports (EDGAR), 92–93
    Web site, 39–43
employment. *See also* careers; job searches
    headhunters, 101. *See also* recruiters
    maintaining, 248–250
    services, 252–257
        advantages, 266–268
encryption, 106. *See also* security
entry-level jobs, 223–224
    College Grad Job Hunter, 232–234
ETA. *See* U.S. government Web sites
ethics, recruiting, 268–271
evaluating interviews, 208–209
Excite, Web site, 22
    city guides, 97
extraction engines. *See* keyword searches

F

face-to-face interviews, 207–219
    evaluating, 208–209
    hypothetical situations, 213–216
    negotiating salaries, 219–222
    questions, 216–219
FAQ (frequently asked questions), 185
fellowships (college students), 225, 240
file transfer protocol. *See* FTP
fonts (resumes), 114
Forbes 500 Largest Private Companies,
    Web site, 93
formatting
    resumes, 86–87, 113–120
        HTML, 147
        spacing (HTML), 153
    RTF (rich-text format), 112–113
    text-only, 112–113
Fortune magazine, 94
forums, online, 64. *See also* newsgroups
free Web servers, 158–159
frequently asked questions. *See* FAQ
frustration, 8
FTP (file transfer protocol), 12
functional format (resumes), 119

G

GeoCities, Web site, 158
GIF (Graphic Interchange Format), 156–157
gophers, 11
GoTo, Web site, 23
grants, college students, 224
Graphic Interchange Format. *See* GIF
graphics. *See also* images
    GIF (Graphic Interchange Format), 156–157

HTML resumes, 145–146
grooming
    men, 244
    women, 246–247

H

headhunters, 101, 257–266. *See also* recruiting
headings
    resumes, 114
    sections (HTML resumes), 153
Hewlett-Packard, 236–239
histories, Web, 11–13
Homefair.com, Web site, 97
Hoover's Online, Web site, 93
HotBot, Web site, 24
HotJobs.com, Web site, 46–47
HTML (Hypertext Markup Language), 143
    tags, 151–153
        adding colors, 152–153
        images, 157
    versions, 157
HTML resumes, 143
    creating, 151–157
    free Web servers, 158–159
    hyperlinks, 144–145
        inserting, 155–156
    images, 145–146
    lists, 154
    preformatted text, 154
    proofreading, 159–160
    publicizing, 160–161
    publishing, 157–159
    resume banks, 158
    samples, 147–151, 161–179
    text-style tags, 154
    Tripod Resume Builder, 158
    writing tips, 186–191
HTTP (hypertext transfer protocol), 11–13
hygiene, for interviews, 245–247
hyperlinks, 11. *See also* links
    HTML resumes, 144–145
    inserting, 155–156
hypermedia, 11
Hypertext Transfer Protocol. *See* HTTP
Hypertext Markup Language. *See* HTML

I

images. *See also* graphics
    GIF (Graphic Interchange Format), 156–157
    HTML resumes, 145–146
    inserting, 156–157

InfoSeek Guide, Web site, 25
inserting. *See also* adding
    colors (HTML tags), 152–153
    GIF (Graphic Interchange Format), 156–157
    hyperlinks (HTML resumes), 154–155
installing AOL, 28–30
Internet
    accessing, 13–17. *See also* AOL, ISPs
    addresses. *See* URLs
    career
        resources, 89–97
        services, 232–236
    e-mail. *See* e-mail
    Explorer. *See* Microsoft Internet Explorer
    interviews, 195–197
        e-mail, 197–201
        videoconferencing, 204–207
        voice e-mail, 203
    netiquette, 191–193
    newsgroups, 64
        Dejanews, 66
    overview, 1–9
    recruiting services, 257–266
    resumes
        HTML, 143
        keyword searches, 121–123
        newsgroups, 78–88
        templates, 124, 126–129
    searching, 20–26. *See also* search engines
    security, 99–103
    service providers. *See* ISPs
    Sites for Job Seekers and Employers, 92
    Student Search System, 223
    telephony, 27–28
internships, 225, 240
interviews, 195–197
    college students, 240–243
    e-mail, 197–201
        negotiating salaries, 219–222
        prescreening, 266–267
        resumes, 197
    evaluating, 208–209
    face-to-face, 207–219
        evaluating, 208–209
        hypothetical situations, 213–216
        interviewers, 212–213
        questions, 216–219
    grooming
        men, 244–246
        women, 246–247
    negotiating salaries, 219–222
    telephone, 201–204
    videoconferencing, 204–207
    voice e-mail, 203
ISPs (Internet service providers), 13–17
    AOL, 28–37
    AT&T WorldNet, 16

blocking spam, 107
Canada, 14–15
CompuServe, 17
ConnectAmerica, 15
Earthlink, 15
MSN (The Microsoft Network), 17
Net4B, 15
newsgroups, 64–66
Prodigy, 16
publishing resumes, 157–158

J

job banks. *See also* job boards
    databases, 54–59
    meta-lists, 59–60
    newsgroups, 63
        accessing, 66–67
job boards, 43–55
    America's Job Bank, 43–45
    Canada's Job Bank, 46
    Careerfile, 51
    CareerMart, 51
    CareerMosiac, 51
    CareerPath.com, 46
    career services. *See* career services
    databases, 54–59
    HotJobs.com, 46–47
    JobNET, 52–54
    JobOptions, 49–51
    Jobs.com, 54
    JOBTRAK, 54
    Monster.com, 47–49
    National Diversity Newspaper Job Bank, 225
    Transition Assistance Online, 55
Job Hunt Manager (Macintosh), 111
JobNET, Web site, 52–54
JobOptions, 49–51, 258–264
job postings, newsgroups, 67–67
    samples, 69–77
Jobs.com, Web site, 54
Job-Search-Engine, 61–62
job searches
    career resources, 91–92
    college students
        career services, 232–236
        internships, 225, 240
        JOBTRAK, 213–232
        recruiters, 236–239
        summer jobs, 225
        University of South Florida, 226–231
    disciplines
        journalism, 225
        math, 224
        physics, 224
        science, 224

entry-level, 223–224
internships, 225
interviews. *See* interviews
JobOptions, 258–264
keywords (resumes), 121–123
netiquette, 181–184
newsgroups, 184–191
recruiting, 251–252. *See* recruiting
security, 99–103
job seekers
Internet overview, 4
interviews. *See* interviews
recruiting services, 257–266
CareerMart, 265
JobOptions, 258–264
Monster.com, 265
resumes. *See* resumes
JOBTRAK, 54, 213–232
JOBWEB, 92
journalism positions, 225

K

keyword searches, 20–26. *See also* searching
resumes

L

language
HTML. *See* HTML
resumes, 117–119
layouts. *See* formatting; templates
legalities, recruiting, 268–271
links, 11. *See also* hyperlinks
HTML resumes, 144–145
resumes to Web sites, 161
lists. *See also* bullets
HTML resumes, 154
Lycos, Web site, 20

M

Macintosh, Job Hunt Manager, 111
magazines
Fortune, 94
Working Woman, 94
maintaining employment, 248–250
MapQuest, Web site, 96
mathematics positions, 224
Media Player, 27
men, grooming, 244
messages, e-mail. *See* e-mail

meta-lists, job banks, 59–60
Microsoft
Internet Explorer, 13, 18
Outlook Express (newsreader), 65
Network. *See* MSN
Word, 110
military, 55
resume preparation, 118
Monster.com, Web site, 33, 47–49, 265
MSN (The Microsoft Network), 17
multimedia, 26–28
HTML resumes, 156
videoconferencing, 204–207
programs, 206
multi-point conferencing, 204

N

National Diversity Newspaper Job Bank,
Web site, 225
National Public School Locator, Web site, 97
National Science Foundation, Web site, 224
navigational links. *See* hyperlinks; links
negotiating salaries, 219–222
Net: User Guidelines and Netiquette, The, 193
Net4B (ISP), 15
netiquette
Internet, 191–193
job searches, 181–184
newsgroups, 184–191
Net Nanny, 108
Netscape Navigator, 13, 18
Collabra (newsreader), 65
networking, 185
newsgroups, 11
job postings, 67–68
job searches, 184
netiquette, 184–191
overview, 63–67
reading, 67
recruiting, 252–257
resumes, 78–88
preparing, 85–87
submitting, 86–88
sample postings, 69–77
selecting, 185
writing tips, 186–191
Nortel Networks, Web site, 40
Northern Light, Web site, 26

O

O*NET, 95
online forums, 64. *See also* newsgroups

onlinecareerguide.com, Web site, 92
opening. *See also* accessing; starting
    newsgroups, 64–65
organizing. *See also* formatting
    HTML resumes, 144–145
    resumes, 120–121
Outlook Express, 65
overview
    Internet, 1–9
    job seekers, 4
    newsgroups, 63–67
    resumes, 112

Job Hunt Manager (Macintosh), 111
    Professional Web Resume, 111
    WinWay Resume V6.0, 111
    You're Hired!, 111
    videoconferencing, 206
proofreading resumes, 159–160
psychological aspects, 7–9
    frustration, 8
    isolation/side-tracking, 8–9
publicizing URLs, 160–161
publishing HTML resumes, 157–159
    ISPs, 157–158

P

paper, selecting (for resumes), 115
part-time jobs, 240
passwords, 106
PGP (Pretty Good Privacy), 106
physics positions, 224
PhysLINK, Web site, 224
placement offices (college students), 226–231
    JOBTRAK, 231–232
    University of South Florida, 226–231
plain-text resumes, formatting, 86–87
point-to-point conferencing, 204
positions, declining, 201
posting resumes
    America's Job Bank, 43–45
    JobOptions, 50
    newsgroups, 78–88
preformatted text (HTML resumes), 154
preparing resumes, 109–111. *See also* resumes
    e-mail interviews, 197–200
    netiquette, 181–191
    newsgroups, 85–87
prescreening interviews, 266–267. *See also* interviews
Pretty Good Privacy. *See* PGP
privacy, 99–103. *See also* security
    anonymous remailers, 106
    e-mail, 106–108
Prodigy (ISP), 16
Professional Web Resume, 111
programs
    applicant-tracking, 126
    Collabra, 65
    CU-SeeMe, 205–206
    Internet Explorer, 13, 18
    Microsoft Word, 110
    Netscape Navigator, 13, 18
    Outlook Express, 65
    PGP, 106
    Restrac, 124–125
    resumes, 111–112

Q

questions, interviews, 216–219

R

reading newsgroups, 67
RealPlayer G2, 27
RealVideo, 27
recruiters (college students), 236–239
recruiting
    advantages, 266–268
    e-mail, 266–267
    employers, 251–252
    legalities, 268–271
    newsgroups, 252–257
    online services, 257–266
        CareerMart, 265
        JobOptions, 258–264
        Monster.com, 265
Recruiting-links.com, Web site, 43
relocation, 96
researching employers, 92–94, 209–210
    SEC reports (EDGAR), 92–93
Restrac, 124–125
resumes
    America's Job bank, 43–45
    applicant-tracking software, 126
    banks, 158
    college students, 239
    CV (Curriculum Vitae), 135–141
    editing, 115–119
    Electronic Disk Resume, 227
    e-mail
        hyperlinks, 155–156
        interviews, 197
        submitting, 86–88
    formats, 119–120
    formatting, 113–115
        text, 86–87

HTML, 143
  creating, 151–157
  images, 145–146
  links, 144–145
  lists, 154
  preformatted text, 154
  publishing, 157–159
  samples, 147–151, 161–179
  tags, 151–153
interviews. *See* interviews
JobOptions, 50, 258–264
keyword searches, 121–123
language, 117–119
military, 118
netiquette, 181–184
newsgroups, 78–88
  netiquette, 184–191
  preparing resume for, 85–87
  submitting resume to, 86–88
online services, 121–123
organizing, 120–121
overview, 112
preparing, 109–111
programs
  Job Hunt Manager (Macintosh), 111
  Professional Web Resume, 111
  WinWay Resume V6.0, 111
  You're Hired!, 111
proofreading, 159–160
Restrac, 124–125
samples, 130–135
scanning, 123–126
security, 110
summaries, 125–126
templates, 124, 126–129
Tripod Resume Builder, 158
writing tips, 186–191
rich-text format. *See* RTF
Riley Guide, The, 92
Rinaldi, Arlene (netiquette Web site), 193
RTF (rich-text format), 112–113

S

salaries
  calculators, 90
  negotiating, 219–222
samples
  HTML resumes, 147–151, 161–179
  newsgroup job postings, 69–77
  resumes, 130–135
scams, 100–101
  work-at-home, 100
scanning resumes, 123–126
science positions, 224

SEARCH.COM, Web site, 61–62
search engines, 20–26
  adding URLs, 160–161
  Ask Jeeves, 21
  Excite, 22
  GoTo, 23
  HotBot, 24
  InfoSeek Guide, 25
  Job-Search-Engine, 61–62
  Lycos, 20
  Northern Light, 26
  SEARCH.COM, 61–62
  Yahoo!, 43
searching
  America's Job Bank, 44
  AOL, 31–32
  Internet, 20–26. *See also* search engines
  job banks, 61–62
    databases, 54–59
  JobNET, 53–54
  Monster.com, 48
  resumes, 121–123
  Student Search System, 223
SEC (Securities and Exchange Commission), 92–93
section headings (HTML resumes), 153
security, 99–103
  adult Web site filters, 108
  anonymous remailers, 106
  e-mail, 106–108
  resumes, 110
selecting
  newsgroups, 185
  paper (resumes), 115
servers, free, 158–159
services
  employment. *See* employment services
  placement offices (college students), 226–231
  recruiting, 257–266
    advantages, 266–268
    CareerMart, 265
    JobOptions, 258–264
    legalities, 268–271
    Monster.com, 265
software. *See* programs
spacing (on HTML resumes), 153
spam, 107–108
starting AOL, 28
STEP (Student Temporary Employment Program), 224
streaming media, 27. *See also* multimedia
students, college. *See* college students
Student Search System, Web site, 223
Student Temporary Employment Program. *See* STEP
Submit It!, Web site, 160

submitting resumes
    adding URLs to search engines, 160–161
    via e-mail, 86–88
success stories, 5–7
summaries (resumes), 125–126
summer jobs, college students, 225
    Cool Works, Web site, 225
Surfwatch, 108

T

tags (HTML), 151–153
    adding colors, 152-153
    images, 157
    text-style, 154
telephone interviews, 210–204
    negotiating salaries, 219–222
Telephony (Internet), 27–28
templates (resumes), 124, 126–129
testing HTML pages, 157
Texas Instruments, Web site, 42
text
    formatting resumes, 86–87, 112–113
    HTML resumes, 144
    preformatted (HTML resumes), 154
    RTF (rich-text format), 112–113
    text-only formatting, 112–113
    text-style HTML tags, 154
TheGlobe.com, Web site, 158
Transition Assistance Online, Web site, 55, 118
Tripod Resume Builder, Web site, 158

U

Uniform Resource Locators. *See* URLs
University of South Florida, Web site, 226–231
uploading. *See also* publishing
    HTML resumes, 157–159
URLs (Uniform Resource Locators), 13
    publicizing, 160–161
U.S. Department of Labor Employment, 94
Usenet newsgroups. *See* newsgroups

V

videoconferencing
    interviews, 204–207
        negotiating salaries, 219–222
    programs, 206
viewing
    databases, 90–91
    newsgroups, 67

voice e-mail, 203
    Bonzi, Web site, 204

W

Web
    accessing, 13–17. *See also* AOL, ISPs
    addresses. *See* URLs
    browsers, 11, 13, 18
    career
        resources, 89–97
        services, 232–236
    e-mail. *See* e-mail
    Explorer. *See* Microsoft Internet Explorer
    free servers, 158–159
    history, 11–13
    interviews, 195–197
        e-mail, 197–201
        videoconferencing, 204–207
        voice e-mail, 203
    multimedia, 26–28
    netiquette, 191–193
    newsgroups, 66
    overview, 1–9
    presence providers, 157–158
    Student Search System, 223
Web sites
    Alternative Work and Career Opportunities, 225
    American Mathematical Society, 224
    America's Job Bank, 43–45
    Angelfire, 158
    Ask Jeeves, 21
    AT&T WorldNet, 16
    BizWeb, 43
    Bonzi, 204
    BridgePath, 234–236
    California state employment, 43
    Canada's Job Bank, 46
    Canadian Career Page, 91
    Canadian government, 96
    Canadian Jobs Catalogue, 91
    Careerfile, 51
    CareerMagazine Online, 91
    CareerMart, 33–35, 51, 265
    CareerMosiac, 51
    CareerPath.com, 46
    citysearch.com, 97
    College Grad Job Hunter, 92, 232–234
    Companies Online, 93
    CompuServe, 17
    ConnectAmerica, 15
    Cool Works, 225
    corporate, 39–43
    Cyber Patrol, 108
    CYBERsitter, 108

Cybertown, 158
Dejanews, 66
Digital Landlords, 157
Disney, 41–42
Dun & Bradsteet Companies Online, 40
Earthlink, 15
Excite, 22
Forbes 500 Largest Private Companies, 93
GeoCities, 158
GoTo, 23
Homefair.com, 97
Hoover's Online, 93
HotBot, 24
HotJobs.com, 46–47
InfoSeek Guide, 25
Internet Sites for Job Seekers and
    Employers, 92
JobNET, 52–54
JobOptions, 49–51, 258
Jobs.com, 54
JOBTRAK, 54, 231–232
JOBWEB, 92
Lycos, 20
MapQuest, 96
Monster.com, 33, 47–49, 265
MSN, 17
National Diversity Newspaper Job Bank, 225
National Public School Locator, 97
National Science Foundation, 224
Net4B, 15
Net Nanny, 108
Netscape, 18
Nortel Networks, 40
Northern Light, 26
onlinecareerguide.com, 92

PhysLINK, 224
Prodigy, 16
Recruiting-links.com, 43
Riley Guide, The, 92
Rinaldi, Arlene (netiquette), 193
Student Search System, 223
Submit It!, 160
SurfWatch, 108
Texas Instruments, 42
TheGlobe.com, 158
Transition Assistance Online, 55, 118
Tripod Resume Builder, 158
University of South Florida, 226–231
U.S. government, 94–97
WebStep TOP 100, 160
Yahoo!, 43
    Careers, 92
WebStep TOP 100, Web site, 160
Windows Media Player, 27
WinWay Resume V6.0, 111
wizards, creating resumes, 110
women, grooming, 246–247
work-at-home scams, 100
Working Woman magazine, 94
World Wide Web. *See* Internet; Web
writing tips, 186–191
WWW (World Wide Web). *See* Internet; Web

Y

Yahoo!, 43
    Careers, Web site, 92
You're Hired!, 111

If You Enjoyed This Book and Want More In-Depth Information About Online Resumes...

Includes details on many cyber-resume topics, including

- Where to find and how to use online resume templates and electronic resume builders.

- Tricks and traps of creating scannable and HTML resumes—with many real-life examples analyzed by the authors.

- Thorough evaluation of over 80 Internet resume sites, rated from outstanding to poor, with details on costs, confidentiality, and more. Learn how to use Internet resume sites that let you post resumes for access by recruiters and employers.

- Interviews with industry insiders on the most effective ways to produce and use your cyberspace resume.

To order, call 1-800-648-JIST, or visit your favorite bookstore.

Best Jobs for the 21st Century

Expert Reference on the Jobs of Tomorrow

By J. Michael Farr and LaVerne L. Ludden, Ed.D.

Whether you're preparing to enter the job market for the first time or simply wish to remain competitive in your current field, this information-packed reference contains data on the latest employment trends.

✦ Contains over 50 lists of jobs with best pay, high growth, and most openings by numerous categories
✦ Describes 686 jobs with fast growth or high pay
✦ Based on expert analysis of labor and economic trends

ISBN: 1-56370-486-2 • $16.95 • Order Code: LP-J4862

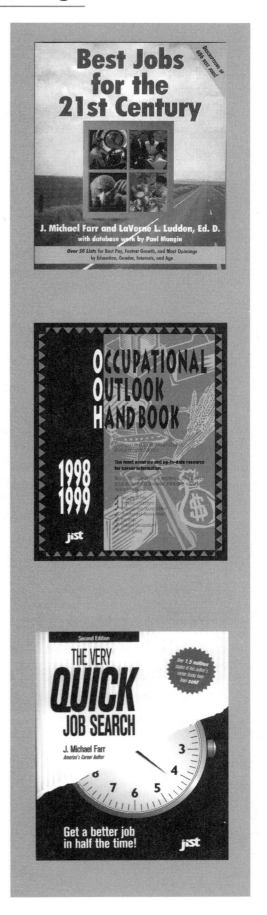

Occupational Outlook Handbook

By the U.S. Department of Labor

The *OOH* is the most widely used career exploration resource. This is a quality reprint of the government's *OOH,* only at a less-expensive price. It describes 250 jobs—jobs held by 85% of the American workforce—making the book ideal for students, counselors, teachers, librarians, and job seekers.

✦ Well-written narrative with many charts and photos
✦ Gives DOT numbers for the occupation and related occupations
✦ Sections on nature of the work, working conditions, training, job outlook, earnings

ISBN: 1-56370-464-1	**ISBN: 1-56370-475-7**
$17.95 Softcover	**$22.95 Hardcover**
Order Code: LP-J4641	**Order Code: LP-J4757**

The Very Quick Job Search

Get a Better Job in Half the Time!

By J. Michael Farr

Mike Farr, one of the most important architects of the self-directed job search, has done it again! Nowhere else will you find such excellent, timeless job search information. This award-winning title has been an important resource for more than 150,000 people just like you!

✦ Thorough coverage of all career planning and job search topics—in one book!
✦ Proven, effective advice for *all* job seekers
✦ Latest information on market trends and results-oriented search techniques

ISBN: 1-56370-181-2 • $16.95 • Order Code: LP-J1812

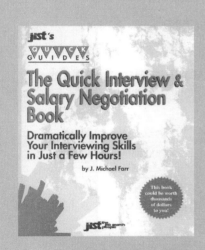
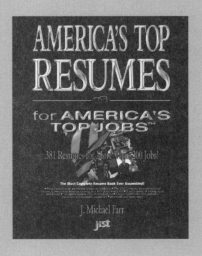

Call 1-800-648-JIST Today!

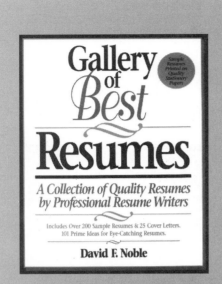

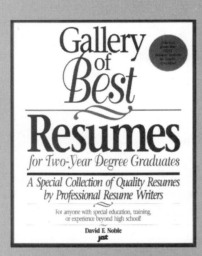

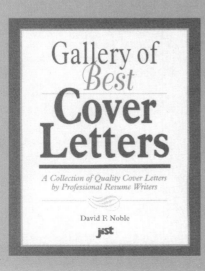

Gallery of Best Resumes

A Collection of Quality Resumes by Professional Resume Writers

By David F. Noble, Ph.D.

This is the best collection of resumes and cover letters you'll ever find! Members of the Professional Association of Résumé Writers offer the best of the best in this wide collection. Sample more than 200 great resumes with an expansive range of styles, formats, designs, occupations, and situations—all arranged in easy-to-find groups. You also get the author's 101 best resume tips—tips on design, layout, papers, writing style, mistakes to avoid, and 25 sample cover letters!

ISBN: 1-56370-144-8 • $17.95 • Order Code: LP-GBR

Gallery of Best Resumes for Two-Year Degree Graduates

A Special Collection of Quality Resumes by Professional Resume Writers

By David F. Noble, Ph.D.

Designed to fit the specific needs of two-year degree graduates, this special collection of resumes provides a wide variety of professional resume examples. Resumes are arranged in occupational groupings, with 229 samples selected from thousands submitted by the Professional Association of Résumé Writers.

ISBN: 1-56370-239-8 • $16.95 • Order Code: LP-J2398

Gallery of Best Cover Letters

A Collection of Quality Cover Letters by Professional Resume Writers

By David F. Noble, Ph.D.

Companion title to the author's popular *Gallery of Best Resumes*. Contains samples from the country's best professional resume writers. A wealth of comments about effective cover letters, plus detailed advice on how to make them error-free.

ISBN: 1-56370-551-6 • $18.95 • Order Code: LP-J5516